How to Cook Everything®

BITTMAN TAKES ON AMERICA'S CHEFS

How to Cook Everything®
BITTMAN TAKES ON AMERICA'S CHEFS

Mark Bittman

Wiley Publishing, Inc.

CONTENTS >

ACKNOWLEDGMENTS > More than anything I have ever published, this book was a team effort. My name may be up front, but from conception to publication I have been far from the only key player. Obviously, thanks go to all of the chefs with whom I cooked, as well as their capable and often heroic assistants. We had fun together, and the results speak for themselves, but they all worked hard to make things come together.

I'm equally indebted to the behind-the-scenes people: On the TV production the mellow Don Barto, effusive Pete McEntyre, ebullient Sam Shinn, and incomparable Lewis Rothenberg were all a gas to work with. And, as you can see and hear, they are amazing at their jobs of arranging for crystal sound, brilliant lighting, stunning camera work, and superb editing.

Peter Meehan proved himself invaluable from the day I met him. His work on the production of the show, on post-production, and on helping put together this book was tireless and—more important—splendid.

Many people at John Wiley & Sons were equally steadfast, but I'd like to single out Linda Ingroia, my indefatigable editor, for special thanks—if there's anyone who has sweated over every word here more than I, it is Linda.

Our copy editor, Anne Rolke, did a fabulous job. Natalie Chapman has been a wonderful colleague and supporter. Other senior management people at Wiley, including Stephen Kippur, Katherine Schowalter, Rob Garber, Larry Olson, Claire Griffin, and Todd Fries, have been behind this project every step of the way, and I'm grateful for that. The book's glorious design is by Alison Lew and Renata De Oliveira; thanks, too, to art director Paul Dinovo, designer Suzanne Sunwoo, production director Diana Cisek, and senior production editor Monique Calello, for all their hard work in shepherding this book. I am lucky enough to have a great ongoing relationship with several other key Wiley folks, including Dean Karrel (and his team), Gypsy Lovett, and P.J. Campbell.

Some people, of course, cross the line between professional and personal, and Angela Miller, in this project as in most others, deserves special mention. Charlie Pinsky is someone I'm happy to have as a friend despite having worked too closely with him; somehow he manages to feel the same way.

Then there are those who have supported me personally in the years it took to develop this series and book, and especially in the couple of years it has taken to pull it all together: John Ringwald, David Paskin, Pamela Hort, Sherry Slade, Fred Zolna, Semeon Tsalbins, Bob and Mary Newhouse, and Shari and Harry Sucheki. My pal Doc remains a long-term source of support, wisdom, and love. And my partner Alisa, who got to have some fun during this process, was a joy to be with.

Finally, my kids—Kate and Emma Baar-Bittman—despite now having big-time lives of their own, were as excited about this project as they could have been, and showed it. I can only imagine how much of a thrill it is for my parents, Murray and Gertrude Bittman, and for that if for no other reason I'm so glad it worked out. Thanks guys—I love you.

NEW YORK, FALL 2004

To Chuck, without whom none of this would have happened

Here, in a nutshell, is the idea behind **How to Cook Everything: Bittman Takes on America's Chefs**: A home cook—that's me—says to a bunch of chefs, essentially, "I may not know what I'm doing in your kitchen, but I know what I'm doing in mine, and I'll put my finished dishes up against yours—I'll show you that simple food cooked at home can taste as good as four-star restaurant cooking." It's a brash concept, and one that might be considered arrogant.

I don't think of myself as an arrogant or even confrontational person—I may be wrong on those points—but for a few reasons I felt I was the right person to challenge the chefs.

I am, or try to be, a straight shooter. This is not because I am a journalist; rather, I became a journalist because of this trait. It might be because I'm a native New Yorker (that's how much of the country sees us—curmudgeonly straight shooters) or because I went to a acclaimed high school where everything was subjected to the rule of the scientific method—prove it!—or simply because I come from a long line of wise guys. All of which has served me pretty well in the food world; I haven't bought into a lot of myths, I question people all the time, and I like to try to figure out the relationships between things.

I also like to challenge authority. And as a young food writer about twenty-five years ago, it seemed to me that chefs had all the authority. The rediscovery of home cooking had reached its zenith with Julia Child's popularity but, except for her, James Beard, and perhaps one or two others, one turned to chefs for ideas and inspiration. Although there was a world of home cooking out there, one far simpler than the one Julia represented, those of us following in her rather large footsteps often had little to do but report on the spectacular inventions of the New American Chefs, even when those spectacular inventions were traditional, exploratory, or even unpalatable.

The roots of **How to Cook Everything: Bittman Takes on America's Chefs** go back to this period, in which I had a professional split personality. I cooked at home, using "non-chef" recipes from all over the world, but I mostly reported about restaurants and their chefs.

WHERE IT ALL BEGAN

Fortunately, the tide turned right about the time I began working on my big basic book, **How to Cook Everything** (this is of course an egocentric view of things, but that doesn't make it less true). The demand for simpler recipes surged, and I found myself in an ideal position to satisfy it. It was at this same time that I proposed my *New York Times* column, **The Minimalist,** and began working with Jean-Georges Vongerichten, among the most important chefs of our time.

Jean-Georges is the uber-chef, the grand poobah, almost universally revered by his peers and critics alike, successful from both artistic and commercial perspectives, and one of the world's most imitated chefs.

Though our work situations could not be more different—he has the resources of an army, I almost never cook with an assistant; he has ingredients flown in from everywhere, I shop in supermarkets; he has a number of multi-million-dollar kitchens, mine is routinely rejected by photographers as unworthy—ten years ago we saw that we understood one another. We shared an openness when it came to flavor, a willingness to combine and experiment but, perhaps more importantly, a reluctance to complicate matters. (Much of this story is reported in our first book together, *Jean-Georges: Cooking at Home with a Four-Star Chef*.)

I say that my work with Jean-Georges led directly to the creation of the television show and this book **Bittman Takes on America's Chefs,** because the concept for our second book, *Simple to Spectacular,* was based directly on our work patterns: Often, we'd start with a simple recipe— mine, his, his mother's, a friend's, a classic—and build on it, turning it into something grand. The bridges between the simple work of the home cook and the more complicated tasks of the grand chef had become apparent to me, and our goal was to demonstrate how those bridges are built.

In "taking on" America's chefs, I had a similar but slightly contrary notion. I'd encourage chefs to do what they do best, and respond by showing that at the heart of their grand creations resided a simple recipe, one that could be prepared on a weeknight by a single person cooking alone at home.

There was another aspect of my work with Jean-Georges that carried over to the show. Over the years, we had become friends, seeing the joys and pains of close relationships begin and end, watching each other's success with admiration (and, it should be noted, a bit of jealousy), traveling together, eating together, and playing together. And over the years, especially in public, he began to good-naturedly tease me about my relative incompetence in the kitchen. (In private, he has always been seriously supportive.)

When Jean-Georges watched me chop a shallot and said, "That's not mincing, it's hacking," Charlie Pinsky—who is both my friend and the producer and director of the TV show that spawned this book—began to believe that **How to Cook Everything: Bittman Takes on America's Chefs** should be part comedy, a cooking version of *The Odd Couple*. In this version, the schlumpy, curmudgeonly journalist (that's me; Oscar; Walter Matthau) meets the sleek chefs who make up the elite cooks of this country. (And let me tell you: Most chefs are such clean freaks they make Felix look like a slob.)

WHAT CHEFS KNOW

I love cooking with chefs and arguing with them and teasing them; they are bound by myths and obscure rules, and often have forgotten how to cook like "real" people do. On the other hand, there's much to learn from them; they're perfectionists and, after all, they cook all the time; they must know *something*.

Whether the chef's are trained in the classic French style, like Daniel Boulud, or essentially self-taught, like Gabrielle Hamilton, or specializes in a cuisine from the other side of the world, like Suvir Saran, they know unique methods, flavor combinations, and dishes and has a personal style. Furthermore, their passion for food is usually what drove them into the field, and that passion is admirable.

As is their work ethic. Chefs—real chefs, not TV star chefs—have burned hands, tough and often broken nails, scarred and sometimes hairless forearms. They sweat, they run up and down stairs, they cut themselves, they drop hot pots, they scorch the meat. This is not the carefree job you see when it's distilled down to run on a TV show, or when you go into a multi-million-dollar restaurant and see the chef drinking a glass of Champagne with a celebrity.

Chefs work. For ninety percent of the world's chefs, it's a job, and one not that much different from being an auto mechanic or a doctor. For our show, of course, we targeted not the guy running the banquet hall at the local Marriott (who, believe me, has an admirable set of skills), but the chefs who appear on national television, who are household names, or close to it.

MEASURING UP

When we proposed **How to Cook Everything: Bittman Takes on America's Chefs,** many chefs were taken by surprise. The concept was new and different and brash. Even some of those chefs who already knew me and (I think) liked me were put off by the idea. The more arrogant acted as if I were challenging Barry Bonds to a home run derby. Some of the less self-assured declined, saying, "Why would I put myself up against Mark and let him make me look like I don't know what I'm doing?"

But the TV show was meant to be fun (so is this book, though the recipes are dead serious, and really good), and was eventually seen that way. I cannot threaten the day-to-day position of any chef. Not only have I never run a restaurant, I have never been to cooking school or even worked in a restaurant, I cannot slice an onion in ten seconds with my eyes closed (neither could a few of our chefs, as I found out), and I certainly have no clue how to manage a staff. My cooking remains straightforward and very much home-style, requires little in the way of real skill, and can almost always be accomplished by a single person, working alone, with fairly little work and—in my case at least—an ever-wandering attention span. (Which turns out to be common. One of our chefs, Gary Danko claims that, "Chefs invented attention deficit disorder; if you're not multitasking in the kitchen, you can't get anything done.")

The show worked like this: Our chefs prepared a dish of their choice, as complicated as they liked, with as much help as they liked, and with whatever ingredients they liked. I followed with a dish that was somehow related—either in concept, spirit, main ingredient, or major flavor—working by myself, as a home cook, with "normal" ingredients and (for the most part, though this was not always possible), normal cookware.

Some chefs took the challenge as a one-on-one thing, and did almost all of the work themselves; this took a long time. If you look at Suzanne Goin's Stuffed Chicken "Poule au Pot" on page 104, you'll see a fairly complicated recipe. Since she worked with very little help, it took her almost all morning to prepare. Usually, in her kitchen, where she might be producing this dish a dozen times a night, it's a team effort. But watching her prepare it solo was very impressive.

Even the great Daniel Boulud, working by himself but with staff support (many of his ingredients were prepared ahead, and he called for new ones at will), spent hours on his dishes. He then proceeded to laugh as I assembled my dish in ten minutes, threw it in the oven, and went out for coffee.

Both of these chefs, and most of the others, teased me mercilessly while they were working (when I offered to dice an onion or brown something, my skills, or lack thereof, were called into question) and even more so when it was my turn. In their world, which smacks of the nineteenth century, one needs a long apprenticeship, or at least a cooking school degree, to pick the leaves off parsley; there's a right way and a wrong way to do everything. But I'd grown up seeing my grandmother hold a potato in one hand and use a butter knife, held in the other, to "chop" it, and I knew that did the job just fine.

There was no question about the chefs' dishes; they'd be terrific. (We handpicked these chefs, eating at scores of restaurants around the country to settle on the thirteen we ultimately chose.) We knew that Chris Schlesinger, Gary Danko, Jean-Georges Vongerichten, and other chefs (well) into their forties, those who'd been successful for decades, would produce great food and great television. We trusted, after much research, that relative newcomers like José Andrés, Gabrielle Hamilton, and Suzanne Goin would do the same, though they've only been on the national scene for a few years. Not surprisingly, we were right.

In fact, though I appeared confident, I was The Great Unknown Factor, and I knew it. Would my Pasta with Ham and Egg measure up to Gabrielle's Pasta Kerchiefs with Poached Egg, French Ham, and Brown Butter? Could I really create a dessert that could rival Jean-Georges's Apple Confit, one of the greatest desserts to grace the New York restaurant scene in the last ten years? Would I get laughed out of the kitchen when I cooked my lamb shoulder with parsley and garlic after watching Daniel stuff a saddle of lamb with exotic ingredients and lasso it like a cowboy?

The answers were mostly affirmative. My pasta measured up, as did my lamb, as did my apple dessert (Jean-Georges and I were both pleasantly surprised by that one), as did all of my dishes. I'm not saying that you'd be as happy paying thirty-five dollars for my roasted stuffed lamb shoulder as you would for Daniel's boned, stuffed, and tied saddle, but that you would be happy eating either.

And you might be happier cooking mine, because as I pointed out during each show, there are distinct advantages to home cooking. Almost always, my dish was faster. Almost always, it required less work (and little or no assistance). Almost always, it used fewer ingredients. And, perhaps most importantly, it required fewer skills. Duplicating chefs' dishes at home is rarely easy; sometimes it's not even feasible, though I do my best to make their recipes accessible to the home cook. And try as we might, no home cook is going to reproduce the look of a top restaurant dish, where the idea of a "garnish" is an assortment of baby vegetables, peeled and shaped, glazed in butter, and finished with reduced lamb stock. Really.

At some point during each show, the chefs would remember that almost anyone could put great flavors into food without a seven-million-dollar kitchen and an army of trained twenty-year-olds. They would start talking about their mother's or grandmother's cooking, or something they, too, used to enjoy cooking at home when they still did. (One of the dirty secrets about chefs is that many almost never cook at home.)

So if there was a point to be made, we made it. People will still go to restaurants for four-star food, and I hope they'll get it there. But my experience with the chefs continues what I've dedicated my professional life to proving: That home-cooked food, prepared by someone with few skills and just a bit of knowledge, can be not just acceptable but a brilliant alternative not only to all the crap that's out there—the fast food, the so-called convenience food, the stuff cooked in central kitchens and shipped to supermarkets in plastic buckets—but even to the really good food that's out there, the things that are prepared with love or at least care by dedicated professionals. People at home cannot cook at their level, but we can produce dishes that rival theirs; you can see that in these pages and on our show: It's as plain as a boiled egg.

I believed this from the start, but I still found the process intimidating, as an experienced hitter might feel every time he faces a great pitcher, or a good student feels before a tough exam. For this reason, we began taping the show in Massachusetts, with Chris Schlesinger, where I was comfortable with both location and chef.

CHRIS SCHLESINGER

I'd lived in Massachusetts for ten years, both in college and immediately afterwards. It was there I'd begun cooking seriously, largely because the food was so terrible I was forced to learn how to cook out of self-defense. And it was while I lived there that I first met Chris.

Chris's cooking is both creative and traditional; it can't be labeled, for which I respect him enormously. When in 1984 he first opened East Coast Grill, his Cambridge restaurant (and now,

improbably, among the oldest of this country's top restaurants; certainly the oldest of the ones at which we taped!), he specialized in a kind of updated southern food. He's from Virginia and made what were far and away the best smoked ribs the Northeast had ever seen. Now he's equally likely to sear tuna and serve it with his own pickled ginger. How do you classify cooking like that?

The East Coast Grill still defies categorization. It's funky, with few of the trappings of upscale restaurants, but damned good food. And its menu is so eclectic: Chris is not in the least bit Frenchified, but he offers oysters and sausage on the menu, a Bretagne staple that makes me drool. At the other end of the spectrum, he'll do shrimp like buffalo wings, and use ridiculously hokey slang like "catch o' the day."

When we cooked together, we began a couple of our long-running arguments—and not just for the camera. Unlike many chefs, Chris knows how to cook for people at home; I've seen him do it. But he maintains the typically perfectionist standards of a professional chef when he does so, an extremely difficult thing to do. And so he's devoted to grilling over wood, and scoffs at me because I use gas (I often throw in a few wood chips for flavor, but to him that's not the point; he likes the risk of incineration). For the cameras, I suppose, we both hammed this up, and the "argument" ended with him throwing me off the dock on which we were grilling.

MICHEL RICHARD

My feet wet in both senses of the phrase, we moved on to another chef I knew well: Michel Richard. Michel runs Citronelle, in the Georgetown section of Washington, DC, and his food comes not only from strict training and his heart, but another planet.

I don't remember the first time Michel and I met, but I do remember a charity event in Las Vegas, where seven of the country's most famous chefs—including Jean-Georges and Daniel Boulud—gathered to cook with Jean-Louis Palladin (since, sadly, departed). The food was incredible; at $250 per head, one might expect that. Jean-Louis acted as head chef, and the scene was frenetic. There were something like eighty guests, and each chef was working to turn out eighty perfect versions of his dish at once; not your typical banquet.

Everyone was working at his or her own station—the huge kitchen was packed—and pretty much ignoring one another. Michel was in charge of dessert, and had taken the challenge seriously, preparing an apple charlotte with poached pear and chocolate-Port sauce, along with a host of petits fours, each of which was a mind-blower. I worked with him for a while, and he had me cementing pairs of small pastry circles together, using egg yolk as the glue. That done, he showed me how to deep fry them, splashing their tops with hot oil until they puffed into small balloons. These, in turn, were rolled in butter, sugar, and nuts, and baked until crisp. This was a garnish!

As I was working with Michel, one by one the other chefs wandered over, until they had all gathered around to see what he was doing. And Jean-Georges said to me, quietly so as not to embarrass any of the others, "Michel is a wizard. Everyone in this room knows that his technique is the best, that no one can do what he does; he makes things no one can think of." Jean-Georges and I discussed this, and I've since talked about it with Michel, and pretty much everyone agrees that because Michel began his career as a pastry chef and then moved on to become a head chef—a very unusual pattern, almost unique in the field—he has a more imaginative, almost painterly approach. Plus he looks like Santa Claus and acts like an elf.

Fast-forward seven or eight years, and I was entering Michel's kitchen not as an assistant but as a would-be competitor. A laughable situation, really, and Michel's dishes—as you might expect—were inconceivably complex.

Or so they seemed, until he demonstrated them. His Lobster Burger (page 74; perhaps the best sandwich in the world at the moment) involves a number of different processes, but nothing especially challenging or unusual. His reconceived Layered Vitello Tonnato (page 50) is trickier, but manageable for the patient cook. His "Breakfast at Citronelle" (see sidebar, 227) is downright insane in its complexity and so funny it makes people laugh out loud; but, again, each element is achievable.

While he was cooking, Michel pranced around, hamming it up, baring his chest, harmlessly flirting with every woman he encountered, making fun of me, and generally acting as if there were a live audience, a real treat for our crew and his kitchen staff.

My complementary efforts—Lobster Roll, Turkey (Tonnato) Sandwiches, Spanish "French" Toast—were in the same spirit, but not on the same plane. At first this made me more than a little uptight, but when Michel bit into my lobster roll (little more than lobster and butter), his eyes lit up. And for the first time, I knew that our show's concept worked.

DANIEL BOULUD

This made me a little more confident at our next stop, the city of my birth and the most challenging place to cook in the United States: New York. Which was not to say I was comfortable: I had friends, associates, and relatives stopping by, and I was going to cook with Daniel Boulud, the starched-white, proper, old-fashioned epitome of a French chef, whose idea of letting it all hang out is not shaving for a couple of days. Though he's younger than Michel (and I), Daniel has a fearsome reputation.

And though I have known him for years, I have never found him exactly playful; I didn't know how he'd take to my teasing. But I did have a secret weapon: I know that he had a soft spot for real peasant food (we'd shared a pig's head at a meal cooked by Jean-Louis Palladin), and that's what I was planning to cook.

In the end, I barely got a chance to do anything. We'd scheduled six dishes, three by each of us (this was the intended plan with each of our chefs) but "one" of Daniel's dishes was four cuts of lamb, each prepared differently. It was a typically magnificent Restaurant Daniel offering: four dishes on one plate. I'd forgotten that when Daniel talks about accessible food, he means dishes that can be done in less than a day, with fewer than forty ingredients, only a modicum of help from others, and a budget of just a couple of hundred bucks.

As we taped, I proceeded to watch him take apart about half a lamb and perform wonders with it. Rather than Daniel and I each cooking three recipes, the episode was becoming The Daniel Boulud Hour. He did a saddle of lamb, a shoulder of lamb, a rack of lamb, and a leg of lamb, excellent recipes all, and each in fact pretty straightforward but for one or two components. His lamb stew (page 154), for example, contains peeled grapes. I remarked on this, and Daniel quipped, "Yes Mark, and if your readers would like to send me a check every month I'll be happy to send a few out to them." Thus I discovered that The Great Chef had a sense of humor, however sardonic.

Literally several hours later and without so much as a minute's break, it was my turn. And, as I implied, I had a trick up my sleeve: A boned shoulder (shoulder, to me, is the best cut of lamb, with more flavor and better texture than any other) stuffed, quite haphazardly, with the classic (and best!) lamb seasonings of all—garlic, parsley, salt, and olive oil.

Though I had to take grief from Daniel about my technique and the paucity of my ingredients, I also took a couple of good suggestions from him, especially in finishing the dish with pan-crisped bread crumbs, using the lamb "juices"—a euphemism for fat—to brown them, a marvelous touch that added a welcome dimension, and one that might never have occurred to me. In the end, Daniel pronounced my spare dish worthy of eating; in fact, as I'd presumed, he would happily eat it any time.

FINDING MORE CHEFS UP FOR THE CHALLENGE

At this point in mid-October, we paused taping the show so that I could scout other chefs with whom we could tape. To me, Chris, Michel, and Daniel had been easy choices, and there were only a couple of other chefs on our grand list who fell into that category.

For the rest, I had to talk with them, eat with them, even cook with them. We were looking for chefs who were not only great cooks but articulate, interesting, and fun. I traveled back to Washington and Boston, to Chicago (twice), and just about the length of the West Coast, from Seattle to south of L.A.

My moods varied from excitement to enervation. My nights were late, my diet necessarily rich (I got so sick of foie gras—not that I expect your sympathy—that I declared it "dead and finished"), my personal time almost nil. The pressure was enormous; choose the wrong chef and I could look forward to a disappointed producer and crew, and a potentially lousy episode of the show.

The easy decision would have been to choose the thirteen most famous chefs in America and call it a day. But taping three shows had shown me the importance of the unpredictable chemistry between each of the chefs and me. There was an increasing sense that our show could be something different, a cooking show with a sense of humor and an edge, a kind of Julia Child meets Larry David, with myself and the chefs performing both roles. In other words, I had to find talented, successful chefs who would not only willingly play along but be good at it; and, of course, their food had to be terrific.

Actually, the last was the easy part. During the course of this month, I ate as well, with as much variation, as I ever had. I checked out Thai, Mexican, and Vietnamese chefs, encountering not only language difficulties but also the problem of family restaurants where there was no real "chef" to identify. I also ate French, Italian, and "new American" food until I could no longer tell the difference; many menus and decors came from the same mold, regardless of the restaurant's stated identity.

Slowly, the priorities became clear, as did the choices. I set up a western swing that included three people cooking in different eclectic American styles; one successful veteran of California cuisine; and a Vietnamese chef, Charles Phan, who runs what might be the most successful Asian restaurant in the United States.

CHARLES PHAN

That successful restaurant is The Slanted Door, which Charles opened a few years ago in San Francisco's Mission District. I've probably written as much about San Francisco restaurants as any East Coaster, and I was an early fan of the restaurant, largely because it overcomes the challenges inherent in Vietnamese food, which—despite its reputation as the French cuisine of Southeast Asia—is pretty limited.

Charles himself is anything but. Born in Vietnam of Chinese immigrants, his family fled during the fall of Saigon in 1975. After several weeks aboard a ship docked outside Singapore, they eventually made their way to Guam and, from there, a couple of years later, to San Francisco. His father worked at an English-style pub (as did Charles when he was young) while the rest of the family went into clothing manufacture, a business still operating in the Mission.

Charles was smart and ambitious enough to attend UC Berkeley and, after spending time in the building trades (he oversaw the construction of the newest version of the Slanted Door), architecture (he designs his restaurants too), and pottery (he doesn't throw his own plates, but he does choose them), he decided to do for Asian food "what Alice Waters did for American."

Like I said, he's ambitious. When Charles moved the restaurant out of the Mission and onto the Embarcadero, a location more acceptable to less-young, less-hip patrons, it became one of the hottest reservations in town. When I visited him in the fall of 2003, he was busy building a new space in the renovated Ferry Building (the vast pre-1906 structure through which walked the vast majority of those who arrived in San Francisco before air travel), re-establishing himself in the Mission, cooking every day, running a restaurant that was doing many hundreds of covers a night, and acting as patriarch (he employs eighteen family members).

I was excited about cooking with Charles not only because I like him but because, though Asian food was my first love and my travels to Vietnam were among the high points of my life, I knew that, as weak as my "normal" cooking techniques were, my expertise with traditional Asian technique was virtually non-existent. I was fascinated by the roaring woks at Slanted Door, and couldn't wait to get behind one of them where, I thought, I would really stir-fry for the first time.

Well, forget that. Stir-frying in the real woks of the restaurant world is not for amateurs; the heat source is, and I'm not kidding, about the same size as that of your average seventy-five-gallon hot water heater. Charles knew how tricky it could be, and eagerly installed me behind a wok, where he gloated while I instantly burned everything in sight. There is a real rhythm and skill set to cooking at this kind of heat, and believe me, none of us is ever going to get it without going to work for Charles, or someone like him.

I surmounted the challenge by reverting to my normal stir-frying technique, which involves cooking in batches over normally high heat. This tactic turns out to be pretty much what the wok-cookers do, only with a lot more control. And I felt a little less insecure when Charles disclosed that he cooks this way whenever he's away from the restaurant's super-woks.

This was not the only challenge in store for me at The Slanted Door. Charles, who is as fond of super-high heat as Chris Schlesinger, has a massive wood-burning grill in the restaurant, which he maintains at about 700°F, or so hot that you can't hold your hand over it even for a second. He expertly and quickly used it to grill a marinated rack of lamb (page 158), and it was all I could to follow up with a simple grilled squid with Vietnamese flavors. In fact, I was overwhelmed by the intensity of the heat on this grill, and though I managed to grill the squid nicely, it was, quite literally, a painful experience. Compared to these two near-disasters, doing summer rolls with Charles (page 42) was a walk in the park.

Despite his teasing (his favorite line, repeated several times off camera, was, "I guess you had plenty of practice with rolling in college, huh?"), we were both pleasantly surprised at my summer roll skills; in this, at least, I'd had practice (see page 43). When it was all over, Charles asked whether I had Asian blood; high and welcome praise, I thought. I left there aglow, though I think in part it was heat stroke.

GARY DANKO

We stayed in the Bay Area for the remainder of that week, and I went to work with Gary Danko, whose restaurant, which bears his name, is usually ranked as the best upscale establishment in the city. It's the kind of place that makes people feel pampered; a lovely room with delicious, carefully prepared food, beautiful flowers, brilliant service, and comfortable seats.

I respect Gary not only for his skills at putting this place together, and for his wonderful palate, but for his teaching ability. He is more articulate than most chefs, more thoughtful, and less myth-bound. He can explain not only the science and technique behind the reasons for doing things the way he chooses to do them, but his feelings about them. (Getting most chefs to talk about their feelings is akin, I imagine, to getting football players to do the same; at least I haven't been able to get many of them to do so.)

Gary gave me a lesson in cooking duck that made me feel like a novice. Though my Crisp-Braised Duck Legs (page 122) are a personal favorite that I have served to many people and prepare with confidence, he spent a couple of hours working a duck over until he'd covered a plate with duck confit hash, seared breast, duck cracklings, and duck essence, (pages 116-120) a majestic dish that perfectly suits his restaurant and can still be done, by the patient cook, at home .

Meanwhile, we talked—about the right amount of salt to use and when to use it, about using your ears to know when food is done, about duck, knives, fish, and the process of thinking through a dish before cooking it—shop talk, I guess, but informative and instructive. Gary not only knows how to cook, he knows how to talk, and intelligently.

The conversation continued on our trip to the Napa Valley, where Gary is really in his element.

He has been cooking in the area for twenty years, and he knows as much about local ingredients as anyone. Non-Californians, myself included, may scoff at the locals' insistence that their products are better and more varied, but spend any time cooking out there and you quickly become a convert.

Even in late October, Gary and I marveled at the bounty of the gardens and orchards at Villa Mille Rose, where our hostess, Maria Manetta Farrow, was gracious enough to let us set up shop.

Ms. Manetti, a woman gracious enough to call me handsome, has baroque taste in furniture and decorating and has a fantastic kitchen. Two kitchens, actually—a work kitchen that is lovely in itself and a bigger, perfectly equipped kitchen with a twelve-foot fireplace replete with electric spit and good, dry wood.

She also farms olives, persimmons, walnuts, almonds, figs, and just about everything else you can grow there, which is a lot. And she collects—and drinks—suitably good wine.

From Gary, I got lessons on pomegranates, kiwis, persimmons, olives, and grapes. Of course every time a cook visits the source of his ingredients there are things to be learned, but in Gary's company the information came as a flood.

We cooked our poultry—Gary, quail; me, chicken—over an open fire in Maria's enormous kitchen. Gary grilled his quail on an iron rack set above the open fire, but I put my chicken in a sauté pan over the fire—I didn't want to lose anything—and indoor wood-grilling is not something that most of us can do.

Things were going to be different in L.A., my next stop. Until now, I had cooked with males only and, with the exception of Charles, men my age. Although Daniel and Michel are Frenchmen, we have a fair amount in common, including mutual friends and some shared history. Plus we have known each other for ten to fifteen years.

SUZANNE GOIN

Here, I was about to cook with Suzanne Goin, one of the rising stars not only of West Coast but national cuisine. Suzanne is twenty years younger than I, ten times more successful than I was at her age (she runs two restaurants, Lucques and A.O.C., and both have been packed every time I've gone), better looking, and a woman.

I wasn't intimidated by her cooking; in fact, I was initially worried that, in its earthiness and simplicity, it was too much like my own, though that turned out to be unwarranted: It was plenty complicated. But it's harder, for me at least, to joust with a woman than a man. Suzanne immediately relieved this tension when she announced, before preparing her first recipe—the ultimate bread pudding (page 218)—that "a good dessert is slutty," a remark my prudishness would probably have kept me from making even if I believed it.

Her bread pudding was typical of top-notch restaurants: It began with making brioche. Only an elite restaurant of our era would even consider the absurdity of making the best possible bread in order to make the best possible bread pudding, a dessert that only exists (or did until recently) to use up leftover bread. And Suzanne's (admittedly wonderful) bread pudding continued from there, until it was no longer recognizable as what I'd call bread pudding.

I love creativity—when it works—but I usually prefer food that is what it's supposed to be. Some things, like bread pudding, pizza, and macaroni and cheese, should remain limited. Put homemade brioche in the first, sliced truffles on the second, or lobster in the third, and what you get may be great, but it's gilding the lily. Call me old-fashioned, but my bread pudding was a bunch of torn-up bread baked with a sweetened egg-and-milk mixture. Suzanne didn't care what I thought; she just blithely proceeded to make the best bread pudding imaginable.

And it was really the least complicated of her dishes. Like many of the new American cooks, Suzanne believes that restaurant food should be the ultimate version of classic peasant dishes.

This explains why I had originally believed her food would be too much like my own; it sounds like my own. (And it is like my own, only taken to another dimension.)

After baking the bread puddings (which included a rather hilarious dispute about water baths, see page 221), Suzanne tackled her Stuffed Chicken "Poule au Pot," which I mentioned earlier. Along with Gary's duck extravaganza, this probably vied for the most elaborate dish of the entire series, and it was a beauty. I was able to counter with a simply stuffed chicken breast, which was roundly enjoyed as a minor relative—exactly my goal.

At that point we retreated to Suzanne's small, attractive house in the Hollywood hills, where we were going to finish Grilled Pork Confit (page 166), a recipe she'd begun a day or two earlier. While she was setting that up, I was nearly panicking about my dish.

Grilling pork was something I could do pretty well, but we already had done a straightforward one with Chris, and cooking "against" Suzanne had a different feel to it. I don't remember what dish I had planned to do to counter her pork—which involved brining a shoulder, then "confiting" it in a combination of duck and pork fat, and finally grilling it (a great dish for a summer cookout, as long as you have plenty of advance time and energy)—but I knew it wasn't going to cut it.

The problem with grilling pork shoulder is that to get it tender you have to set up an elaborate indirect grilling system (not unlike what Chris Schlesinger does with his ribs) and be prepared to wait for a few hours. It's great, but there was no time for that (not only was it getting dark, we had a schedule to keep). Furthermore, because we were no longer at the restaurant but at Suzanne's home, my options and resources were limited; her kitchen was well equipped but her cupboards and fridge nearly bare. (Remember when I wrote that few chefs cook at home? Suzanne's home kitchen is akin to that of a disinterested bachelor.)

I decided to mimic her dish, simply and quickly. I began to wing it. While Suzanne was gently warming the fat in which she would dunk her brined pork, I cut my piece of shoulder into chunks and braised it with whatever I could find in Suzanne's house, plus whatever I could steal from her preparations. Once I started opening cupboards, it turned out there was plenty of stuff, and soon I had a nice braise going on top of the stove, one that included a couple of bottles of dark beer, which gave off a sweet, yeasty aroma that contrasted beautifully with that of the meat. When it was tender, I browned it over the dying coals of the grill, and, at dusk, we all—Suzanne, myself, the crew, and a couple of hangers-on—feasted on meat and side dishes, a long and successful day concluded.

JAMES BOYCE

At twilight, we drove down to Laguna Beach, to the kind of resort we all dream about, a place called Montage, right on the beach. Though we might have agreed to cook at Montage if Hannibal Lecter ran the kitchen, we were here because its restaurant, Studio, is run by the talented and distinctly non-homicidal James Boyce, whom I'd met about six months earlier. James had received some national acclaim and Studio was doing well, but the nature of things means that even a destination restaurant in Laguna Beach is not going to get the same kind of attention as a similar place in a major city.

I was lucky to find him, and not only because I like his food, which features international flavors combined in very logical, "French" ways. He'd worked, years ago, with Daniel Boulud and, like many of Daniel's disciples, he has a brilliant palate, one that rarely leads him wrong. He can put together a dish like skate with *beurre noisette,* dates, preserved lemon, and fresh porcini—which at first sounded to me like an utter hodgepodge, the kind of thing clueless chefs do when given access to too many ingredients—and make it memorable. (In fact, this was the dish that made me fall in love with James's food.) To cater to a largely wealthy, conservative, counter-hip clientele (Orange County is the part of California that feels most like Florida), and deliver praiseworthy and innovative food…well, I had to admire that.

There were other things about James and Studio that made the visit appealing. Both restaurant and kitchen are gorgeous. Picture the most spectacular restaurant kitchen you've ever seen in a Caribbean-like setting, overlooking the beach. The interior of the restaurant is perfectly nice, but when the weather is good enough to allow you to sit outside, the whole situation is idyllic.

I liked this. Did you think I was stupid? (Maybe I am; not too many days later I was trudging through the slush to cook in a tiny, cramped kitchen on New York's Lower East Side.)

Plus, James is funny, witty, sarcastic, and self-deprecating. At about forty, he's cooked all over the country and—the Daniel credential will do this—with the best. He's seen and lived through the dark, difficult side of restaurant life: the repeated sixteen-hour days, the overeating, and the alcoholism, and he's willing to talk about it. And he's come out the other side, to become a man who values life and lives it, who works really hard and cares deeply about the quality of his work, but also knows that a good bike ride at eleven in the morning may be more important than haggling with the fish guy.

We had a great time, as one does at resorts. James and I woke up early and went for a swim in the Pacific, which was labeled cold by the locals (it was the same temperature as the North Atlantic in July). After warming up in the hot tub, we went to a yoga class, largely for the cameras; each of us has the flexibility of a new dress shoe.

And after James made truffle-laden scrambled eggs for me and the crew, we went to work. The cooking was fun, or would have been, were it not for James's furnace of a stove, some $100,000 job imported from France, which could have doubled as a smelter. Simply putting a pan on the flattop turned my arm bright red; by the end of the morning, I had little hair left on my right arm. I recalled the stories of the ironworkers wearing many layers of clothing in order to keep their body temperatures at 98.6 degrees, because the alternative was so much hotter, so I switched to wearing long sleeves, as did the chef (he complained about it even more than I did).

James made his skate dish, which I happily ate, even though it was only 10 a.m. and the memory of the eggs was fresh. I countered with a pared-down version of same. He produced a lovely halibut and white beans, a kind of fish cassoulet, and I mimicked it with well-seasoned scallops on quick-cooked lentils. Finally, he devised a contemporary surf-and-turf, featuring a superb lobster salad, and I made a Thai-style beef-and-shrimp salad of which I was more than a little proud. No one was in a rush to leave idyllic Laguna, but our next stop was Las Vegas and we were driving. It was time to hit the road.

KERRY SIMON

In Vegas, we were to cook with Kerry Simon, an old friend who was Jean-Georges Vongerichten's sous-chef back in the eighties, when all of us were just getting started. Kerry was a part of Jean-Georges's break-out period at Lafayette, where vegetable juices, infused oils, and exotic ingredients—especially Asian ones (Jean-Georges lived in Asia for five years before moving to the States)—began to enter the mainstream of upscale restaurants.

In the late nineties, Kerry, Jean-Georges, and I traveled to Thailand, Vietnam, and China together, and it was the kind of bonding experience one never forgets. Like Jean-Georges (and myself), Kerry has a particular fondness for Asian flavors, and there was no way I was going to do a cooking series featuring "America's top chefs" without him, especially since his restaurant— Simon Kitchen and Bar—is one of the few Vegas joints in which the famous chef in the name actually spends time in the kitchen.

By now, I knew what I was doing—or at least I thought I did—and with Kerry there was no need for a feeling-out period. We knew what to expect, and since he began teasing me about my

cooking ten years ago, he needed little prodding from Charlie to deride my technique, ingredients, and even equipment. (We were traveling with pots and pans that were part of a line designed by Jamie Oliver, with his name on them. Since Mr. Oliver is presumably a competitor of mine, this was seen as bizarre. But I didn't care; the pans were as good as any I'd ever owned, so I kept using them.) I was so mellow from my time in Laguna I decided to regard Kerry's caustic comments as signs of love.

Kerry did an Asian-flavored beef tartare (page 138), typical of his style, and fantastic; I responded with a barely-cooked burger with classic tartare spices (page 140). He conjured up a magnificent plate of tandoori-style salmon (page 78), bypassing the making of his tandoori paste, which probably takes one of his cooks two days to assemble, and I some thinly sliced salmon slices with chickpea raita (page 80). (That raita has become a staple in the kitchen of everyone who's tried it, so be sure to check it out.) Finally, he summoned his pastry chef (don't think I didn't ride him about that; as I've said, many chefs have no clue when it comes to desserts) to make an extravagant banana cake with several toppings (page 212). My counteroffer couldn't have been simpler: frozen banana on a stick (page 216). (Thank you, Ms. Smith.)

Though I've never liked Vegas, I decided that in these circumstances it was an experience to be savored. While this did not mean I was about to start gambling or hanging out with showgirls, I did go with the flow more than usual. And when I found myself standing in the heavily planted median right on the Strip opposite the Bellagio, with three cameras focused on me, and a producer who was ruthlessly readjusting the city's lighting system to provide us with enough illumination to shoot my standup narrative, I became downright giddy, as if I'd become a part of all the surreal fakery around me. Afterwards, we bar-hopped through a couple of hotels, ate some really bad food that was supposed to be good, and began to plan the rest of the show, to be taped back east.

Where, in the course of our two-week absence, it had become winter. Yet a new set of hazards surfaced in this unfolding adventure.

GABRIELLE HAMILTON

Strolling down Melrose Boulevard or the boardwalk on Laguna is one thing; navigating Orchard Street filthy with snow in sub-freezing weather is another. But there I was on a December afternoon, after spending the morning cooking with Gabrielle Hamilton at Prune, a tiny Lower East Side restaurant that would fit neatly in James Boyce's kitchen.

I was insistent that we include Gabrielle in the show; although we are nearly twenty years apart in age, in cooking and eating we are soul mates. If I were running a restaurant, I would want it to be much like Prune. This is not to say it's the best restaurant in the country in my opinion (or in Gabrielle's, for that matter) but that it is real, and you know exactly where the food is coming from.

There's more to my history with Gabrielle: When my younger daughter, Emma, was nine, she went to a summer camp in the Berkshires. If you don't know what the food is like at summer camps, picture a boarding school with no budget and you've just about got it. So when it came time for "parents' lunch" on the day we dropped off Emma, I figured we'd have some greasy salami on bad Massachusetts bread with bright yellow mustard, and stop at McDonald's on the way home; I saw that as a step up.

When I approached the buffet, though, I was stunned: There were Vietnamese summer rolls, couscous salad with apricots and pine nuts, pasta with arugula, a good-smelling meat stew, a potato salad that looked promising, real desserts…I can't remember what else, but enough to blow me away. When I marched into the kitchen and asked who was responsible for this, I was introduced to Gabrielle Hamilton. She'd taken the job as a lark, to see what she could do with mass production and no money. (Emma had one of the great summers of her life, and I swear Gabrielle had more to do with what will undoubtedly become a lifelong love of food than I ever could have. You have to hate what your parents do, after all, don't you?)

I had been worried at first that Gabrielle's simple cooking and tiny Lower East Side restaurant would pale in comparison to the elaborate cooking and glamorous establishments of some of the other chefs. But there is so much life in what Gabrielle does, and her food is so instantly likable—she really cooks from the heart—that I was really looking forward to this one.

So we crammed the crew and their equipment into a space the size of your bedroom (unless you have a big one), while Gabrielle and I cooked in a space the size of your kitchen (unless, ditto). Bearing in mind that she spends a third of her life in this space, I kept my mouth shut. I don't know how she does it, but somehow she and her staff produce great food for a hundred people or so a night without murdering one another.

For the two of us, it was easy. Gabrielle made fresh pasta and cooked flat squares of it ("handkerchiefs") with poached eggs, ham, and arugula (page 178), a regal dish and one I especially like late at night. I followed up with dried pasta with ham and egg (page 180), a simpler but equally legitimate version that she liked enough to threaten to add to her menu.

Her duck breast pastrami omelet with rye crumbs (page 132) recalled my youth's Lower East Side dish of salami and eggs (page 134; I grew up in this neighborhood), so I prepared that, for probably the first time in twenty years, after a quick (and very cold) run over to Katz's (a classic deli in business since 1888), where the garlic-laden salami is as good as I remember it. Finally, she demonstrated a bar dish of pickled shrimp (page 46), and I a tapa of shrimp cooked in olive oil and garlic (page 48). We actually clashed over mojitos (pages 56 and 58; I believe mine, though not exactly traditional, is the best), but once the crew started drinking those the shoot was over.

JOSÉ ANDRÉS

Then back to DC—this time to cook with José Andrés, a young Spaniard whom I'd met a few years ago when pursuing a story—as all dutiful food writers must—about Ferran Adrià, the eccentric, intense, ultra-creative chef of El Bulli, a restaurant outside of Barcelona that for a while was proclaimed the world's best. No matter what you think about his food, Adrià is indisputably fascinating: He closes his restaurant for half the year and experiments, coming up with things like Parmesan ice cream, raw egg in gelatin, drinks made of mushrooms, squid ravioli wrapped around coconut milk, and wafers of deep-fried chicken feet.

José is a protégé of Ferran's. Like him, José can cook traditional food, and very well. Unlike Ferran, he is running a number of commercially successful restaurants in addition to working daily on what he calls, simply, "creative cuisine." The first day, José and I prepared two different versions of paella—his vast and grand, mine small and humble—and a couple of lovely crab dishes.

The next morning, bright and early, we gathered upstairs at Café Atlantico, at the six-seat bar José has dubbed the Mini Bar, a kind of sushi bar where the "sushi" are tiny dishes prepared *à la minute* by a team of three chefs, one of whom is often José himself. Given that there are six seats, the chef-to-client ratio rivals that of any place in the world (though I do believe at El Bulli it approaches one-to-one). You sit at the bar and, leisurely but without much pause, the chefs ply you with dishes…like forty dishes.

And before José and I cooked our last dish together, I was to eat all forty for the cameras.

I wasn't exactly dreading this.

Yet by about 9 a.m., I was cranky from hunger (yes, I admit it), eager to begin (and finish; a snowstorm was on the way, and we were scheduled to be back in New York that night), and José was nowhere in sight. It turned out he was cooking "properly fried" eggs—José's arrogance makes me look like a shrinking violet—some croissants with ham, and *torrijas* (page 230) for the crew. Starving (I use the word freely), I had what I thought were a few bites, but what really amounted to not only a full but a luxurious breakfast by most standards—even my own—only to find that the crew was now ready to begin shooting and José's team had readied the Mini Bar. On a full stomach, I then proceeded to eat (and nearly finish):

- "Cones" of tomato and basil; tuna and sesame; lox, capers, onions, and cream cheese; avocado and tomato sorbet; trout roe
- Watermelon with balsamic vinegar and olive oil; with tomato seeds; with balsamic and trout roe; with Parmigiano-Reggiano
- Foie gras with cotton candy; with corn; with chocolate truffle and tamarind
- Jicama rolls with tuna; with salmon and orange powder; with avocado; with tomato and Altoids (yes, grated on top); with tuna, sesame, nori, and soy gelatin; with apples and *cabrales* (Spanish blue cheese)
- Oranges and limes with radish sprouts; watermelon and mint with Campari gelatin; crabmeat, avocado, sesame seeds, and nori
- Deconstructed Caesar salad (I can't remember this one but I believe I drank it)
- "Injections" (you squirt liquid from a plastic ampoule directly into your mouth, while eating, for example, some tomato), one of tomato with mozzarella soup and basil, the other of lobster américaine
- Mango "ravioli," with anchovy mousse; with trout roe; with avocado and chile pepper
- Jicama "ravioli," with guacamole; with tuna seviche; with salmon
- Pineapple "ravioli," with avocado and plantain powder; with trout roe; with cured salmon and crispy quinoa
- Hot and cold asparagus soups with dill
- Sardines in bread
- Conch fritters with a liquid center
- Potato mousse with American caviar and vanilla
- Tuna with rice mousse, crispy rice, and soy sauce
- Caviar with avocado
- Guacamole with tomato sorbet

- Deconstructed New England clam chowder
- Meat and potatoes

Even the last of these (I count forty-two, though José might have omitted a couple out of pity, or I might have forgotten a couple out of food-induced stupor) was not what it sounds like. I believe it was a frothy mousse of potatoes with a few nicely cooked slices of rare tenderloin on top. The clam chowder, I think, was a clam with a potato and some bacon and whipped cream. To tell you the truth, my head was spinning, and I am what I like to think of as a veteran eater.

José then dazzled me with a few insane proclamations. I believe he announced that Spanish olive oil is "healthier" than any other; that Spanish salt is "saltier" than that sold in the States; that Antonio Adrià, Ferran's brother, is "the greatest chef in the world, no question about it"; and that I was a pain in the neck for countering these claims (this last is true of course, though not for that particular reason). But then, in making his Deconstructed Gazpacho (page 34) he dazzled me with something I'd never seen before: tomato seeds.

Well, not that I'd never seen tomato seeds. But I'd spent much of my career arguing against chefs who insisted that, of the three parts that made up a tomato—skin, seeds, and flesh—the first two were to be discarded whenever practical, because they were bitter or didn't taste good or were of objectionable consistency.

My position, as a home cook, was that (a) the seeds tasted just fine, if you ask me and (b) the skin and seeds were a hassle to remove, so why bother unless absolutely necessary? (It goes further than this, of course. By insisting that home cooks skin and seed tomatoes, most chefs make their recipes unnecessarily inaccessible, forgetting, as is their wont, that home cooks don't have free or $6-an-hour apprentices to peel and seed their tomatoes.)

Now here comes this chef who is intentionally serving the seeds as if they were jewels! José figured out that you can remove the seed packets intact, and they retain their integrity. When you

plop them on a plate, they look like little pouches of caviar and, they taste, not surprisingly, like tomato. I'd be shocked if this were the first time this has been done, and neither is it the first time a hotshot chef has taken a normally rejected ingredient and served it. But this is the equivalent of serving parsley stems or cabbage cores…and it works.

I was impressed. José is a windbag, and even more of a pain in the neck than me, but I love him—he's funny, generous, smart, and talented—and he really knows what he's doing. I left DC in a great mood, which I managed to maintain despite enduring a seven-hour drive back to New York, through what turned out to be the storm of the year on the East Coast.

ANNA KLINGER

I grew up just a few miles from our next stop—Park Slope, Brooklyn—but it was across the river, and when I was young, Brooklyn might as well have been Newark. Or Pittsburgh. Manhattan was affordable then, a place where working-class families didn't think twice about living and, though my parents were both born and raised in "the boroughs"—my dad in the Bronx, my mom all over the city (I believe she lived in every borough but one)—to me, they were places where one went for two reasons: unwillingly, to visit relatives, or willingly, to go to Coney Island or other beaches.

So the first time I took the subway to Al di Là, to chat with Anna Klinger and her Italian husband Emiliano, I got off at the wrong stop and ended up walking about three miles through an industrial zone that was visually interesting (in fact I took pictures) but definitely wrong. It was August, and ninety degrees, and I was late; not fun. Once I cooled down a bit, I fell in love with the young couple and their infant son, Sasha. Their attitude was at once adorable and efficient; Emiliano compared running the restaurant to running a ship, and he would be a good captain.

By the time Anna and I cooked together, I had my subway act straightened out and the temperature had fallen fifty or sixty degrees.

It was now the New Year (2004) and the snow was mostly gone, but there was a steady, light drizzle and near-freezing temperatures, which made getting around fairly unpleasant. Inside Al di Là, however, it was cozy and even dreamy. Because we were cooking Italian food, and because we kept it pretty simple, we accomplished everything in one day.

At first, I was more than a little reluctant to include Italian cooking on the show, for a number of reasons. I first traveled to Italy in 1976, about the same time I began writing about food and, like all my friends and colleagues, was astonished by how wonderful true Italian food was. (I still remember my first bowl of mussels and my first plate of linguine all'Amatriciana in Rome.)

But at this point almost anything I say about Italy will sound canned and trite, largely because much of cooking in America is now focused on Italian cooking. Not that there's anything wrong with that, and it's certainly an improvement on a steady diet of beef stew and American chop suey (a Massachusetts specialty of overcooked macaroni with overcooked tomato sauce and ground beef), but to me it seems that a disproportionately large percentage of all cookbooks and cooking shows and even discussion about food is Italian oriented. And, as we know, there are other cuisines to explore; even French food feels underrated now.

By winter, however, after taping on and off for four months, after exploring a number of different cuisines, and after being about as adventuresome as I care to be (I'm guessing you're going to be blown away by some of the recipes in the following pages), I began to see the appeal of a plate of pasta and some pan-roasted chicken, not just to eat (I'd never stopped eating this food) but to talk about.

And Anna was a perfect choice. Her restaurant is like home, the ideal neighborhood place that's so good that people travel to it from out of the neighborhood (I have several friends in Manhattan who eat at Al di Là routinely). The dish I most wanted to cook with Anna was her ribs, which are braised and then grilled, but I had been through that routine with Suzanne and felt we had enough pork on the show (and in this book) to satisfy any carnivore.

So we began with my second favorite of her dishes, a complex and wonderful beet ravioli (page 172). This dish itself can be simplified, but I chose to follow up with pasta and cabbage (page 174), a related preparation I'd been craving to cook (and eat) for a couple of weeks.

Next came Anna's rustic Braised Rabbit with Olives (page 128); I made Chicken alla Cacciatora (page 130), a dish in the same spirit, but a little more straightforward. The food was so good we didn't break for lunch, but went straight into dessert, a simple pear-chocolate cake (page 222) on Anna's part and, from me, Poached Pears with Chocolate Sauce (page 224). It was a great day of winter cooking.

SUVIR SARAN

I was glad things went so smoothly, because the following day we were cooking again, this time with Suvir Saran, a young Indian chef whose restaurant, Amma, was the talk of the town. It's located in a real hole-in-the-wall in midtown Manhattan—if anything a bit smaller than Prune—but that didn't stop Suvir and his co-chef, Hemant Mathur, from installing a real tandoor oven, and it sure as hell didn't stop them from preparing the best Indian food I've had in the States.

Suvir had been in the back of my mind from the beginning, but I hadn't had a chance to eat at Amma until just before Christmas, when New York is at its crowded and cold worst. (The crowded and hot summer isn't so great either, but nothing beats the couple of weeks before Christmas, when tourists outnumber residents, or so it seems.) On that day, the streets packed with filthy snow, I wandered around the city, hitting three different restaurants in hopes of one of them working out. Amma was the obvious choice; in fact my companions and I agreed it was mind-blowing.

As this isn't a restaurant review, I won't bore you with the details, but let's just say that it was difficult to figure out what to cook with Suvir, because so many of the dishes were delicious, unusual and, as it turned out, not especially difficult. We settled on his Manchurian-style cauliflower (made with a ton of ketchup, yes!), his amazing fried okra salad (though his crunchy spinach salad is just as good) with tandoori prawns, and a lamb *paratha* (page 186). I countered with stir-fried cauliflower, Indian-style, sautéed okra with shrimp, and a funky tortilla stuffed with mashed potatoes (page 188), a kind of simplified *aloo* (potato) paratha that Suvir assured me was not unlike a "frankie," something they serve on the streets of Bombay.

I've not been to Bombay, but I have spent a little time in northern India, and I remain astonished at how few inroads Indian cooking has made in the States, especially given how simple it is. Of course I believe, and long have, that the daily food of every country, the food that people cook at home, is simple enough to be replicated in the American kitchen by anyone with a few skills. It isn't only Italian food that you just throw in the oven; when you think about it, there are only a few basic cooking techniques, and they're used by everyone around the globe.

Much Indian cooking is, in fact, dead easy, and you get more flavor per minute of work than you do in many cuisines, thanks to the skillful use of spices. Given that many of these spice mixes can be premade or even bought (the *chaat masala* that is the "secret" ingredient in Suvir's fried okra is an Indian equivalent of Old Bay or Mr. Salt, only better tasting), I just don't get why people are intimidated.

Cooking with Suvir reinforced this notion. We breezed through the dishes, each enjoying one another's cooking, both impressed by how much flavor we were coaxing out of a few ingredients. Suvir is from an upper-crust Indian family, but has lived in the States since he was quite young (he's just into his thirties now), so part of this may be that he has a different, less traditional attitude toward cooking, that he "gets" that today's cooks are impatient and more interested in flavor than in tradition.

JEAN-GEORGES VONGERICHTEN

Speaking of which. It was time for our grand finale, and we were set to finish as I had begun, teaming up with Jean-Georges. Having said enough about him and our partnership, the cooking itself is easy to describe. Jean-Georges began with one of his classic made-on-the-spot spice and nut mixes for fish, prepared a mushroom-based broth, and simply browned the fish and served it in the broth; it was a typical Jean-Georges recipe, one that could be pared down or jazzed up, one that had flavor combinations that you would not find elsewhere, and one that worked perfectly.

The vaguely Asian nature of that preparation encouraged me to look back to a recipe I'd devised for my first book, *Fish,* in which I'd used plain sesame seeds to give a fish fillet a super-crunchy sauce. I finished the dish, as I describe on page 93, with a sauce inspired by Jean-Georges, a combination of soy sauce and butter that I knew he'd love.

We then played around with candy-coated poultry (why should José Andrés have all the fun?), he using Jordan almonds and squab (page 124), I employing Red Hots and Cornish hens (page 126); both dishes are easy, and both are worth trying (really!). We finished, at my insistence, with his Apple Confit (page 208), one of my favorite all-time desserts, and my Tartless "Tarte Tatin" (page 210), a not dissimilar dish on which I'd been working all fall, and one that Jean-Georges (to my delight) found successful.

Pleasing him was not the goal of the show or of this book or even of that day, but it was a nice way to finish things off. Though I'd expected a sense of relief at ending the near-constant travel and pressure, there were many aspects of the show I'd loved—the camaraderie, the challenge, the learning.

I'm ready to have at 'em again.

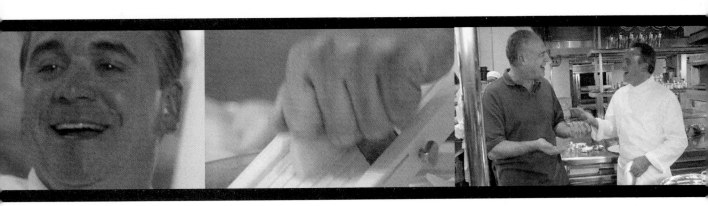

THE CHEFS AND THE DISHES

NEW YORK

Al di Là
248 5th Avenue Brooklyn, NY 11215 718-636-8888

Anna Klinger	**Mark**
Beet Ravioli with Butter and Poppy Seeds (*Casunziei*)	>> Pasta with Savoy Cabbage
Braised Rabbit with Olives	>> Chicken alla Cacciatora
Chocolate Pear Cake	>> Poached Pears with Chocolate Sauce

Jean-Georges
1 Central Park West New York, NY 10023 212-299-3900

Jean-Georges Vongerichten	**Mark**
Sea Bass Fillets with Mushroom Beurre Noisette	>> Sesame-Crusted Fish with Soy, Butter, and Ginger Sauce
Broiled Squab with Jordan Almonds	>> Broiled Cornish Hens with Red Hots
Apple Confit	>> Tartless "TartTatin"

Devi
8 East18th Street New York, NY 10003 212-691-1300

Suvir Saran	**Mark**
Manchurian-Style Cauliflower (*Lahsuni Gobi*)	>> Indian-Style Cauliflower Stir-Fry
Tandoori Shrimp Crispy Okra Salad (*Kararee Bhindi*)	>> Stir-Fried Shrimp with Okra and Lime
Parathas Stuffed with Lamb, Chiles, and Cilantro (*Keema Ke Parathe*)	>> Faux Potato (Aloo) Paratha

Prune
54 East First Street New York, NY 10009 212-677-6221

Gabrielle Hamilton	**Mark**
Rye Omelet with Duck Pastrami	>> Salami and Eggs
Pasta Kerchiefs with Poached Egg, French Ham, and Brown Butter	>> Pasta with Ham and Egg
Pickled Shrimp	>> Shrimp with Garlic
Classic Mojito	>> Bittman's Minty Rum Drink

Restaurant Daniel
60 East 65th Street New York, NY 10021 212-288-0033

Daniel Boulud	**Mark**
Stuffed Saddle of Lamb; Leg of Lamb with Beans and Mushrooms; Brochette of Lamb Chops, Summer Squash, and Zucchini; Braised Lamb Shoulder	>> "Too-Simple" Stuffed Lamb Shoulder

WASHINGTON, DC

Citronelle The Latham Hotel
3000 M Street, NW   Washington, DC 20007   202-625-2150

Michel Richard	Mark
Lobster Burger	>> Lobster Roll
Layered Vitello Tonnato	>> Turkey (Tonnato) Sandwiches
"Fried Egg" (Apricots with Sweet Cheese)	>> Spanish "French" Toast (*Torrijas Castellanas*)

**Café Atlantico & Minibar
Zaytinya**
701 9th Street, NW   Washington, DC 20004   202-638-0800

José Andrés	Mark
Mushroom and Chicken Paella (*Paella de Setas y Pollo*)	Fast and Easy Shrimp "Paella" (*Arroz de Gambas*)
Stuffed Fresh Crab (*Txangurro*)	>> Garlic Soup with Crab
Deconstructed Gazpacho	>> Traditional Gazpacho

BOSTON/CAMBRIDGE, MA

East Coast Grill & Raw Bar
1271 Cambridge Street   Cambridge, MA 02139   617-491-6568

Chris Schlesinger	Mark
Grilled Tuna with Soy, Wasabi, and Pickled Ginger	>> Tuna Teriyaki
Chris Schlesinger's Slow-Grilled Ribs	>> Bittman's Faster Grilled Ribs
Grilled Clams and Oysters with Barbecue Sauce	>> Clams "Johnson," Southeast Asian Style

SAN FRANCISCO

Restaurant Gary Danko
800 North Point Street   San Francisco, CA 94109   415-749-2060

Gary Danko	Mark
Lemon-Peppered Duck Breast	>> Crisp-Braised Duck Legs with Aromatic Vegetables
Grilled Quail with Bitter Greens Salad	>> Sautéed Chicken with Green Olives and White Wine
Persimmon Pudding	>> Frozen Persimmons

The Slanted Door
1 Ferry Building, No. 3   San Francisco, CA 94111   415-861-8032

Charles Phan	Mark
Summer Roll	>> "Unrolled" Summer Roll
Wok-Cooked Chicken with Nuts and Fruits	>> Stir-Fried Chicken with Broccoli and Walnuts
Lemongrass-Grilled Rack of Lamb	>> Skewered Squid with Black Pepper and Sesame-Lemon Sauce

LOS ANGELES

Lucques
8474 Melrose Avenue   Los Angeles, CA 90069   323-655-6277

A.O.C.
8022 W. Third Street   Los Angeles, CA 90048   323-653-6359

Suzanne Goin	Mark
Stuffed Chicken "Poule au Pot"	>> Chicken Breasts Stuffed with Prosciutto and Parmigiano-Reggiano
Grilled Pork Confit	>> Braised and Grilled Pork Shoulder
Brioche Bread Pudding	>> Easy Bread Pudding

LAGUNA BEACH, CA

Studio Montage Laguna Beach
30801 South Coast Hwy   Laguna Beach, CA 92651   949-715-6420

James Boyce	Mark
Skate Wing with Tamarind Gastrique	>> Skate with Brown Butter and Honey
Lobster Salad with Corn and Tomatoes	>> Thai-Style Shrimp and Beef Salad
Seared Tenderloin with Root Vegetables and Balsamic Vinegar	
Halibut with White Beans	>> Seared Scallops with Curried Lentils

LAS VEGAS

Simon Kitchen & Bar Hard Rock Hotel and Casino
4455 Paradise Road   Las Vegas, NV 89109   702-693-4440

Kerry Simon	Mark
Steak Tartare	>> Good Burgers with Tartare-Like Seasonings
Salmon Tandoori	>> Flash-Cooked Curried Salmon
Banana Bread	>> Frozen Chocolate Banana on a Stick

Starters

Many people who regularly dine out swear that first courses are always more interesting than main courses. There are several reasons for this, ranging from the obvious (we're all *hungrier* when we eat our first courses than later in the meal) to the more subtle.

Two important factors, I think, are that smaller portions leave us wanting more, and that first courses are cleaner—they make a simple statement, and they come unsullied with side dishes. Finally, I think chefs, consciously or not, try harder with first courses. Not only are they aware of the power of first impressions, they themselves grew up eating first courses that were more interesting than the food that followed.

Our chefs ran the gamut in this field. José Andrés's Deconstructed Gazpacho (page 34) is among the most outrageous recipes in this book (mine is a simple, quite traditional version), and Gabrielle Hamilton's Pickled Shrimp (page 46) is a barroom classic among the most traditional and straightforward (my shrimp dish is among the most frequently seen and wonderful tapas). In between, we have a few stunning salads, a traditional Vietnamese summer roll (and my easier version), and even a couple of cocktails. Good starters, all.

Deconstructed Gazpacho

JOSÉ ANDRÉS | Makes: 4 SERVINGS Time: AT LEAST 1 HOUR

An aggressively modern treatment, this is gazpacho pulled apart, re-imagined, and reassembled, with trout roe and mango "ravioli" thrown in for good measure. There is a stunning minimalist sensibility to this dish when it's on the plate in front of you, with each element separate from the other, and each tasted separately, but the execution is about as maximal, effortwise, as you can get.

José is one of the culinary field's mad geniuses, as evidenced by his "discovery" of tomato seeds—the part of the tomato that just about every chef discards—as a precious item, a bundle of glistening pearls. The gelatin of vinegar, the mango–trout roe ravioli, even the bell pepper, each becomes a design as well as a flavor element. When you eat this, delicious at it is, you feel you are wrecking a tableau.

Finally, when I say, "cut into the tiniest, most even dice you can manage," I'm translating what's called a brunoise cut. Brunoise are little cubes of food, about $\frac{1}{16}$ of an inch on each side, and usually, when done by a skilled knife technician, quite square. I can't do that to save my life, but if you can, more power to you. Otherwise—as I say—cut the food into the tiniest, most even dice you can manage.

1 envelope (1 tablespoon) unflavored gelatin

¼ cup sherry vinegar

4 medium tomatoes

¼ cup diced decent white bread (like a Pullman loaf), cut into the tiniest, most even dice you can manage

¼ cup extra-virgin olive oil

16 thin slices taken from 2 near-ripe, peeled mangoes, cut on a mandoline

1 small jar (about ½ cup) trout or salmon roe

¼ cup finely diced cucumber (the tiniest, most even dice you can manage)

4 teaspoons finely diced bell pepper, preferably orange (the tiniest, most even dice you can manage)

2 scallions, white parts only, slivered

Coarse sea salt

1 Dissolve the gelatin into the vinegar in a small saucepan over low heat, stirring frequently. Transfer to a small bowl and refrigerate for at least 2 hours. (You can make this vinegar jelly as far in advance as you like.)

2 Cut about ⅛ inch off the top and bottom of each tomato, then assess where you'll make your next cut: There will be 2 or 3 chambers of seeds separated by 1 or 2 walls of tomato flesh. Make a cut through the outside flesh of the tomato where it meets one of the walls, then gently pull the flesh away from the seed packet. Detach the seed packet with a spoon from the center wall it's attached to and reserve. Repeat for remaining seed packets in each tomato. You want at least 2 seed packets per serving.

3 Preheat the toaster oven or oven to 200°F. Cut about ¼ cup of the resulting tomato flesh into ¼-inch dice and reserve. Puree the rest in a blender or food processor and pass the resulting puree through a fine-meshed sieve or strainer; discard the solids.

4 On a toaster oven pan or baking sheet, toss the cubed bread in 1 tablespoon of the olive oil and toast in the oven until evenly browned and crisped. Reserve.

5 Make the "ravioli": Lay 2 slices of mango on a cutting board in front of you, overlapping them slightly in the middle. Put 1 tablespoon roe on the overlap, then fold the mango slices up, one over the roe and the other over it. Fold the sides underneath and reserve; repeat with remaining mango and roe.

6 Per plate, arrange 2 tomato seed packets, 2 trout roe and mango ravioli, two ½-tablespoon piles of diced tomato, 1 tablespoon diced cucumber, 1 teaspoon diced bell pepper, and two ½-tablespoon piles of jellied sherry vinegar. Scatter each pile with mini-croutons and slivered scallions. Top each tomato seed packet with a pinch of salt and drizzle each plate with 1 tablespoon olive oil (or more, if desired). Serve, saucing each portion lightly with the strained tomato juice at the table.

SHOP TALK: Is José Andrés a Culinary Terrorist?

MB: I like this dish but I'm not sure it counts as cooking... .

JOSÉ: Well, if it's not cooking, then we're going to have to compare the Rolling Stones to Antonio Vivaldi. Do you like them both?

MB: Yes.

JOSÉ: They are different. And at the end, these things are either good or not good, which is what's important. I think we need to have both traditional restaurants that continue the identity of regions or countries, along with chefs who keep pushing the envelope.

MB: Agreed. And it's worth pointing out that traditional dishes sometimes aren't necessarily even that old.

JOSÉ: And sometimes not even well done. It seems sometimes like creative cooking is some kind of terrorism in the food world. On the contrary, we need to remember that the creative and modern dishes of today are going to be the traditional dishes of tomorrow.

Traditional Gazpacho

MARK BITTMAN | **Makes:** 4 SERVINGS **Time:** ABOUT 20 MINUTES

This version is quite a bit more traditional than José's Deconstructed Gazpacho. It belies my prejudice for a gazpacho with enough vinegar to make it lively but not so much that you feel like you're drinking it straight from the bottle. The anchovy fillets were José's suggestion, and are absolutely optional, but they make a great addition to the dish.

1 pound tomatoes, roughly chopped, or 1 (14-ounce) can tomatoes (don't bother to drain)

1 medium cucumber, peeled and diced

2 or 3 slices bread, a day or two old, crusts removed, torn into small pieces

¼ cup extra-virgin olive oil, plus more for garnish

2 tablespoons sherry vinegar or red wine vinegar

1 clove garlic, chopped, or more to taste

Salt and black pepper to taste

8 anchovy fillets (optional)

1 Combine the tomatoes, cucumber, bread, oil, vinegar, and garlic with 1 cup water in the container of a blender; process until smooth. If the gazpacho seems too thick, thin with additional water.

2 Taste and add salt and black pepper as necessary. Serve immediately (or refrigerate and serve within a couple of hours), garnished with the anchovies, if using, and a drizzle of olive oil.

What's Gazpacho?

There are so many "authentic" gazpacho recipes that there might as well be none. Some people say a soup must have bread in it to be gazpacho; others insist it must contain vinegar. I'm from the school that says gazpacho must be cold (hot gazpacho is no more desirable than cooked sashimi, though I've seen both), almost drinkable, and refreshing—a cooling, portable, nutritious meal that could serve as lunch for travelers and laborers under the hot Spanish sun. I think, too, that the "refreshing" part of this definition is what leads to the addition of vinegar. Sweet soups, or very rich, creamy ones, are not as clean as lean ones, especially those on the acidic side.

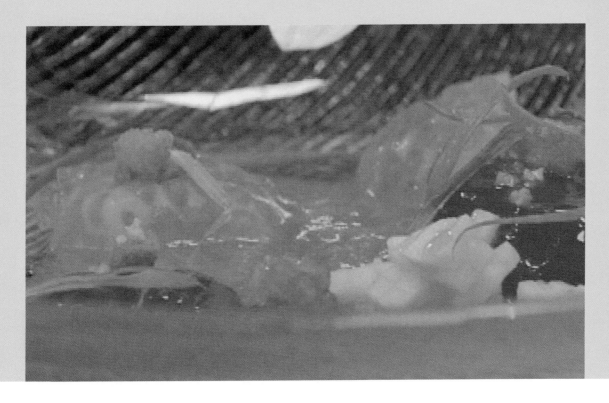

Stuffed Fresh Crab (Txangurro)

JOSÉ ANDRÉS | Makes: 4 SMALL OR 2 GENEROUS SERVINGS Time: 1 HOUR

This dish, pronounced "chan-gurr-o," is a Basque tradition that José learned from his mother. In Spain they'd make this with a crab called buey mar *("beef of the sea") though both Dungeness and blue crabs are good stand-ins.*

José presented this dish with the crabmeat stuffed back into the shells. Very elegant, but he also served a big plate of it to the crew sans shells, so I feel comfortable saying you can elect to skip the last step if you're so inclined (or if you're using blue crabs) and just serve the sautéed meat with crusty bread to soak up the juices. You can also make this with prepicked crabmeat, which is what most people would do, replacing the crab shells with ramekins.

4 leeks, white parts diced, green parts reserved

10 black peppercorns

1 bay leaf

2 Dungeness crabs, 8 blue crabs, or about 12 ounces picked crabmeat

2 tablespoons Spanish extra-virgin olive oil, plus extra for garnish

2 tablespoons butter

1 green bell pepper, stemmed, seeded, and diced

1 small Spanish onion, diced

1 dried red chile or crushed red pepper flakes to taste (just a little, though)

2 teaspoons minced garlic

½ cup tomato sauce

Salt

2 ounces brandy, preferably Spanish

¼ cup fresh bread crumbs

1   Preheat the oven to 500°F. Bring a large pot of salted water to a boil with the leek greens, peppercorns, and bay leaf. Add the crabs and cook for 15 minutes, until they are bright red (blue crabs take only 6 minutes). Transfer the crabs from the pot to a cutting board and remove the meat, making sure to reserve the juices. (If you're using dungeness crabs, you should be able to remove the bottom shell easily enough to keep the top shells intact, so you can serve out of them if you like; this will not be possible with blue crabs, however.)

2   Put the oil and butter in a wide skillet and turn the heat to medium-high. Wait a minute or so, until the oil is hot, then add the green pepper, white parts of the leeks, onion, chile, and garlic and sauté until softened, about 5 minutes.

3 Add the tomato sauce, a pinch of salt, and the crabmeat. Warm through, then add the brandy and reduce by half, about 5 minutes. Spoon the mixture into the reserved crab shells (if using), sprinkle with bread crumbs, drizzle with additional olive oil, and bake for about 5 minutes, or until the crumbs are lightly browned. Serve hot or warm.

SHOP TALK:
Txangurro

MB: What's it called again?

JOSÉ: Can I spell it for you? T X A N G U R R O. Chan–gurr-o!

MB: And it means stuffed crab?

JOSÉ: Crab. It's a type of crab. You know, in Spain it's not like here where you can get the picked crabmeat everywhere. When you get a crab, it's something unique, and you bring them home and the whole family gathers around the table and helps pick the meat from the shell and make the dish.

MB: I can't imagine the whole family carefully stuffing the crab back into the shells though.

JOSÉ: Hey! At home it's done more simply—we might not even stuff it. But I have a profession here—cooking!

Garlic Soup with Crab

MARK BITTMAN | Makes: 4 SERVINGS   Time: ABOUT 1 HOUR

Freshly picked crabmeat is about as good as ingredients get, but good lump crabmeat, sold in all high-quality fish markets and many supermarkets, is a nearly identical stand-in. The irony is that even without crab, this is a great soup.

3 tablespoons extra-virgin olive oil

4 heads garlic, separated into cloves, peeled, and thinly sliced (you can do this with a mandoline, the slicing blade of a small food processor, or a sharp knife)

2 teaspoons fresh thyme leaves

6 cups chicken stock

Salt and black pepper to taste

2 eggs

2 tablespoons fresh lemon juice, or more

1 small container (about 1 cup) picked jumbo lump crabmeat

½ cup chopped fresh parsley leaves

1   Place the oil in a 3- or 4-quart saucepan and turn the heat to medium; add the garlic and thyme. Cook, stirring occasionally, until the garlic has a translucent appearance and begins to soften, about 10 minutes. (If you taste it at this point it will already be quite mild.)

2   Add the stock and bring to a boil over high heat. Turn the heat down to medium—you want the soup to be bubbling, but not furiously—and cook, stirring occasionally, until the liquid is somewhat reduced and the garlic very tender, about 15 minutes.

3   Add salt and black pepper to the soup and turn the heat as low as possible. In a small bowl, beat the eggs with the lemon juice, then gently whisk the mixture into the soup; the eggs will cook in shreds and thicken the soup. Add the crabmeat, cook until heated through, then taste, adding more salt, black pepper, or lemon juice as necessary. Garnish each portion with a healthy sprinkle of parsley and serve immediately.

SHOP TALK: A Better Boiled Water

JOSÉ: This is very similar to traditional Spanish garlic soup.

MB: Yeah? What's the story with that?

JOSÉ: You use bread—old bread, garlic, water, and eggs that you add at the end.

MB: A poor people's soup.

JOSÉ: Exactly. But really an amazing soup when it's done right. And when you said eggs and garlic, it made me think of it.

MB: Except I'm using crab instead of bread.

JOSÉ: That's even better.

MB: I think it's okay for people to use canned stock or even water in place of the stock you've so kindly provided for me. In some languages isn't the traditional garlic soup called boiled water?

JOSÉ: Is this a trick question? You know, Mark, I'm just a cook. I can't know about everything. I can't be the *Britannica Encyclopedia*.

Summer Roll

CHARLES PHAN | Makes: 8 ROLLS, 4 TO 8 SERVINGS Time: ABOUT 1 HOUR

Charles's "super lean, super clean" summer roll is the classic, with one variation: the addition of aioli (a trick his mother learned working with French people in Saigon), which adds both flavor and moisture. You can consider it an optional restaurant fillip, especially since the Peanut Dipping Sauce achieves the same results, and in spades. The basic guidelines: Don't overfill (as Charles says, "This isn't a burrito"), and wrap as tightly as you can—really squish the thing as you roll; this is a technique that will come to you quickly.

Use any leftover meat you have for the filling, or omit it entirely.

8 (10-inch) sheets rice paper

2 to 3 cups tender lettuce, like Boston, washed, dried, and torn

8 tablespoons (½ recipe) Aioli (page 244)

2 cups cooked rice vermicelli (see sidebar, page 45)

16 to 24 small slices roast pork, or leftover roast chicken

24 small fresh mint sprigs

16 shrimp, peeled, poached, and cut in half the long way

Peanut Dipping Sauce (page 247)

1 Have all the ingredients ready before you start to roll (you can make the peanut sauce after you make the rolls, if you like). Set a large pot of water on the stove and heat it until it is steaming, not boiling. Set a damp towel on a counter; dip a sheet of rice paper about one-third of the way into the water for about 2 seconds. Turn it and dip the remaining section of the rice paper and lay it on the towel.

2 Working on the bottom third of the rice paper, spread about ⅓ cup lettuce, topped with 1 tablespoon Aioli, about ¼ cup noodles, a couple of slices of pork, and 2 or 3 sprigs mint. Fold up the bottom edge to cover, then fold in the sides. Add 4 shrimp halves, pink sides up (this makes a nicer presentation). Then roll tightly (don't worry too much about rips; the rice paper is tough, and there is enough of it to cover those rips), using both hands and as much pressure as you dare.

3 Serve right away, or store the rolls, lightly covered and refrigerated, for up to 2 hours if you like. Cut straight across each roll to make 2 or 3 pieces, then serve with Peanut Dipping Sauce.

Yes, White Men Can Make Summer Rolls

On a trip to Vietnam's Mekong Delta about five years ago (among my traveling companions were Kerry Simon and Jean-Georges Vongerichten), I visited the small ancestral village of one of my companions. A dinner was being prepared for us, and I wandered into the room where five or six women sat, making summer rolls much like the ones Charles Phan serves at Slanted Door. I'd already produced a few summer rolls in my life, so I asked if I could join the party.

I was nearly laughed out of the room, whether because I was a man or because I wasn't Asian, I couldn't figure out. (Charles said "probably both.") But I proceeded to roll a few pathetic summer rolls; they got better with each attempt, though none were as neat as those rolled by the women. But I kept at it, that night and in the years that followed—it's really a matter of practice—and, by the time I made a summer roll next to Charles in San Francisco, my technique was pretty good. For a white man, at least.

"Unrolled" Summer Roll

MARK BITTMAN | Makes: 4 SERVINGS   Time: 20 MINUTES, WITH PREPARED INGREDIENTS

Especially after I succeeded in making a decent summer roll when cooking Charles's version, I was concerned that my simplified summer roll, devised so that you wouldn't have to deal with rolling, would be just a footnote. But he declared my "creation" to be a venerable and legitimate Vietnamese salad (called bun), and suggested that (a) I grill the shrimp and b) I serve it with a little Scallion Oil (opposite). Both are good ideas.

By the way, the Vietnamese phrase for Thai basil—the fragrant, super-minty basil that is quite unlike the more common Italian kind—is "beautiful smelling herb," which indeed it is. Look for it at Asian markets.

DRESSING
¼ cup fish sauce (nam pla or nuoc mam)

1 tablespoon sugar, or more to taste

1 tablespoon peeled and minced fresh ginger

1 teaspoon Vietnamese chili-garlic paste, or to taste, or chopped fresh chiles to taste

Salt and black pepper to taste

4 to 6 cups lettuce, washed, dried, and torn or chopped

1 to 1½ cups cooked rice noodles (see sidebar)

½ cup shredded peeled carrots

¼ cup fresh mint leaves, left whole or barely torn

¼ cup fresh Thai (or other) basil leaves, left whole or barely torn

¼ cup fresh cilantro leaves, left whole or barely torn

12 small slices cooked pork or 12 poached or grilled shrimp, split lengthwise in half

Scallion Oil (optional, recipe follows)

1   First, make the dressing: In a small bowl, combine the fish sauce, sugar, ginger, and chili-garlic paste with about ¼ cup water, to produce a thin sauce. Taste and adjust seasoning, adding salt and black pepper if necessary.

2   Divide the lettuce among 4 plates. Top each with a quarter of the noodles, carrots, herbs, and pork or shrimp. Drizzle the dressing over all, and, if you like, top with Scallion Oil.

Scallion Oil

Makes: ABOUT ¼ CUP **Time:** 10 MINUTES

As Charles Phan says, "Vietnamese food can be so lean that sometimes you need a little added fat." This will do just the trick, for Vietnamese food and beyond, adding richness and great flavor to salads and stir-fries. It'll keep a day or two, refrigerated, but is best eaten soon after being made.

¼ cup neutral oil, like corn or canola

¼ teaspoon salt

½ teaspoon sugar

2 or 3 scallions, trimmed and minced

1　Put the scallions in a small bowl; stir in the salt and sugar.

2　Heat the oil in a small pan until it is thin and fragrant. Pour the oil over the scallions; they should sizzle (if they do not, the oil wasn't hot enough). Cool and use by the spoonful.

Rice Noodles

Rice noodles look and taste different from their counterparts made of wheat, and they require different handling. There aren't nearly as many shapes, which makes buying them easier; the most useful shape is vermicelli, which is thin.

To use rice noodles, soak them in hot water for about a half hour (you can change the water once or twice to hasten the process). If you're going to cook them further, in a stir-fry for example, this will suffice. But to use them in spring or summer rolls or salads, the soaked noodles should then be plunged into boiling water for 30 seconds, or a little more, until tender. At this point they can be drained and rinsed, then held for a few hours before incorporating them into the summer rolls.

Pickled Shrimp

GABRIELLE HAMILTON | Makes: 6 SERVINGS Time: 30 MINUTES PLUS MARINATING TIME

Despite the diminutive size of the bar at Prune, in New York—there are only four seats—it has its own menu, including a great collection of cocktail food like deviled eggs, sardines with Triscuits, and fried burrata (a super-creamy fresh cow or buffalo milk cheese) masquerading as mozzarella sticks. These classic shrimp, made with Gabrielle's own spice mix, may be cooked the day before serving, so they're perfect for entertaining. Just make sure to let the dish come to room temperature first, otherwise the oil may be cloudy and the flavor muted. Gabrielle puts the pickled shrimp on her menu only when Ruby Red shrimp from Maine are around—usually in summer. Unlike most shrimp, these come to New York unfrozen, so they are quite special. (They're good because they're fresh, tender, and very tasty—mostly that's the freshness. But also because they're from cold water.) But the technique and the Ruby Boil Spice Mix can be used with any shrimp.

Salt

1 recipe Ruby Boil Spice Mix (recipe follows) or ¼ cup Old Bay

1½ pounds large (21–30) shrimp, peeled and deveined

1 cup extra-virgin olive oil

2 lemons, washed and sliced paper thin

1 red onion, sliced paper thin

¼ cup fresh lemon juice

¼ cup rice wine vinegar

6 crushed cloves garlic

1 tablespoon black peppercorns

1 tablespoon coriander seed

1   Bring a pot of heavily salted water to a boil (use about 2 cups salt for 8 quarts water) with the Ruby Boil Spice Mix or Old Bay. Have a large bowl of ice near the stove. When the water reaches a rolling boil, drop in the shrimp and poach them just until they are firm, not more than 45 seconds (the water probably won't even return to a boil). Using a fine-meshed strainer, transfer the shrimp (and whatever of the Ruby Boil Spice Mix comes with them) into the bowl of ice. Toss them with the ice to stop them from cooking further.

2   Combine the oil, lemon slices, onion, lemon juice, vinegar, garlic, peppercorns, coriander, and 1 tablespoon salt in a large bowl. When the shrimp have cooled, remove them from the (now) ice water, shaking or brushing off any of the spices clinging to them from the boil, and transfer them to the bowl. Toss and taste, adding more salt or vinegar as necessary. Refrigerate at least 8 hours or preferably overnight. Serve at room temperature.

Ruby Boil Spice Mix

Makes: ENOUGH FOR A 6- TO 10-QUART BOIL **Time:** 5 MINUTES

The quintessential spice mix for a seafood boil. Feel free to double or triple the recipe and use in place of Old Bay or the like whenever you're boiling seafood.

1 large bunch fresh thyme

15 to 20 bay leaves

¼ cup paprika

1 head garlic, unpeeled

2 tablespoons mustard seeds

1½ tablespoons cardamom seeds

1 tablespoon allspice berries

1 tablespoon celery seed

1 cinnamon stick

Combine the ingredients in a medium bowl, then transfer the mixture to a sealable container. This keeps, sealed, more or less indefinitely.

SHOP TALK: Are You Veining in Vain?

MB: Let's talk about deveining shrimp, which I know is a sore subject between us.

GABRIELLE *(holding a shrimp vein on the tip of her knife):* You wanna eat that?

MB: Yeah. I have friends who argue that shrimp doesn't taste as good if you take the vein out.

GABRIELLE: Who are they? Name names.

MB: Well . . . I've met a lot of people from the South who think that. Shrimp is kind of a controversial thing, you know. There are a lot of people who hate the flavor of iodine in shrimp, and there are others, especially southerners, who say that if shrimp doesn't taste like iodine it has no flavor. It's the same with veins. I understand that some people are grossed out by shrimp veins; others argue that that's where a lot of the flavor is. My argument is that nine out of ten people couldn't tell the difference if they ate them blindfolded.

GABRIELLE: I have to say that I don't mind the flavor. But the texture—

that gritty line—that's unsavory to me. Texture is part of the whole experience...

MB: Right. But when you cook lobster do you take the vein out?

GABRIELLE (laughing): No!

MB: Hey, it's practically the same animal and the same vein.

GABRIELLE: Fine. I don't have a leg to stand on...I mean, this *is* tedious.

MB: Well, give me a paring knife and I'll help you.

Shrimp with Garlic

MARK BITTMAN | **Makes:** 4 SERVINGS **Time:** 10 MINUTES

This classic Spanish tapa isn't as ornate as Gabrielle's pickled shrimp, but it's comparably delicious. And it would be even easier to prepare and serve—and possibly even better tasting—if you cooked the shrimp shell-on and shucked them as you ate. (I like to be kind to my guests, so I shell the shrimp in advance.)

In any case, serve this with crusty bread to sop up the flavorful oil, and plenty of wine, Sangria (page 61), or Mojitos (page 56) to wash it all down.

½ cup extra-virgin olive oil

6 cloves garlic, slivered

1 bay leaf

Pinch to ¼ teaspoon cayenne or good paprika, or to taste

1 pound large (21–30) shrimp, peeled

Salt

Chopped fresh parsley leaves, for garnish

Lemon wedges

1   Put the oil in a medium skillet and turn the heat to medium. A minute later, when the oil is warm, add the garlic, bay leaf, and cayenne and cook until fragrant, 2 to 3 minutes.

2   Raise the heat to high and add the shrimp; cook, stirring occasionally, until cooked through, about 5 minutes. Transfer the entire contents to a shallow bowl, season to taste with salt, and garnish with chopped parsley and lemon wedges. Serve warm or at room temperature.

A Recipe Is Like a River...

While cooking the Shrimp with Garlic with me, Gabrielle started rattling off (good) ideas about ways to vary it, like adding chopped tomatoes at the end, or saffron at the beginning, and when I rebuffed her, saying I didn't want to make the dish complicated, she proclaimed saffron to be "expensive but not complicated."

She was right, of course. But I explained to her that one of my concerns when creating recipes for home cooks is that not everyone knows—I haven't always known—that when a recipe calls for saffron it doesn't mean you can't make the dish without saffron. It means that the dish might be better with saffron.

She empathized and we got back to cooking but then I started thinking out loud about how the dish would taste if we had started with toasted cumin.

It's not that I'm a hypocrite, really—it's just that listing more ingredients than you really need to make a dish taste good can be counterproductive, and making many ingredients optional can be confusing. As you cook more and more, you realize that most recipes are guides, ideas caught on paper—a chef once said to me, "A recipe is the product of a moment in time; you know, you can never step in the same river twice."—and records of something that happened and can be (usually imperfectly) reproduced, rather than hard and fast instructions. So, within limits, please, omit or add ingredients as seems appropriate and suits your taste and convenience.

Layered Vitello Tonnato

MICHEL RICHARD | **Makes:** 8 SERVINGS **Time:** 4 HOURS, SOMEWHAT UNATTENDED

There is more than a little work involved here, both in shopping and in preparation, but you cannot find a more impressive starter. When completed, these perfect appetizers look like gorgeous little napoleons in layers of red and white. And the work is manageable as long as you're patient. Not coincidentally, Michel's accompanying Caesar Salad Dressing is the paradigm.

2 pounds center-cut veal loin

Salt and black pepper to taste

½ bottle (about 1½ cups) white wine

2 quarts chicken broth, preferably homemade (page 249), or more as needed

2 sprigs fresh thyme

2 sprigs fresh rosemary

2 shallots, peeled and chopped

2 pounds sashimi-grade tuna loin (see headnote, page 82)

SAUCE
1 recipe Caesar Salad Dressing (page 53)

2 ounces capers, drained

1 head frisée, dark green tips and hard white roots removed, cut into ½-inch pieces

1   Preheat the oven to 225°F. Split the veal loin in half horizontally and season both cut sides with salt and black pepper. Place pieces back on top of one another and tie the loin with butcher's twine, forcing it into as cylindrical a shape as possible.

2   Nestle the tied veal loin in a pan just large enough to hold it and cover it with the wine and chicken broth (add water if you don't have enough broth). Bring to a boil, then reduce to a simmer and add the thyme, rosemary, shallots, and salt and black pepper to taste; transfer the pan to the oven. Cook the loin at a slow simmer until the internal temperature reaches 140°F (use an instant-read thermometer), about 2½ hours.

3   When the veal is ready, remove it from the broth and let it rest on a cutting board until cool enough to handle. Wrap tightly with plastic, using the plastic to help shape it into a cylinder. Put in the refrigerator to chill.

4   Prepare the tuna: Trim the loin into a cylindrical shape, removing the dark bloodline and the skin with a paring knife, then wrap in plastic the same way you did the veal, using the plastic wrap to help form the loin

SHOP TALK:
The Chef as Artist

Michel Richard is considered a wizard by many of his peers, and it's at least in part because he began his career as a pastry chef; he is more visually oriented than most. I asked him what accounted for this.

MB: I think many of your peers are in awe of your creativity. I know this is partially because of your background in pastry and partially because you have an artistic inclination; I've seen some of your paintings, and you've told me you want to finish your life painting when you're done being a chef. I'm wondering how you design dishes, and how you use your creativity to invent new things.

MICHEL: It's easier for me to be a chef if I think of myself as an artist. If I draw a recipe or draw a dish—I draw tomato, I taste tomato.

MB: So just drawing it brings it all out for you?

MICHEL: And sometimes you try and you draw a dish on paper and because, you know, all that's going on in the kitchen, you might not think about putting those things together. And because I am an artist I try to design the look of the dish, then when I'm in the kitchen I can take things out or add them. You know, when I was a kid I used to draw the food of my grandma and even today I can see those dishes right there in front of me....

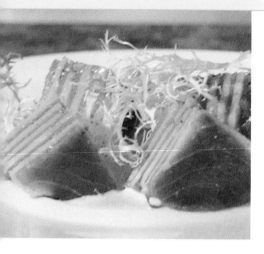

into a cylindrical shape. Place the tuna roll in the freezer for 20 to 30 minutes, until very firm.

5 Make the sauce: Put the Caesar Salad Dressing and capers in a blender or food processor and puree; add salt and black pepper as needed and set aside.

6 When ready to serve, remove the tuna roulade from the freezer and, with a very sharp serrated slicing knife, cut the tuna as thinly as possible into 32 slices (reserve ends and scraps for another use). Repeat with the veal roulade, cutting it as thinly as possible into 24 slices (use any leftovers as a substitute for turkey in my turkey tonnato, page 54). This is probably easiest if you first cut the rolls in half, then cut each half into half again, then proceed to slice.

7 Now build 8 little towers: Start each with a slice of tuna, season with salt and black pepper, top with a slice of veal, and repeat—each portion will comprise 4 slices of tuna and 3 slices of veal. Transfer the towers to a non-stick baking sheet and put in the freezer, so they have a chance to firm up, about 20 minutes. Once set, use a serrated knife to cut each stack into quarters. Allow them to sit at room temperature until they lose the chill from the freezer.

8 Lay out 8 plates and spoon 2 tablespoons of the caper-Caesar sauce onto their centers. Using a spatula and your opposite hand, transfer each tuna and veal tower to a plate on top of the sauce. Garnish with pieces of frisée and serve.

Caesar Salad Dressing

Makes: ABOUT 1 CUP OR 8 SERVINGS **Time:** 20 MINUTES

1 clove garlic, halved

3 eggs

¼ cup fresh lemon juice

¾ cup extra-virgin olive oil

¼ cup minced anchovies, or to taste

¼ teaspoon Worcestershire sauce, or to taste

Salt and black pepper to taste

1 Rub the inside of a salad bowl with the garlic clove; discard it.

2 Bring a small pot of water to a boil. Pierce a tiny hole in the broad end of each of the eggs with a pin or a needle and boil them for 60 to 90 seconds; they will just begin to firm up. Crack them into the salad bowl, making sure to scoop out the white that clings to the shell.

3 Beat the eggs with a fork, gradually adding the lemon juice and then the olive oil, beating all the while.

4 Stir in the anchovies and the Worcestershire. Taste and add salt, if needed, and plenty of black pepper. Cover and refrigerate until needed.

Turkey (Tonnato) Sandwiches

MARK BITTMAN | **Makes:** 4 SERVINGS **Time:** 30 MINUTES WITH PRECOOKED TURKEY

Neither Michel Richard nor I made a true vitello tonnato on the days we cooked together, but my version is more closely related to the classic Italian appetizer than his—it remains true to the idea of a strong mayonnaise moistening and flavoring slices of meat that, well, might need it, because they've become dried out from overcooking or relatively long storage, or because they were not super moist to start out.

But instead of calling for slices of roast veal—which would take some work—I went for white-meat turkey, an easily found option (I bought mine at a deli), and one that doesn't differ all that much in taste and texture from cold veal.

1 recipe Mayonnaise (page 244, without the ginger) or prepared mayonnaise

1 (6-ounce) can tuna packed in olive oil (preferably imported from Italy)

¼ cup fresh parsley leaves

2 tablespoons capers, drained

2 tablespoons minced shallots

6 anchovy fillets, minced

About ¼ cup olive oil or hot water

Salt and black pepper

8 slices sandwich bread, toasted if desired (or use French bread)

8 (¼- to ⅜-inch-thick) slices white-meat turkey

1 Combine the Mayonnaise with the tuna, parsley, capers, shallots, and anchovies. Whisk in enough olive oil (or water), a little at a time, to achieve a creamy consistency. Taste, and add salt and black pepper as necessary.

2 Lay out 4 slices bread. Top each with a thin layer of sauce; cover with a slice of turkey, then more sauce, then another slice of turkey, then finally more sauce and top layers of bread. Slice the sandwiches in half to display the interior layers, and serve.

SHOP TALK: Le Grand Chef

Some chefs played into the "competitive" aspect of our cooking challenge better than others, but none as spiritedly as Michel Richard. When he helped me make my turkey and tuna sandwiches, he needled me every step of the way.

MB: I don't think this mayonnaise is going to need any salt—it's got plenty of capers and anchovies.

MICHEL *(throwing some shallots into my sauce):* I think this sauce is going to need a lot of things!

MB: You haven't tasted it yet!

MICHEL: I'm going to taste it. I think it's very strange, the way you cook. I don't think you will ever be *un grand chef.*

MB: I have no aspiration to be *un grand chef*—having you and your friends is plenty. Please, get out of my way and let me taste this....

MICHEL: Mix it first!

At that point, le grand chef grabbed the spoon from me, stirred, and tasted a spoonful, eyes closed, with a mock contemplative look on his face.

MICHEL: It's good!

I was relieved—not that I thought it was going to be bad. He then appended his appraisal.

MICHEL: And it's the extra shallots I added that did it. They made it super-delicious!

There is no way to win when you're cooking with French chefs.

Classic Mojito

GABRIELLE HAMILTON | **Makes:** 1 DRINK **Time:** LESS THAN 5 MINUTES

This is a beautiful and arguably traditional mojito, though I believe Gabrielle makes a mistake calling for Bacardi instead of a better rum like the Barbancourt I use in my drink recipe (see sidebar, page 59). I'm obviously partial, so you'll have to try both and sort it out for yourself. Meanwhile, she remains steadfast in making this the way she learned it.

A note on "muddling" the mint: Mash it until it's aromatic but not until it's a paste or oxidized and black. If your first mojito isn't suitably minty, up the amount of mint, not the time you spend muddling.

About 1 cup crushed ice

About 2 tablespoons fresh mint leaves

Juice of 1 lime plus 2 or more lime wedges

2 teaspoons superfine sugar, or more to taste

¼ cup Bacardi white rum

Soda water

Dash Angostura Bitters

1 In the glass of a cocktail shaker, combine the ice, mint, lime juice, and sugar. Muddle (crush) with a wooden spoon or masher until the mint is bruised and aromatic and the sugar has dissolved.

2 Add rum and a couple more ice cubes and shake until frosty. Strain into a glass, then finish with lime wedges, a splash of soda, and a dash of bitters. Serve at once.

The Original Mojito

Is the name an appropriation of "mojo," meaning that the cocktail, therefore, was dubbed a little spell or curse? Was it originally created at one particular club (Sloppy Joe's?) in Havana? Did the bartender use cane sugar or simple syrup in that primordial mojito? Did the original use white rum as in Gabrielle's version?

Any question about the mojito's history will yield multiple answers. Mint, sugar, lime, and spirits were all friendly before rum came into the picture, and it's likely they had ended up in the same glass before.

It's just that very few dishes or cocktails throughout history have a clearly demarcated point of "invention"—Caesar Cardini's salad is one that does, more or less—but even the recipe for an original Caesar salad is besieged with questions: Did he use Worcestershire sauce or anchovy fillets? Garlic or no?

My advice is not to worry about what the mojito looked like the first time someone made one. Try Gabrielle's recipe, try mine, and decide which you like. Then make up your own and the name of a long-shuttered bar in old Havana where you can swear they made the mojitos just like you do.

Bittman's Minty Rum Drink

MARK BITTMAN | Makes: 4 SERVINGS   Time: LESS THAN 10 MINUTES

Gabrielle made fun of this drink, declaring it "not a real mojito." Maybe not, but it's better than most of what you get in bars.

Make the sugar syrup in advance, and use plenty of mint. Add the best dark rum you can find—I like Barbancourt and Saint James, but there are many good ones out there.

My ingredients may be a little "fancier" here, but I don't muddle the mint and sugar, making my method faster and easier.

1 cup sugar

About ½ cup fresh lime juice

1 cup fresh mint leaves, washed, dried, and roughly chopped

6 ounces dark rum, or more to taste

Plenty of ice

1   Combine the sugar with 1 cup water in a small saucepan. Heat until the sugar dissolves, then let cool. (This syrup will keep indefinitely in your refrigerator.)

2   Combine about ½ cup each sugar syrup and lime juice in a pitcher. Add the mint and rum and stir. Taste and adjust seasoning; it should be plenty strong, but also sour and minty, and you should taste the rum. Add whatever seems missing, pour over ice, and drink.

A Little about Rum

Rum has a fascinating history, tied up with politics and trade in a way that can be said for only a few other products.

Sugarcane was first cultivated in East Asia and, although sugar and molasses ferment easily, there were no refined or codified spirits made from sugarcane until the large colonial-era plantings in the West Indies were sowed. That's when the immediate antecedents of the sugarcane spirit we know as rum today were born, and began to figure prominently in the transatlantic slave trade (you made more money off your sugar crop if you processed the molasses into rum).

Eventually rum was held as a point of national pride for the many diverse island cultures that did—and still do—produce it.

Methods of production diversified, distillers got particular about where the barrels in which they'd age the rum would come from, and different islands still argue today that their soil or strain of sugarcane produces a better rum.

The basic styles of rum are:

White: The cheapest and least complex member of the rum family; regularly used in cocktails. Gabrielle noted that Bacardi was originally made in Cuba and therefore a likely constituent of the earliest mojitos. (The company relocated to Bermuda in the sixties.) Today, mojitos in Havana use Havana Club, the product of Cuba's nationalized rum industry, but it's not imported into this country. Most of the flavored (not spiced) rums are white rums infused with citrus or other flavors.

Gold or Aged: These spend anywhere from three to twenty years in wood casks and can cost as much as (and have comparable complexity to) a good bottle of Scotch. My favorite, Barbancourt Reserve Especial, comes from the French-speaking island of Haiti, where it spends eight years in Limousin oak casks before it's bottled. And though I use it in my rum drink, it's super neat or on the rocks.

Spiced Rums: Spiced rums are often made from a blend of young and aged rums, then flavored with a proprietary blend of spices. Though you wouldn't likely drink these rums on the rocks, nor use them in classic Cuban cocktails like the mojito, they regularly are used in rum punches and rum and Cokes.

White Sangria

JOSÉ ANDRÉS | **Makes:** 6 SERVINGS **Time:** 15 MINUTES

"Things that are new today are the classic dishes of tomorrow," was José Andrés's mantra over the two days I spent cooking with him in Washington. And while only time will tell if José's Deconstructed Gazpacho (page 34) will be part of the canon in a few years, updates of classic cocktails and drinks seem like a safer bet. Case in point: this white sangria from José's bar at Jaleo in Washington, DC.

⅓ cup cut fruit, like strawberries, peaches, or seedless grapes, plus extra for garnish

About 2 tablespoons fresh mint leaves, plus extra for garnish

⅔ bottle (about 2 cups) dry sparkling wine, like Cava or Prosecco

1 shot (2 ounces) Liquor 43, any vanilla liquor, or Grand Marnier, or more to taste

1 shot (2 ounces) brandy, or more to taste

1 shot (2 ounces) white grape juice

1 teaspoon sugar, or more to taste

1   Fill a pitcher halfway with ice, then add the fruit and mint. Add the wine, pouring very slowly to avoid losing too much of the wine's sparkle.

2   Mix together the Liquor 43, brandy, grape juice, and sugar in a cocktail shaker and add to the pitcher.

3   Stir with a long spoon, taste, adding more sugar or spirits to taste. Serve in glasses garnished with additional cut fruit and mint sprigs, if desired.

Red Sangria

JOSÉ ANDRÉS | **Makes:** 6 SERVINGS **Time:** 15 MINUTES PLUS 2 HOURS MARINATING TIME

Bolder and stronger than José's white sangria, but equally refreshing.

⅔ bottle (about 2 cups) red wine

⅔ cup cut fruit, like oranges and apples, plus extra for garnish

1 shot (2 ounces) vodka, or more to taste

1 shot (2 ounces) brandy or Grand Marnier, or more to taste

1 shot (2 ounces) fresh orange juice

Splash Rose's lime juice

1 teaspoon sugar, or more to taste

1 cinnamon stick

Ice

Splash Sprite

1   Combine the wine, fruit, vodka, brandy, juices, sugar, and cinnamon stick in a pitcher and let macerate in the refrigerator for 2 hours.

2   Add ice to fill the pitcher, the splash of Sprite, and more sugar or spirits to taste. Serve in glasses garnished with additional cut fruit, if desired.

Sangria

Sangria is a likely place for cheap or leftover wine to end up. The addition of fruits and spirits like Grand Marnier cover many flaws, and the temperature it's served at—chilled, often over ice—does plenty to mask any inherent deficiencies in the wine.

But the difference between sangria made with jug wine and sangria made with inexpensive but decent wine (that you'd drink without fruit and ice) is considerable. If you start with a soft, fruity, drinkable wine from a reputable store—even that in the $6 to $9 a bottle range—your sangria will be superior to any you've had in a restaurant.

Fish

Chefs love seafood because—with the possible exception of vegetables—it contains a greater variety of choices than anything else they serve. They can execute a menu change simply by switching a given preparation from lobster to shrimp or tuna to swordfish. And if a shipment comes in with one fish substituted for another, it can be an opportunity rather than a disaster; finding yourself without tuna but with halibut is not quite the same thing as finding yourself without beef.

Furthermore, seafood recipes can be quite straightforward: Fish has enough intrinsic flavor to allow chefs to treat it minimally yet still make an interesting dish.

I like fish for the same reasons. If I'm in the mood for a certain preparation, I go to the fish market (or supermarket) and see what's good, knowing that the chances are I can fit something they have that looks good into the dish I feel like making.

Another thing about fish: It cooks quickly. Note that when a recipe in this chapter is a lengthy one, it's because the sauce or garnish is complicated or slow-cooking. The fish itself can almost always be cooked in a half hour, and usually far less than that.

These days, it seems that chefs simply must have lobster on the menu—everyone sees this as a luxury, so serving it makes a statement. Tuna is equally popular because it has become, for many diners, the new beef.

Really, it was all I could do to keep all of our chefs from focusing on these two items. But I insisted that we broaden our scope, and as a result we have, I believe, almost all of the really popular fish here, including—of course—shrimp and salmon, as well as a couple of less common items, like sea bass (for which you can substitute red snapper) and skate.

Grilled Clams and Oysters with Barbecue Sauce

CHRIS SCHLESINGER | **Makes:** 6 FIRST COURSE SERVINGS   **Time:** 15 MINUTES,
PLUS TIME TO PREHEAT THE GRILL

This is a straightforward, easy-to-execute dish, providing you've got your clams and oysters shucked. Unfortunately, shucking either intimidates or frustrates pretty much every home cook I know, including me; see the sidebar, and also my recipe (page 66), which requires no dexterity.

It's not so much the combination of clams and oysters that is important here, but the freshness of the mollusks you buy. So if the oysters look better than the clams at your fish market, do all oysters; if the oysters look raggedy, load the grill up with clams (mussels will work too, or scallops on the half-shell if you can find them). And don't fret about the varieties you're buying: Freshness is the only imperative. Whether you get local littleneck clams, or fist-size oysters from the Gulf of Mexico, this recipe will work perfectly. Serve with cold beer.

36 clams, oysters, or (preferably) a combination	1 tablespoon Tabasco sauce, or to taste
8 tablespoons (1 stick) unsalted butter	The juice of ½ lemon
1 tablespoon minced garlic	Salt and black pepper
	Lemon wedges for serving

1   Build a multilevel fire in your grill (using hardwood charcoal, if possible): Leave one-quarter of the bottom free of coals; in the rest of the grill, bank the coals so that they are about 3 times as high on one side as the other. When the coals are all white and the temperature has died down to medium, 20 to 30 minutes after you light the fire (you should be able to hold your hand about 5 inches above the hot part of the grill for a few seconds), you're ready to cook. Meanwhile, scrub the clams and oysters with a stiff brush, then shuck them and detach them from their bottom shells.

2   Make the barbecue sauce: Combine the butter, garlic, Tabasco, lemon juice, and salt and pepper to taste in a small saucepan and simmer over low heat (you can do this on the grill; see Pans on the Grill sidebar), cooking the sauce until the flavors have melded and the garlic has lost its raw bite, 5 to 10 minutes.

3   Arrange the mollusks over the hot part of the grill and baste each with a little of the sauce. Cook until the sauce bubbles and simmers for just a minute, then carefully transfer the clams and oysters to a platter and serve at once (be careful; the shells are hot), with the lemon wedges.

How to Shuck Clams and Oysters

The difficulty of shucking mollusks is more in the effort required rather than because it's a dangerous process; just learn the technique, protect your hands, and work carefully until you get the hang of it, and you'll be fine.

To shuck a clam, hold the clam in the palm of your hand, hinge facing toward you (you might want a towel underneath the clam to protect your hand; or wear a heavy glove). Wiggle the edge of a clam knife in between the two shells, then work it around the edge to separate the two shells. Open the clam and use the knife to scrape the meat from the top shell into the bottom shell, then to separate the meat from the bottom shell.

To shuck an oyster, protect your hand with a towel or glove. (An oyster may take more effort to open than a clam, so protecting your hand is essential here.) Then take an oyster knife, a can opener—an ordinary church key, which some people swear by, and works pretty well for beginners—or any sturdy (but preferably not too sharp) knife. Put the oyster, cupped side down, on a flat surface; insert the point of the knife into the hinge. Press and twist the knife until the oyster shell pops, or use the church key as you would on a bottle (some adjustments are inevitable; unfortunately, it's not as easy as it sounds). Twist off the top shell, trying to keep as much juice inside as possible. Use a paring knife to detach the meat from the bottom shell.

Clams "Johnson," Southeast Asian Style

MARK BITTMAN | **Makes:** 6 FIRST COURSE SERVINGS   **Time:** 20 MINUTES, PLUS TIME TO PREHEAT THE GRILL

Steve Johnson is a great chef, a high school buddy of Chris's, and a friend of mine. His recipe for grilled clams in sauce is a modern classic; this was my take on it the day Chris and I cooked together, and it's a good one. Note that there is no shucking involved!

This will work equally well with oysters (make sure the shells are very well scrubbed) and mussels. Serve with Sticky Rice (page 236) or crusty bread.

½ cup dry white wine

4 tablespoons (½ stick) unsalted butter

1 tablespoon trimmed and chopped lemongrass (see page 161)

1 tablespoon peeled and chopped shallot

1 tablespoon peeled and minced fresh ginger

1 small chile, minced

Salt and black pepper to taste

36 or more littleneck or cherrystone clams, well scrubbed

Chopped fresh cilantro leaves, for garnish

Lime wedges

1   Start a gas or charcoal grill; the core of the fire should be quite hot—you should only be able to hold your hand a few inches above the flames for a couple of seconds—and the rack about 4 inches from the heat source. In a pan large enough to hold a few of the clams at a time, combine the wine, butter, lemongrass, shallot, ginger, chile, and salt and pepper to taste. Place over a medium-hot part of the grill and bring to a boil. Move to a cooler part of the grill so the mixture just simmers.

2   Meanwhile, put the clams on the grill rack over the hottest part of the fire and close or cover the grill. When the clams begin to open, transfer each to the sauce pan, turning it a few times to coat with the sauce. When the pan becomes crowded, transfer the coated clams to a warm platter; continue until all are finished.

3   For each serving, top the clams with a sprinkle of cilantro, a squeeze of lime juice, and few spoonfuls of the sauce.

SHOP TALK: The Grill Master Meets Everyman

Chris and I have argued the not-too-fine points of cooking since he started cooking school (long enough ago so that I can't figure out when it was). One of our most common arguments is about grilling. I acknowledge that Chris is a serious Grill Master—one of the best in the country—but I find his slavish devotion to hardwood charcoal at times excessive. And he, not to put too fine a point on it, thinks I'm a slouch. (Note that this particular discussion took place just before he threw me in the water off the dock on which we were grilling, in Westport, MA.)

CHRIS: Mark, why are you cooking on a gas grill? Don't you find that the natural flavor of a real-wood charcoal is superior?

MB: Actually, what I'm looking for here is the natural flavor of the clams, and we're going to get that in both of our recipes, whether we use wood or gas.

CHRIS : I think that the flavor of wood charcoal really adds something, something important.

MB: Maybe, but Chris, gas grills outsell charcoal grills four to one. I am a man of the people; I cook on a gas grill because most of my readers and viewers cook on gas grills. Also because I'm lazy. You turn it on and it works.

CHRIS : I like recipes that capture a lot of smoke, and I also like the risk involved in real fire. I mean, if you screw something up, you have a problem. It's always an adventure.

MB: I get it. You're looking for a primitive experience. I'm just looking to cook the damned clams.

Tandoori Shrimp

SUVIR SARAN | **Makes:** 4 SERVINGS **Time:** ABOUT 30 MINUTES, PLUS 2 HOURS MARINATING TIME

Suvir does a great job of taking Indian street food and making it appeal to everyone. This is a spectacular example of this, a combination tandoor dish and salad that would shine no matter where it was served.

Suvir says he uses colossal shrimp for this recipe because smaller shrimp would overcook in the time it takes for the tandoori paste to turn into a delicious glaze. That makes sense to me, though I have since tried the recipe with smaller shrimp and the results, while less glorious, were good.

As Suvir does not use food coloring, his tandoori dishes do not have the bright red color of those in most Indian restaurants. On the other hand, they have amazing flavor, even when made in a conventional oven or on a grill.

Suvir serves this with the Crispy Okra Salad (page 70), but it would also go beautifully with the Chickpea Raita (page 81).

1 tablespoon cumin seeds or 2 teaspoons ground cumin	½ cup fresh lemon juice
3 tablespoons peeled and minced fresh ginger	2 cups plain yogurt, drained over a bowl in a cheesecloth-lined strainer or a coffee filter for at least 1 hour (if longer, refrigerate)
3 tablespoons minced garlic	12 colossal (about 2 pounds) shrimp, shelled
3 tablespoons toasted chickpea flour (besan) or all-purpose flour	Salt
1 teaspoon ground white pepper	3 tablespoons butter, melted
1 teaspoon Garam Masala (page 248)	1 lemon, halved
½ teaspoon ground turmeric	Crispy Okra Salad (optional, page 70)

1   If you're using whole cumin, toast the seeds in a dry frying pan over medium heat, shaking the pan, until fragrant and lightly browned, 2 to 3 minutes. Grind 2 teaspoons of the cumin seeds to a powder in a coffee grinder or mortar and pestle and set aside.

2   Stir together the ginger, garlic, flour, ground cumin, pepper, Garam Masala, and turmeric in a bowl large enough to hold the shrimp. Stir in the lemon juice and then the yogurt, a bit at a time, stirring until smooth after each addition. Add the shrimp and toss to coat with the marinade. Refrigerate, covered, for at least 2 hours; overnight is fine.

3   Preheat the oven to 550°F, or as near that temperature as you can get it. Put the shrimp in a single layer on a rack in a foil-lined baking pan, sprinkle with salt, and roast 10 minutes. Remove from the oven and let rest 15 minutes, then brush with the melted butter and roast another 10 minutes, until cooked through.

4   Arrange the shrimp on a platter, sprinkle with the reserved toasted cumin seeds and squeeze the lemon juice over all. Serve hot.

Grilled Tandoori Prawns: When you're ready to cook (Step 3 above), start a charcoal or gas grill; the fire should be very hot—you should barely be able to hold your hand over the core of it—and set the rack about 4 inches from the heat source. Grill the shrimp for 3 minutes on each side; let rest 15 minutes off the grill, then brush with the butter and grill 5 to 10 more minutes, until cooked through.

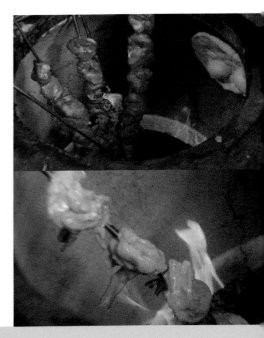

The Tandoor

Tandoors are top-loading, wood-fired, clay ovens used across India and, with slight variation in construction and name, in many parts of southwest Asia. Breads like *naan* are hand stretched and slapped against the sides of the tandoor, where they stick until they're done, minutes later. Marinated meats and vegetables are skewered on long metal poles and stood in the center of the oven, where the intense, dry heat roasts them quickly.

I thought it was hard enough to handle a real wok in Charles Phan's kitchen (see page 10 for more about that) or to stand next to James Boyce's smelting furnace of a flattop, but tandoors are in a class by themselves—neither Suvir nor I could even hope to cook in the one at his restaurant. His co-chef Hemant Mathur, who handles all the tandoor cooking, just smiled amusedly when I tried to see how long I could hold my hand over it—microseconds. Hemant is

so well acclimated he deals with it unfazed.

But it's the often spicy and frequently yogurt-based marinade used for foods headed to the tandoor that have given way to the looser and more colloquial usage of "tandoori," generally referring to dishes that are marinated in a tandoori style—like this Tandoori Shrimp or Kerry Simon's Salmon Tandoori (page 78). And though the heat of the tandoor imparts a distinctive flavor, anyone can produce tandoori-style foods at home.

Crispy Okra Salad

SUVIR SARAN | **Makes:** 4 SERVINGS **Time:** 25 MINUTES

I love this salad (called Kararee Bhindi *in Hindu) of very thinly sliced (julienned) fried okra mixed with onions, tomatoes, and seasoning (including the magical chaat masala), and so, it seems, does everyone else who has tried it. It isn't a traditional dish, but something Suvir and his family's chef, Panditji, came up with together. Suvir says that no one slivers okra like this in India, that it is instead cut crosswise, and he asserts that the dish's lack of trademark okra sliminess (which I happen to like) is a result of the way it's cut (see sidebar, page 73).*

This is a great dish on its own or together with the Tandoori Shrimp, as Suvir often serves it.

Neutral oil, like corn or canola, for frying

1 pound okra, stemmed and julienned lengthwise

½ small red onion, thinly sliced

2 small or 1 medium tomato, cored, seeded, and julienned

¼ cup chopped fresh cilantro leaves, for garnish

½ lemon, or more as needed

1½ teaspoons Chaat Masala, store-bought or homemade (page 71), or more to taste

½ teaspoon salt, or more to taste

1   Heat at least 2 inches oil to 350°F (you can check this with a deep-fry or instant-read thermometer) in a countertop deep fryer or in a heavy pot on the stove.

2   Fry the julienned okra in batches small enough not to crowd your pan or fryer and make sure to let the oil return to temperature (350°F) between batches. Fry it until crisp, 5 to 7 minutes—the seeds will swell and it will be deeply colored at the edges—then transfer to drain on paper towels.

3   Toss the okra together with the onion, tomato, and cilantro, squeeze the lemon juice over all, and season to taste with Chaat Masala and salt.

Chaat Masala

Makes: ABOUT 2 TABLESPOONS   **Time:** 5 MINUTES (PLUS TIME TO SHOP!)

There are dozens of spice blends, perhaps hundreds, in India, including this one, which Suvir favors and I came to love. It's called Chaat Masala, *which translates loosely as "mouthwatering spice mix" because it's traditionally used on street foods and snack foods—just the type of foods that make your mouth water.*

Chaat masala is delicious—sour, sulphurous, sweet, and beguiling—and is properly made from a mix of ground dried mango peel, pomegranate seed powder, toasted cumin seeds, asafetida, black salt (which contributes the sulphurous note), cayenne, coriander, ginger, and cardamom. I buy it packaged, and so does Suvir (look for quality premixed packages and the individual spices in Indian markets, well-stocked food stores, or spice websites), but if you want to try making some, here's a recipe for a simple version.

2 tablespoons amchoor (dried mango powder)

1 teaspoon ground cumin

1 teaspoon ground black salt

1 teaspoon ground coriander

1 teaspoon ground ginger

¼ teaspoon hing (asafetida)

¼ teaspoon cayenne

Pinch salt

Combine all ingredients and store in a tightly sealed container.

Stir-Fried Shrimp with Okra and Lime

MARK BITTMAN | Makes: 4 SERVINGS   Time: 20-25 MINUTES

Here, the juices exuded by the okra (its sliminess, if you prefer) combine with the sugar, lime juice, oil, and butter to produce a simple but delicious sauce in no time flat. I used chopped colossal shrimp in my dish—that's what we had on hand—but you can make this with any size shrimp.

1 pound shrimp, shelled and deveined

The juice of ½ lime

1 tablespoon sugar

Salt

1 tablespoon canola oil

2 tablespoons unsalted butter

1 pound okra, trimmed and chopped or slivered

¼ cup fresh cilantro, chopped

Lime wedges for garnish

1   Place the shrimp in a bowl with the juice, sugar, and a pinch of salt. Toss to coat and let marinate for 5 minutes.

2   Put the oil and butter in a non-stick skillet and turn the heat to high. When the butter foam subsides, add the shrimp and marinade and cook, stirring or tossing, until the shrimp is lightly browned, about 3 minutes (this will happen rapidly because the sugar will caramelize quickly).

3   Use a slotted spoon to transfer the shrimp to a plate, then return the pan to the stove. Add the okra and cook 3 to 5 minutes, stirring occasionally, until lightly browned and crisped. If it looks like the okra is going to crowd the pan you're working with, cook in batches.

4   Add about ½ cup water to the pan and, over high heat, scrape to loosen any browned bits. Add the cilantro to the pan, stir everything together briefly, then transfer the okra and cilantro to a serving platter. Top with the sautéed shrimp and pour the pan sauce over all. Salt to taste, garnish with lime wedges, and serve immediately.

A Sliver of Truth?

I well remember the first time a chef told me a bit of cooking dogma that made me respond, "Nonsense." It was Jean-Georges Vongerichten, and he told me that you stuck cloves in onions when making stock because there was "a chemical reaction between the two" that made them both taste better.

After my epithet, I suggested that perhaps it simply made it easier to keep track of the cloves.

Chefs are trained to believe what they're told, and often this dogma is passed on from one generation to another. Almost every chef I have cooked with has some little nugget of kitchen "wisdom" that, though well intentioned and sometimes functional, was more than a little unscientific. They are founts of kitchen superstitions, and it's amusing that few chefs question their own rules, so they don't know whether they're actually true.

Suzanne Goin demanded that sugar left mixed with egg yolks too long would somehow negatively affect her custard and that bread pudding cooked without a water bath would scramble—neither of which happens to be true. José Andrés blamed a lack of salt in a dish of his on the clearly indisputable fact that "American salt is less salty."

And, case in point: Suvir Saran said that cutting okra pods into slivers instead of round slices was the secret to the crispness of his fried okra salad. If true, this would be a revelation to legions of people who fear okra because of the slimy texture (which many people happen to like).

I took this on faith (forgive me; I was busy), slivered the okra I was going to use in my dish (it wasn't easy), and got cooking. Then, while stirring the slivered okra I was sautéing, Suvir counseled me to let it cook undisturbed until lightly crisped, or else it would turn slimy.

In the end, it turns out that okra, cooked over high heat with enough room for it to brown instead of stew, loses the juices that cause the slimy texture—whether slivered or sliced. You want crisp okra? Fry or stir-fry it. Soft, moist okra? Stew it. It doesn't matter how you cut it.

Lobster Burger

MICHEL RICHARD | **Makes:** 4 BURGERS **Time:** 45 MINUTES

Michel's wonderful lobster burger is simple, but not exactly easy; still, it may also change your mind about nonmeat burgers, because it is amazing. But even if you don't opt to make your own buns, you must take your time to put the "burger" together.

The best way to approach it would be to break up the cooking into two sections: Cook the lobsters, extract their meat, and make the patties, tomato confit, and mayonnaise early in the day, or even the day before, then impress your guests by just cooking the patties and building the burgers at the last minute. (This is essentially what Michel does at Citronelle.)

Many fish markets, especially those in the Northeast, sell picked lobster meat; this would save you a lot of time and should not, in theory, cost you a lot of flavor.

Michel served this with Pont-Neuf Potatoes (page 194).

Salt

4 (1-pound) lobsters, 2 or more larger lobsters, or 1 pound lobster meat

Large bowl ice water

2 ounces bay or sea scallops

Freshly ground black pepper

3 tablespoons extra-virgin olive oil

4 brioche buns, or any hamburger-size rolls

Softened butter as needed

4 ounces mâche or similar tender greens

½ lemon

½ cup Ginger Mayonnaise (page 244) or prepared mayonnaise flavored with 1 tablespoon grated fresh ginger and ½ teaspoon soy sauce

1 recipe Tomato Confit (page 243)

1 Bring a large pot of water to boil and salt it. Drop the lobsters in and cook for 30 to 60 seconds—just enough time to firm up the meat. Plunge the lobsters into a bowl of ice water. When they're cool, break them apart and extract their meat.

2 Puree the scallops in a small food processor (or chop them very finely with a knife), then pass the puree through a fine-meshed strainer. Combine the scallop puree with the lobster meat, season lightly with salt and pepper, and form the mixture into 4 equal patties. (These patties can be made up to 24 hours in advance. Wrap them individually in plastic and refrigerate.)

3 Preheat the oven to 300°F. Heat 2 tablespoons of the olive oil over high heat in an ovenproof non-stick sauté pan with an oven-safe handle, and quickly sear the patties on both sides, about 1 minute per side. Transfer the pan to the oven to barely cook them through, about 5 minutes more; they're done when firm and hot throughout.

4 Meanwhile, split the brioche buns (Michel insists that the slice for the top should be one-third the thickness of the bun, the bottom slice the remaining two-thirds, to help keep the sandwich together when the bottom is soaked with juices from the burger, and this makes some sense). Lightly butter and toast the insides of the buns on a grill, grill pan, or, using tongs, directly over a gas burner.

5 Toss the mâche with the remaining 1 tablespoon olive oil and a squeeze of lemon juice. Spread both sides of the buns with the Ginger Mayonnaise, then add a slice of Tomato Confit, a lobster patty, and a little of the dressed mâche. Top with the other half of the bun and serve.

Clarified Butter

Removing the white milk solids from the golden butterfat is the "clarification" behind clarified butter. It's a useful trick, because it is these same solids that burn at high temperatures. (If you control their browning you make Beurre Noisette; see page 97.)

Clarified butter, unlike whole butter, can be used for sautéing over very high heat or even to fry in, as Michel does for his Pont-Neuf Potatoes (page 194). But most of us first encountered clarified butter as "drawn" butter alongside simply boiled lobster or shrimp.

To make clarified butter at home, melt a stick or more of unsalted butter over low heat, and cook it over the lowest possible heat for three to five minutes, skimming the clusters of white milk solids off the top of the butter as you do, then let the pan stand off the heat for a minute or two. Pour off the golden liquid, leaving the milk solids at the bottom of the pan, where they will have settled. Use immediately, or store in an airtight container in the refrigerator for up to one month.

Lobster Roll

MARK BITTMAN | **Makes:** 4 LARGE LOBSTER ROLLS (you may want to eat more than one)
Time: 30 MINUTES, INCLUDING COOKING THE LOBSTER

Though I look for great ingredients, this is one place where the sweet softness of a hot dog bun-from-a-bag really plays an important role.

Salt

4 (1- to 1¼-pound) lobsters or
1 pound lobster meat

Large bowl ice water

4 hot dog buns

8 tablespoons (1 stick) melted
unsalted butter, warm

1   Put about 2 inches water in a large pot, salt it, cover, and bring to a boil. Plunge the lobsters into the pot, cover, and cook about 10 minutes, or until the lobsters are bright red. Plunge into ice water until cool enough to handle, then remove all the meat; shred with your hands or roughly chop it. Work quickly so the meat stays warm.

2   Split and lightly toast the hot dog buns. Portion the lobster meat among the 4 buns, spoon 2 tablespoons melted butter over each sandwich and sprinkle with salt. Eat with napkins near at hand.

Quaint but Spectacular: The Lobster Roll

I'd eaten Michel's lobster burger a few times, and it wasn't easy to come up with something comparable. Fortunately, my show's producer, Charlie Pinsky, reminded me, "When in doubt, go simple." So I determined to make the always-reliable lobster roll.

I once lived in Massachusetts, and fondly remembered trips to the north shore, where, in the towns of Ipswich and Essex, there were clam shacks galore, whose specialties were fried clams and…lobster rolls. There was nothing simpler than these: Cooked lobster was piled on a hot dog bun, the worst kind of commercially made one, by the way, not one made from brioche. The meat was drenched in melt-ed butter; lemon was barely an option. Salt was imperative. Of course the lobster itself was ter-rific, and perfectly fresh. I went with that—the most primal, ele-mental lobster roll conceivable—no mayo, no Old Bay; nothing but lobster, bun, and butter. And it paid off. When I was done, both Michel and I regretted that I had made just one.

Salmon Tandoori

KERRY SIMON | **Makes:** 4 SERVINGS **Time:** 15 MINUTES PLUS MARINATING TIME

Kerry says that this is a dish that tries to "recreate the vibe of the tandoor." To replicate the clay oven's intensely high, dry, and direct heat, he uses a scorching hot skillet.

In a gracious and unchefly concession, Kerry allows that you can use store-bought tandoori paste (or substitute Suvir Saran's from page 68) instead of preparing your own blend of garlic, ginger, onion, oil, cumin, paprika, coriander, cloves, cardamom, cinnamon, cayenne pepper, turmeric, black pepper, tomato puree, and tamarind paste, like they do at Simon Kitchen & Bar in Las Vegas. (The length of the ingredient list alone makes me cringe.)

This recipe is lovely, with bright and contrasting colors, especially when served with Fresh Mango Chutney (page 240), and Red (or Yellow) Pepper Oil (recipe follows). You can serve it with any and all of these things, or with a simple salad; you can even grill the fish over hot coals on a lightly oiled grill. Look for the tandoori paste and the pappadum (lentil crispbreads) in Indian markets.

4 ounces Patak's Tandoori Paste

¼ cup low-fat yogurt

4 (6-ounce) salmon fillets

1 or 2 pappadum, lightly toasted and broken into quarters

Sprigs of fresh cilantro, for garnish

Red (or Yellow) Pepper Oil (recipe follows), for drizzling (optional)

1 Stir the yogurt and tandoori paste together and slather each of the salmon fillets with some of the mixture. Marinate the salmon, refrigerated, for at least 8 hours or, preferably, overnight.

2 Preheat a dry non-stick pan or well-seasoned skillet over high heat for 2 minutes or so, or until the pan is searing hot. Wipe off any excess (but not all) marinade from the salmon fillets and add them to the pan skin sides down. The skin sides should color and get crisp in about 2 minutes; flip the salmon over and cook it 2 to 3 minutes more, until just medium-rare.

3 Serve the salmon, if you like, over ½ cup Black Bean Salad, then top each portion with a spoonful of Fresh Mango Chutney, a piece of the pappadum, and a sprig of cilantro. Dress the plate with a swirl of the pepper oil if you're using it.

Red (or Yellow) Pepper Oil

Makes: ABOUT ¼ CUP   **Time:** 10 MINUTES

Kerry Simon served this with his Salmon Tandoori (opposite), garnishing the dish with rings of red and yellow pepper oils. You can use this to decorate (and add flavor to) almost any strong-flavored dish you like, especially meat, poultry, or meaty fish like salmon. Pepper oil will keep for up to a week, covered and refrigerated.

1 red or yellow bell pepper

6 tablespoons olive oil

1   Put the pepper through a juicer, then put the juice in a deep, heavy-bottomed saucepan over medium-high heat. Boil the juice until it reduces to the thickness of a glaze, about 20 minutes.

2   Add the oil and use an immersion or standard blender to combine until the sauce is emulsified. Use immediately, or cover and refrigerate for up to 2 weeks.

Flash-Cooked Curried Salmon

MARK BITTMAN | **Makes:** 4 SERVINGS **Time:** 10 MINUTES

Faster than a fried egg: Thinly slice salmon, throw it in a hot, non-stick pan—no fat is necessary—then flip it almost the second it hits the heat. I added the curry powder to make the salmon akin to Kerry's Salmon Tandoori, but you could just as easily omit the curry powder and finish it with lemon to serve it alongside any kind of traditional American or European side dish.

4 (6-ounce) salmon fillets

2 tablespoons curry powder or
Garam Masala (page 248)

Salt to taste

Chickpea Raita (recipe follows)

1   Preheat the oven to 200°F. Cut the salmon fillets in half horizontally to make 8 thinner pieces: Hold your knife parallel to the cutting board and use your other hand to apply pressure on the salmon so the knife glides through evenly. Dust each piece with the curry powder and salt on both sides. Put 4 plates in the oven to warm.

2   Preheat a large non-stick pan over medium-high heat for 1 minute—the salmon should sizzle when it hits the pan—then add the fillet halves. Cook for 45 seconds to 1 minute on each side. You'll see the opaque pink color salmon turns as it cooks climbing up the sides of the fillets almost as soon as it hits the pan, and the idea is to serve it just a touch rare in the middle. You'll need to cook the fish in batches, but as each will take only 1 to 2 minutes, that shouldn't be much of a problem.

3   Put the salmon on the warmed plates as it finishes. Serve immediately, with Chickpea Raita.

Chickpea Raita

Makes: 2½ CUPS **Time:** 10 MINUTES, WITH COOKED CHICKPEAS

It's worth your while to seek out a yogurt that's not overly processed for this raita (and, for that matter, any other use); national brands often add thickeners to their yogurts, which significantly change the yogurt's natural consistency. If they're all that's available to you, just whisk the yogurt with a little water to thin it out.

1½ cups plain yogurt, preferably full fat

1 cup cooked chickpeas, drained (canned are fine)

¼ cup minced cucumber (leave the skin on if it's unwaxed)

¼ cup minced red onion

1 teaspoon sugar

¼ teaspoon ground cumin

¼ teaspoon ground mustard

1 teaspoon crushed red pepper flakes, or to taste

Salt and black pepper

1   Combine the yogurt, chickpeas, cucumber, onion, sugar, cumin, and mustard in a bowl.

2   Add red pepper flakes, salt, and pepper to taste and serve immediately.

The Salsa Called Raita

Chutney has well-deserved and widespread fame, but the lesser-known raita, a cooling side dish that combines aspects of salad, salsa, chutney, and sauce, is just as frequently served as an accompaniment to Indian meals. (There are similar preparations in the Middle East—think of *tzatziki*, the Greek preparation of yogurt and cucumber.)

Raita is almost always tart, because it's yogurt based; this means it's usually cooling, too, though it may be spicy as well. Usually there is a component of herbs and spices, and sometimes the sourness is balanced by sweetness. The Chickpea Raita, which I served with my salmon fillets, is a good basic raita, but you could just as easily prepare the dish made with tomato, chile, and cilantro or mixed cut-up vegetables and cumin or cooked cubed potatoes and minced chiles. You get the idea.

Grilled Tuna with Soy, Wasabi, and Pickled Ginger

CHRIS SCHLESINGER | **Makes:** 4 SERVINGS   **Time:** 20 MINUTES, PLUS TIME TO PREHEAT THE GRILL

This signature East Coast Grill dish is nearly raw tuna, seared on the grill for extra flavor. The tuna Chris uses here is sold as "#1" or "sashimi" quality—safe and flavorful enough to be eaten raw. (In his dish, the tuna is cooked, but only just until rare.) It's a deep, rich red, with a sweet, slightly briny odor and a high price. Though it isn't seen everywhere, almost any fish market can order it for you, because it is sold (to the highest bidder) on the open market. But if you're not itching to spend $20 plus per pound for tuna, or the fish markets near you aren't outbidding the buyers at Tokyo's world-famous Tsukiji market, you'll probably want to cook your tuna beyond the near-raw stage; check out my recipe for Tuna Teriyaki (page 84).

4 (8-ounce) sashimi-grade tuna steaks, each about 2 inches thick

¼ cup sesame oil

Salt and white pepper

¾ cup Pickled Ginger (*Gari*, page 242)

6 tablespoons wasabi powder mixed with water to a paste or 6 tablespoons real wasabi paste (see sidebar)

½ cup top-quality soy sauce

1   Start a charcoal or gas grill; the fire should be quite hot (you should barely be able to hold your hand over it) and place the rack about 4 inches from the heat source. Brush the tuna steaks lightly with the sesame oil and season with salt and pepper to taste.

2   Put the tuna on the grill and cook 4 to 5 minutes on each side, or until a dark-brown crispy skin forms. Now cook the steaks for 2 to 3 minutes on each edge (holding it on its side with tongs, if necessary), until they are cooked on the outside and very rare inside.

3   Transfer the steaks from the grill to a platter, and serve with the pickled ginger, wasabi, and soy sauce for dipping.

What's "Real" Wasabi?

The little mound of sinus-clearing green paste you used to spike your soy sauce at the sushi bar is not actually wasabi, but powdered horseradish, artificially colored and reconstituted with water. In fact, unless you've eaten in the kind of Japanese restaurant where they likely made a big deal about how their wasabi is actually wasabi, there's a good chance you've never tasted it.

Why? There are relatively rigorous limitations on the kind of environment you need to grow true wasabi, and it can take up to two years for the rhizome to mature to the point where it can be harvested. Not surprisingly, this makes it expensive and rare.

Horseradish, on the other hand, is an easy-to-grow root vegetable that performs well in even inhospitable climes (ask any gardener who's tried to get rid of it). Add the fact that the dyed horseradish paste is really pretty close to real wasabi, and you can understand why you're almost never offered the original.

But if you'd like to taste the difference for yourself and really replicate the dish Chris serves at the East Coast Grill, check out the offerings from Pacific Farms at www.freshwasabi.com.

Tuna Teriyaki

MARK BITTMAN | **Makes:** 4 SERVINGS **Time:** 20 MINUTES, PLUS TIME TO PREHEAT THE GRILL IF YOU'RE USING IT

Chris's dish is great as long as you can get spanking fresh, sushi-quality tuna, but home cooks may have a hard time finding it—or paying for it. My alternative recipe is less "pure" but works quite well with ordinary supermarket tuna, which is likely not fabulous enough to eat raw or very rare, but still good. You can use the grill or stovetop for this method, both with great success. Serve this with Seaweed Salad with Cucumber (opposite) and rice.

⅓ cup sake or slightly sweet white wine

⅓ cup mirin (or use 2 tablespoons honey mixed with 2 tablespoons water)

⅓ cup soy sauce

2 tablespoons sugar

4 (6-ounce) tuna steaks

1a If you're grilling, start a charcoal or gas grill; the fire should be moderately hot, and the rack should be about 4 inches from the heat source. Combine the sake, mirin, soy, sugar, and 2 tablespoons water in a small saucepan and heat gently, stirring to dissolve the sugar. Grill the fish on one side until brown, then begin brushing it frequently with the sauce and turn it once or twice more, until nicely browned on both sides and cooked to the stage of doneness you prefer. Brush once more with the sauce, then serve.

1b If you are cooking on a stovetop, preheat a large non-stick skillet over medium-high heat for about 2 minutes, then add the tuna. Brown quickly on both sides, not more than 2 minutes per side. Transfer the fish to a plate and turn the heat to medium. Add 2 tablespoons water, followed by the sake, mirin, sugar, and finally soy sauce. Stir to blend and, when the mixture is producing lively bubbles and beginning to thicken, about 10 minutes, return the tuna to the pan.

2b Cook about 2 minutes more, turning the tuna a couple of times to glaze it with the sauce. By that time the fish will be adequately cooked (it should still be slightly rare in its center, but you can cook it longer if you prefer). Serve hot or at room temperature.

Seaweed Salad with Cucumber

MARK BITTMAN | **Makes:** 4 SERVINGS **Time:** 20 MINUTES

You can use any kind of seaweed you like for this simple salad, which is lovely with either of the tuna dishes on the preceding pages. Many Japanese markets sell 1-ounce packages of mixed dried seaweeds—an easy way to get varied color and flavor—but wakame seaweed (the most common) is good all by itself.

1 ounce wakame or assorted dried seaweeds

1 small cucumber, preferably thin-skinned, like Kirby, English, or Japanese

2 tablespoons minced shallot, scallion, or red onion

2 tablespoons soy sauce

1 tablespoon rice wine vinegar or other light vinegar

1 tablespoon mirin or a pinch or 2 sugar

2 teaspoons sesame oil

Salt, if necessary

1   Rinse the seaweed and soak it in at least 10 times its volume of water. Wash and dice the cucumber; do not peel unless the skin is waxed or bitter. When the seaweed is tender, 5 minutes later, drain and gently squeeze the mixture to remove excess water. Pick through the seaweed to sort out any hard bits (there may be none), and chop or cut up (you can use scissors, which you may find easier) if the pieces are large.

2   Combine the cucumber and seaweed mixture in a bowl. Toss with the shallot, soy, vinegar, mirin, and oil, then taste and add salt or other seasonings as necessary, and serve.

Halibut with White Beans

JAMES BOYCE | Makes: 4 SERVINGS Time: 45 MINUTES

When James was cooking this dish I was struck by his combination of herbs, wine, bacon, and beans; it screamed cassoulet to me. Pairing them with a meaty fish like halibut makes this dish a spa version of that meaty, mid-winter French stew, if there was ever to be one.

Though there's a little advance preparation here, the presentation is a little complicated—typically chefy, if you ask me—so be sure to read through the recipe once before tackling it. Having said that, it's not a tough dish to execute.

Soaking the beans is not essential, but they'll take longer to cook if you don't soak them—figure at least an hour. And if you cannot find halibut fillets, you can make this dish with fillets of black sea bass, red snapper, or grouper. Cooking time will vary according to the thickness of the fillet, of course.

¼ cup extra-virgin olive oil, plus extra as needed

2 ounces slab bacon, cut into ¼-inch cubes

1 shallot, peeled and sliced

½ cup diced onion

Salt and black pepper to taste

1 pound white beans, rinsed and soaked overnight, or for at least a few hours, then drained

¼ cup chopped fresh parsley leaves

Sprig fresh thyme

½ cup white wine

2 to 3 cups chicken stock, preferably homemade (page 249)

4 (6-ounce) halibut fillets

Handful frisée, trimmed, washed, and dried

1 preserved lemon, skin only, sliced as thinly as possible (optional)

4 tablespoons (½ stick) butter

2 teaspoons sherry vinegar, or to taste

1   Put 1 tablespoon of the oil in a large saucepan and turn the heat to medium; a minute later, add the bacon and cook, stirring, for 2 to 3 minutes, until the bacon starts to color and render. Add the shallot and onion, season with salt and pepper, and cook the mixture a few minutes more, until the shallot and onion are softened but not colored.

2   Turn the heat up to high and add the beans, about half the parsley, and the thyme sprig. Cook, stirring, without any additional liquid, for 1 minute or more, until you hear the beans start to sizzle. Add the wine and reduce by half. Add enough stock to barely cover the beans and bring to a boil; reduce the heat to low. Cook the beans, partially covered, at a steady simmer for 20 to 30 minutes, until soft, replenishing the cooking liquid with stock or water, if necessary.

3   When the beans are nearly done, put 2 tablespoons of the oil in a large skillet over medium heat. Pat the halibut fillets dry with paper towels and season with salt and pepper. When the oil shimmers, add the fillets (skin sides down, if they have skin) and sear for 5 to 7 minutes, until nicely browned, then flip and sear on the second sides. Meanwhile, make a small salad to garnish the dish by tossing the frisée with the remaining tablespoon oil, the preserved lemon skin, and a pinch of salt.

4   Add 3 tablespoons of the butter to the pan and, once it has melted, baste the fish with it almost constantly until the fish is just cooked through, about 3 minutes longer. Add the remaining 1 tablespoon butter to the beans along with a splash of olive oil if you like and the sherry vinegar. Taste and adjust the seasonings, then finish with the remaining parsley.

5   Arrange the fillets on a large platter with a mound of the beans between them and perch the salad on top of the beans. Garnish the plate with a few additional strands of preserved lemon zest, if using, and circle the plate with a drizzle of olive oil if desired. Serve immediately.

Stock 'n' Beans

There are a few ways to make beans taste really, really good—rich and completely appetizing. Unfortunately, two of them involve huge amounts of fat: butter (which you see a lot in India) and cream (which you see a lot in France). But cooking this dish with James reminded me of how much I love beans cooked in stock, which is another terrific technique and one that, combined with a little extra-virgin olive oil and perhaps a bit of garlic, turns white beans (or the pale green beans known as flageolets) into a luxury dish.

Cook your beans in water until just about tender, as usual; if you have some fresh thyme, throw it in there. Then replace the water with good stock (this is the right time to add salt, too) and cook them, adding some more stock if necessary, until they are really soft, though not falling apart. About three minutes before you're going to serve them, add a teaspoon to a tablespoon of minced garlic and, just before serving, a drizzle of extra-virgin olive oil and salt to taste.

Seared Scallops with Curried Lentils

MARK BITTMAN | **Makes:** 4 SERVINGS **Time:** 30 MINUTES

To counter James's wonderful Halibut with White Beans, I wanted to come up with some strong flavors simply, and to shorten the cooking time. After all, his beans needed soaking, or at least long cooking, and finding preserved lemons can be a challenge. So I settled on red lentils—the fastest-cooking of all legumes—and scallops, two quick-cooking and easy-to-find ingredients, and seasoned them with curry powder. The results make a terrific and quick weeknight meal.

2 tablespoons extra-virgin olive oil or any neutral oil, like corn or canola

1 large onion, roughly chopped

⅓ cup peeled and finely chopped carrot

1 stalk celery, trimmed and roughly chopped

2 tablespoons curry powder or Garam Masala (page 248)

¾ cup red lentils

2 tablespoons currants or raisins

2 tablespoons butter (or use more oil)

1½ pounds sea scallops

Salt and black pepper to taste

About 1 tablespoon lemon zest, for garnish

1   Put the oil in a large skillet or casserole over medium-high heat; a minute later, add the onion, carrot, and celery and cook, stirring occasionally, until the mixture starts to take on a little color. Stir in 1 table-spoon of the curry powder, then 2 cups water. Bring to a boil and add the lentils. Bring back to a boil, add the currants, then cover and adjust the heat so the mixture simmers steadily. Cook until the liquid has evaporated and the lentils are tender, about 20 minutes.

2   Meanwhile, put the butter in a large non-stick skillet and turn the heat to medium-high; begin to dredge the scallops lightly in the remaining 1 tablespoon curry powder. When the butter foam subsides, add the scallops swiftly but not all at once. Turn them individually as they brown, allowing 2 or 3 minutes for the first sides and 1 to 2 minutes for the second sides. Season with salt and pepper as they cook.

3   Uncover the lentils and, if necessary, boil off any excess water. Season to taste with salt and pepper. Serve the seared scallops on a bed of the lentils, garnishing each serving with a little lemon zest.

SHOP TALK: A Real Chef…

A discussion with James Boyce that took place while I was cooking my scallops:

JAMES: "I was hoping you would use a spoon to turn your scallops, like a real chef would do."

MB: "Why does a real chef use a spoon to turn scallops?"

JAMES: "Because a real chef can't keep track of his spatula."

Sea Bass Fillets with Mushroom Beurre Noisette

JEAN-GEORGES VONGERICHTEN | **Makes:** 4 SERVINGS **Time:** ABOUT 1 HOUR

The vegetarian mushroom jus in this dish is a lesson in combining a few simple flavors to produce something rich and almost luxurious without meat or much time. Really, most of the work goes into this component and the vegetable garnish; the fish requires only a few minutes to cook. Like many of Jean-Georges's dishes, it demonstrates that simplicity can pack a real wallop.

Beurre noisette is simply butter cooked until it browns. As long as you don't overcook it, it's simple stuff (and, if you do overdo it, it becomes beurre noir, or black butter—a legitimate variation).

8 ounces white mushrooms, washed and sliced

7 tablespoons butter

1½ tablespoons honey

1 tablespoon fresh lime juice

1 tablespoon sherry vinegar

1 tablespoon soy sauce

2 hazelnuts

2 almonds

1 tablespoon coriander seeds

1 tablespoon sesame seeds

½ tablespoon black pepper

Salt

10 pearl onions, peeled and halved

20 lima or peeled fava beans

4 (6-ounce) sea bass, red snapper, or other fillets

Large bowl ice water

Pinch cayenne pepper

½ cup cream

20 cherry tomatoes, halved

2 tablespoons minced fresh marjoram or oregano

1 Combine the mushrooms and 2 tablespoons of the butter in a skillet and turn the heat to high. Cook for about 2 minutes, stirring occasionally, then drizzle with the honey. When the mushrooms brown—the natural sugars in the honey will cause this to happen quickly—add the juice, vinegar, and soy sauce, and pour into a small saucepan.

2 Add 1 cup water to the skillet in which you browned the mushrooms and cook over high heat, stirring occasionally, for about 1 minute. Transfer the water to the saucepan and simmer this mixture over medium-low heat for about 30 minutes; a thin-bladed knife will meet little or no resistance when inserted into the thickest part. Then strain; reserve the liquid and discard the solids.

3 Meanwhile, combine the nuts, coriander, sesame seeds, and pepper in a small dry skillet; turn the heat to medium. Toast, shaking the pan occasionally, until the spices are fragrant, just a minute or two. Grind to a powder in a mortar and pestle or spice or coffee mill.

4 Bring a medium pot of water to a boil and salt it. Add the onions and cook for about 5 minutes, or just until tender. Remove with a slotted spoon and add the lima beans and cook for about 2 minutes, or just until tender. Remove with a slotted spoon and set aside.

5 Put 3 tablespoons of the butter in a small saucepan over medium heat. Stir, scraping down the sides with a rubber spatula, until the butter foam subsides and the butter turns nut brown. Immerse the bottom of the pan in a bowl or pan of ice water to stop the cooking (this will only take 30 seconds or so), then keep warm over the lowest possible heat.

6 Put the nut and seed powder onto a plate, season the fillets with salt and cayenne and brush with cream on all sides. Dredge the flesh sides in the spice mixture and set aside.

7 Put the remaining 2 tablespoons butter in a skillet large enough to hold the fish in 1 layer (work in batches if you have to; you'll need a little more butter). Turn the heat to medium-high. When the butter melts, add the fish and turn the heat to high. Cook 3 to 4 minutes per side, turning once, until the fish is cooked through.

8 Combine the mushroom stock and the beurre noisette and heat through; season to taste, then stir in the onions, beans, and tomatoes. Put each fish fillet in a bowl and surround with the broth and vegetables. Garnish with the marjoram and serve.

How a Master Seasons Fish

I've never seen Jean-Georges use black pepper on fish. As a matter of routine, at this point unconscious, when he seasons fish he does so with salt and cayenne, not salt and black pepper.

I once asked him why. His response: "I think cayenne complements fish better; it's a little more complex than black pepper, and, if you don't use too much—usually a tiny pinch per fillet is enough; you can almost count the grains—it's actually far milder. Black pepper is very assaultive, and far more fragrant, and these are qualities I think are better with big, fatty, rich foods like meat. Fish needs something a little more subtle, but still with flavor."

The logic, to me, is elusive, but there's no question that in practice he's right, and I've followed his lead on this one for a long time—at least for some dishes; when cooking Vietnamese food, I revert to black pepper for everything. (Interestingly, Michel Richard often uses ground coriander in place of black pepper on fish.)

Sesame-Crusted Fish with Soy, Butter, and Ginger Sauce

MARK BITTMAN | Makes: 4 SERVINGS Time: 15 MINUTES

This dish is a breeze, largely because of the sesame seed crust, which guarantees both flavor and crunch. And the sauce takes about 3 minutes to make.

Use any firm white fillets you like here, from sea bass to red snapper or grouper.

1 cup sesame seeds, more or less

Salt and black pepper

3 tablespoons neutral oil, like corn or canola

4 (6-ounce) skinless fillets black sea bass, red snapper, or the like

2 tablespoons butter

1 tablespoon peeled and minced fresh ginger

2 tablespoons soy sauce

1 Preheat the oven to 200°F. Preheat a large, heavy skillet over medium heat while you prepare the sesame seeds. Put them on a plate and season with salt and pepper; add the oil to the skillet. When the oil shimmers, begin to turn the fillets in the seeds, encouraging them to coat the fillets as fully as possible, and add the fillets to the skillet.

2 Brown the fish on 1 side for a couple of minutes, then turn and brown on the other side, another minute or two. Remove the skillet from the heat and transfer the fish to a plate (don't worry if it's done); put the plate of fish in the oven to keep warm.

3 When the skillet has cooled slightly, return it to the stove over medium heat. Add the butter and, when it melts, the ginger. About 30 seconds later, add the soy sauce and ¼ cup water and stir to blend. Return the fillets to the skillet, along with any of their accumulated juices.

4 Turn the heat to medium and cook the fillets for a total of about 4 minutes, turning 3 or 4 times. (If at any time the pan seems to dry out entirely, add 2 or 3 tablespoons water.) At this point, the fish should be done (a thin-bladed knife inserted into its thickest point will meet little resistance). Serve with the pan juices spooned over the fish.

Fusion That Works

I'm not a huge fan of so-called fusion cuisine, but some ingredients from the East and the West were married for the first time late in the last century (a couple of them, arguably for the first time, by Jean-Georges Vongerichten) and they'll never again be separated. Chief among these, in my opinion, are soy sauce and butter.

Until well after World War II, butter was considered disgusting by the Japanese (probably still is, in many circles). And until ten years ago, if you wanted to buy soy sauce in Paris, well let's just say it was easier to buy pig's ears. But in the last few years, the combination of soy and butter has gained favor in many culinary circles, including those in France and Japan, largely because it is a magical one.

It's one I was introduced to by Jean-Georges, the adventuresome and open-minded French chef who has spent a great deal of his career cooking and eating in Asia. I love the combination (and the combination of nam pla and butter, which I'm quite sure was "invented" by Jean-Georges) and I know he does too, so I think of my simple fish dish—which he obviously enjoyed—as a kind of tribute.

Skate Wing with Tamarind Gastrique

JAMES BOYCE | **Makes:** 2 SERVINGS **Time:** 30 MINUTES

James's food bears the mark of the formal French training he had, first at the Culinary Institute of America and later in the kitchen at Le Cirque (where he worked for Daniel Boulud), but he's not afraid to incorporate new ingredients into his dishes. Since he has a wonderful palate, the results are often fabulous.

This fancified version of the classic Skate with Brown Butter and Honey (see page 96 for my more basic recipe), with the exotic flavors of tamarind, ginger, and anise—served over porcini mushrooms—grabbed my attention the first time I ate it. With its gastrique—essentially a sweet-and-sour sauce—and exotic ingredients, it's a quite miraculous transformation of a once-simple dish.

You could cook it as James does, with three or more pans going at once, but I've broken it down into easier-to-execute steps. Still, if your skate wings are exceptionally large, you may need to cook them sequentially, or use two pans.

For Tamarind Sauce, follow Charles Phan's procedure on page 160.

½ cup sugar

2 tablespoons anise honey or regular honey mixed with ½ teaspoon ground anise or fennel

20 dates, halved and pitted

1 cup tamarind sauce

1 tablespoon peeled and minced fresh ginger

½ lemon, juiced

3 tablespoons extra-virgin olive oil

8 ounces fresh and preferably small porcini or shiitake mushrooms, halved lengthwise (if you use shiitakes, discard the stems)

Salt and black pepper to taste

4 tablespoons (½ stick) butter

2 (12-ounce) skinless skate wing fillets

¼ cup walnuts, toasted and chopped

1   Combine the sugar and honey in a small saucepan with 1 tablespoon water and cook over medium heat until the mixture liquefies and browns. Add the dates and cook them, stirring, for 1 minute or so. Add the tamarind paste, ginger, and lemon juice; stir to incorporate and taste (making sure to let the sauce cool on the spoon for a minute before tasting) for seasoning. Adjust with more lemon juice or tamarind, as necessary, and keep warm over low heat.

2 Heat 1 tablespoon of the olive oil in a small sauté pan over medium-high heat and after 1 minute or so, when the oil is shimmering, add the mushrooms, cut sides down. Cook them on the first side for 2 to 3 minutes, until nicely and rather deeply browned, then flip them over and season with salt and pepper. Turn the heat down to medium, add 2 tablespoons of the butter, and cook them another 3 to 5 minutes, until aromatic and cooked through. Keep warm over low heat.

3 Heat the remaining 2 tablespoons olive oil in a 12- to 14-inch sauté pan, preferably non-stick (or split it between 2 smaller non-stick pans), over medium-high heat. After 1 minute or so, when the oil is shimmering, add the skate wings. Season them with salt and pepper and let them cook for 3 to 5 minutes—the idea is to finish about two-thirds of the cooking on the first side, ensuring a beautifully crisped and browned presentation side. When the first side is colored but short of being ready to flip, add the remaining 2 tablespoons butter, cook 30 seconds more, and flip the wings over (use two spatulas if necessary to keep the skate from breaking). Cook about 2 minutes more; the fish is done when a thin-bladed knife inserted into its thickest part meets little resistance. Remove from the heat.

4 Divide the mushrooms among 4 plates, lay a portion of the skate on top, and spoon the gastrique over all. Garnish with the toasted walnuts and serve immediately.

Skate Skills

Whole, fresh skate is not only ugly, it's hard to handle. To remove the skin, you need a super-sharp knife and a lot of skill, or a pair of pliers—and even then it won't be easy. (Trust me: Don't buy skin-on skate.)

The central cartilage (skate is a member of the shark family and has no bones) is actually edible if cooked long enough to soften it.

But few novices are going to go in that direction, so you have one of two choices: You can buy skate that has been filleted, that is, removed from its central cartilage, which is the most common solution, and the one I strongly recommend.

Or, you can leave the cartilage intact and cook the skate considerably longer than indicated in the recipe. You're essentially cooking two fillets in a sandwich, so it takes the heat a while to reach the center—in which case, once it's done, remove it from the cartilage in two separate pieces (this is most easily accomplished with a spatula).

Skate with Brown Butter and Honey

MARK BITTMAN | **Makes:** 4 SERVINGS **Time:** 20 MINUTES

Poaching skate is a classic French technique but, like James, I prefer sautéing. Unlike James, I never thought of making the brown butter that typically accompanies it even sweeter by using honey, but I've also never been above appropriating a good idea, and I do think my simpler version captures some of the spirit of James's more elegant (and more complicated) dish.

Flour, for dredging

Salt and black pepper to taste

3 tablespoons extra-virgin olive oil

2 (12-ounce) skinless skate wing fillets

4 tablespoons (½ stick) butter

½ cup honey

2 tablespoons capers, drained, or to taste

2 tablespoons white wine vinegar

Chopped fresh parsley leaves, for garnish

1   Put a large skillet over medium-high heat. While it is heating, put the flour on a plate and season it with salt and pepper. Put the oil in the skillet—it should coat the bottom well—and turn the heat to high. When the oil shimmers, dredge the skate lightly in the flour, shaking to remove the excess, and add it to the pan. (You may have to cook in batches; if so, keep the skate warm in a low oven while preparing the sauce.)

2   Cook until the skate is nicely browned on the first side, about 5 minutes, then turn (use 2 spatulas if necessary to keep the skate from breaking). Cook on the second side, adjusting the heat so the fish does not burn, until it is firm to the touch, another 3 minutes or so. Reduce the heat to medium and transfer the skate to a warm platter.

3   Add the butter and honey to the pan and cook until bubbly, 1 to 2 minutes. Add the capers and swirl them around, then pour the butter over the fish. Immediately add the vinegar to the pan that the butter was in, swirl it around, and pour it over the fish. Garnish with parsley and serve immediately.

Better Butter: Beurre Noisette

Used here and in the Jean-Georges recipe on page 90, beurre noisette is browned, or nut-colored, butter, a French classic that fully qualifies as a sauce yet contains only one ingredient. Get over your fear of butter—about 1 tablespoon per serving is all you need, not really that much—and you might find yourself using it all the time, especially over fish.

I integrate making of the beurre noisette into my skate dish, but it's usually done separately.

For 4 servings, put 3 or 4 tablespoons of butter in a small saucepan over medium heat. Stir, scraping down the sides with a rubber spatula, until the butter foam subsides and the butter turns nut-brown. Immerse the bottom of the pan in a pan or bowl of ice water to stop the cooking, then keep warm over the lowest possible heat until you're ready to use it (use it within ten minutes).

Poultry & Eggs

Most home cooks automatically think "chicken" (and these days, even "chicken breast") when they hear the word "poultry," but the category drives chefs in many different directions. In fact, only a minority of the recipes here are chicken; we have squab, Cornish hen (my contribution), quail, rabbit (not exactly poultry but closer to chicken than to beef), and duck.

Here, you'll find only one chicken breast recipe, which doesn't mean that the recipes are all exotic; the assortment ranges from quick stir-fries from Charles Phan and me to a fairly complicated but accessible duck recipe by Gary Danko (countered by a very straightforward one from me) and a simple but very unusual squab from Jean-Georges Vongerichten. For good measure, we've included a few egg recipes, all but one useful for quick weeknight dinners.

Wok-Cooked Chicken with Nuts and Fruits

CHARLES PHAN | **Makes:** 4 SERVINGS   **Time:** 20 MINUTES

Charles Phan was born in Vietnam, but his parents came from China, and he's an all-time pro stir-fryer. In this basic dish, he combines a number of semi-exotic ingredients but is quick to point out that, as in all stir-fries, you can substitute freely.

This is fortunate, because you may have a hard time finding fresh gingko nuts, which are soft and meaty; you should, however, be able to find dried Chinese dates (also called jujubes) in most Asian markets. In any case, the idea here is to use a few different types of nuts and dried fruit, so each bite tastes different. I wouldn't hesitate to include raisins, "regular" dates, or filberts (hazelnuts).

Serve this, of course, with plain white rice.

½ cup peanut oil (preferred), or neutral oil like corn or canola, as needed

1 pound boneless chicken meat, preferably from the thigh, thinly sliced

1 tablespoon minced garlic

½ cup chicken stock

¼ cup sake or rice wine

2 tablespoons fish sauce (nuoc mam)

1 tablespoon sugar

1½ cups mixed nuts and dried fruit (Charles used fresh gingko, dried Chinese dates, raisins, cashews, and walnuts)

½ cup trimmed and chopped scallions

Salt and black pepper if necessary

1   Heat a wok or large frying pan over very high heat until smoking. Add half the oil and, a few seconds later, as much chicken as will fit in one layer (you may have to cook the chicken in two batches). Cook, stirring infrequently, until the meat loses its pinkness, 2 to 3 minutes. Remove from the pan with a slotted spoon, drain out most of the oil, and return the pan to the heat.

Cooking at Super-High Heat Ain't Easy

I'd never cooked over *really* high heat before, so I welcomed the chance to cook on one of Charles Phan's woks, 168,000 BTUs of fire, fed by a two-and-a-half-inch gas line (the one feeding your kitchen is probably a half inch).

What amazed me, apart from the *noise* (the roar of the gas fire makes you raise your voice), was that even with that much heat Charles cooked in batches during my lesson—much as I normally do when stir-frying. The differences are the speed with which he was able to cook (we were at the wok for *maybe* three minutes) and the resulting "breath of the wok" (see sidebar, page 103).

"You cook these dishes fast, and you'd better eat them fast," said Charles. "Their shelf-life is about three minutes."

When it was my turn, I couldn't keep up. I burned garlic, I burned scallions, I almost burned chicken. I certainly overheated the oil, and nearly sprained my wrist trying to get the wok-shaking motion right (Charles rotates his cooks through this station, because the constant motion is a frequent cause of repetitive motion injuries.) Just about the only thing I did get right was the trick of turning the gas on and off with my knee.

I was glad to return to a normal stove, which I did for my dish.

2 Add the garlic and stir once, then immediately add the stock, sake, fish sauce, and sugar. Stir once or twice; if the mixture dries out (at this or any other point) add a splash of water. Add the nuts and fruit and stir for 30 seconds. Return the chicken to the pan, along with the scallions. Taste, adjust seasoning with salt and pepper if needed, and serve.

Stir-Fried Chicken with Broccoli and Walnuts

MARK BITTMAN | **Makes:** 4 SERVINGS **Time:** 20 MINUTES

This is the basic technique for stir-frying without a huge wok, one I've used for twenty years or so, and Charles agrees that it's pretty much the only way to go for home cooks.

In fact, his one criticism of my dish (during the making of which he commented that I must have had "Asian blood") was the hoisin—he said it robbed the dish of subtlety (something for which I've never been known). So let's consider it optional, though I'll continue to use it.

Salt

2 cups broccoli florets, cut into small pieces

3 tablespoons peanut oil, or neutral oil like corn or canola, as needed

1 pound boneless chicken meat, preferably from the thigh, thinly sliced

1 tablespoon peeled and minced fresh ginger

1 tablespoon minced garlic

½ cup chicken stock

1 cup walnuts

½ cup trimmed and chopped scallions

1 tablespoon hoisin sauce (optional)

Black pepper if necessary

1   Set a medium pot of water to boil and salt it. Poach the broccoli in the water until it turns bright green and begins to become tender, just a couple of minutes. Drain.

2   Heat a large frying pan over very high heat until smoking. Add 2 tablespoons of oil and, a few seconds later, as much chicken as will fit in one layer (you may have to cook the chicken in two batches). Cook, stirring occasionally, until all the meat loses its pinkness, 2 to 3 minutes. Remove from the pan with a slotted spoon.

3   Add the broccoli and cook, stirring occasionally, until it begins to brown a bit, then remove with a slotted spoon. Add the remaining oil, along with the ginger and garlic. Stir for 30 seconds; return the broccoli and chicken to the pan, along with the stock.

The "Breath of the Wok" Comes Home

Stir-frying at home uses the same principles as it does in restaurants, but each stage takes a bit longer, and sometimes precooking is necessary. You'll almost always need to parboil hard vegetables like broccoli, asparagus, cauliflower, carrots, and so on, even if you cut them fairly small. Just cook them in boiling salted water until they're about half done, then drain (you can do this up to a day in advance if you like). If you want to avoid precooking, use vegetables like red bell peppers or onions or both; they need no parboiling and become tender and sweet in three or four minutes.

Be sure, too, to cut the meat in small cubes or thin slices; it should just about cook through in the time it takes to brown (this will often mean cooking in batches so the meat doesn't steam in its own juices). And although nuts aren't essential, I like them for their flavor, their chunkiness, and the fact that they need no preparation time.

Charles agreed that, using these techniques, you get a bit of what he calls "the breath of the wok"—a certain firmness and smokiness that high stovetop heat can give. The key is to keep the heat as high as you can and the cooking time as short as you can, so the food is almost shocked by the heat, but not burned.

4 Cook for about 1 minute, then add the nuts. Stir once or twice; if the mixture dries out at this or any other point, add a splash of water. Stir in the scallions and, if you're using it, the hoisin. Taste, adjust seasoning with salt and pepper if needed, and serve.

Stuffed Chicken "Poule au Pot"

SUZANNE GOIN | **Makes:** 6 SERVINGS **Time:** 1½ HOURS (OR 4 HOURS INCLUDING TIME FOR SUB-RECIPES), PLUS A FEW HOURS RESTING TIME

When Suzanne and I first talked about this dish, she made it sound simple: "It's just a stuffed chicken leg served with a little broth, inspired by the traditional poule au pot." And, to her credit, when it's on the table in front of you, it seems an honest creation, a barely dandified version of that French classic.

But as I saw in her kitchen (and you can tell from the supplementary recipes here) this dish is a labor of love. The good news is that each of the components has uses beyond just this dish, so they're worthwhile additions to your culinary repertoire; taken individually, they're really not difficult.

6 large chicken legs, deboned, with the skin on

1 tablespoon fennel seed, toasted in a dry skillet until fragrant, then crushed or ground

1 teaspoon minced garlic

1 teaspoon minced lemon zest

6 (6 x 6-inch) pieces caul fat, available at most good butchers, about 1 pound (see sidebar)

1 recipe Herb-Garlic Butter (page 245)

Salt and black pepper

1 recipe Fennel-Sage Stuffing (page 234)

1 recipe Sage Broth (page 106)

1 recipe Cornichon Sauce (page 246)

1 recipe Fried Sage (page 241)

1 In a large resealable bag or bowl, marinate the chicken legs with the fennel seed, garlic, and lemon for at least 6 hours, or overnight, refrigerated.

2 Preheat the oven to 450°F. Lay the squares of caul fat out on a work surface. Place ½ tablespoon Herb-Garlic Butter in the center of each piece. Season both sides of the chicken legs with salt and pepper and lay one skin side down on top of each pat of butter. Nestle little ½-cup balls of stuffing onto the center of each chicken leg, then gather up the caul fat and bring it over the top of the chicken, using the membrane to help shape each chicken leg into a rough "ball," enclosing the stuffing. Twist the caul fat at the top so that it will hold the chicken balls closed. Then carefully turn the little packages over, seal sides down, onto a rack set over a baking sheet. (There should be some stuffing remaining.)

The Facts on Caul Fat

Caul fat is the thin, lacy membrane that encases a pig's internal organs. This fact is not a particularly good selling point and—given today's attitudes about any animal part other than muscle—has kept caul fat from establishing any prominence in the larder of the contemporary home cook.

But caul fat is inexpensive to the point of being nearly free (it costs around a dollar a pound, which is more than you'll need for any one recipe) and it performs its main function—holding things together—quite admirably. (It also adds a pleasant meatiness to the food it surrounds.) Traditionally, it has been used as a wrap for *crepinettes*, sausage patties, and pâtés, and Suzanne's recipe here is another wonderful application.

Caul fat is usually frozen when you buy it (typically, finding it will take a trip to a real butcher, though a supermarket can order it for you). You can keep if frozen for months before thawing, which is most easily done in cold water; change the water a few times to remove any gamy smell. It will usually adhere to itself when you use it to wrap something, but if it does not you can easily tie its ends; it's very strong.

The most amazing feature of caul fat is that by the time you've sautéed, roasted, or grilled whatever you've wrapped in it, the caul fat will have melted away, leaving barely a trace of itself. So you don't have to explain anything to your guests about pig membranes.

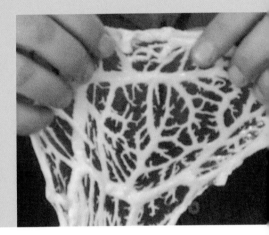

3 Transfer the chicken legs to a pan and roast for 30 to 40 minutes, or until the meat is done, the skin crispy, and the caul fat melted (it will virtually disappear). If there's still a little nubbin of caul fat on the seam side of the chicken, snip or slice it off before serving your guests.

4 Let the chicken legs rest for a few minutes before you assemble the dish and, in that time, run about 1 cup of the remaining stuffing under the broiler, until crisp on top. Add the blanched vegetables back to the broth (see Sage Broth recipe) and bring it to a boil.

5 To serve, put 2 tablespoons stuffing at the center of each of 6 large shallow bowls. Ladle ½ cup or more broth into each bowl, portioning the vegetables evenly, and then perch the chicken on top of the stuffing. Spoon 1 tablespoon Cornichon Sauce over the chicken, garnish the bowl with Fried Sage, and serve immediately.

Sage Broth

Makes: 2 QUARTS **Time:** 20 TO 30 MINUTES, WITH PREMADE OR CANNED STOCK

Use this as in the preceding recipe or add some egg noodles along with some shredded leftover chicken or turkey and the cooked vegetables for a warming fall lunch or evening meal.

6 cups Chicken Stock (page 249) or use canned broth

1 bunch sage stems (leaves reserved for Fried Sage, page 241), tied into a small bundle

1 leek, quartered lengthwise, then cut into 1½-inch pieces

1 bunch Swiss chard, stemmed and chopped

2 large carrots, peeled and roughly chopped

1   Bring the stock to a boil and add the sage stems bundle.

2   Add the leeks and blanch them in the broth until soft, 5 minutes or less depending on their thickness; use a strainer or slotted spoon to remove them to a platter. Blanch the chard for 1 minute and remove; drain excess liquid, transfer to a cutting board and chop finely. Blanch the carrots until tender, 5 to 10 minutes; remove with a strainer. Remove and discard the sage stem bundle.

3   Use the broth alone as needed or if serving as a soup, return the vegetables to the broth and heat through.

"Much Easier" Chicken Legs with Stuffing

SUZANNE GOIN | **Makes:** 4 SERVINGS **Time:** 30 MINUTES, WITH PREMADE STUFFING

After Suzanne demonstrated her admittedly complex Stuffed Chicken "Poule au Pot" (page 104), we took a break while the legs cooked. She had marinated a couple of extra chicken legs and without fanfare or flourish, threw them in a pan, skin sides down, put a slightly larger pan on top of them, and walked away from the stove. A couple minutes later she flipped them, and five minutes later, topped them with a scoop of that delicious Fennel-Sage Stuffing (page 234)—our meal was ready.

This is unquestionably the way to go if you want to combine this wonderful stuffing with boned chicken legs for a weeknight meal.

4 large chicken legs, deboned (see sidebar), preferably with skin on

1 tablespoon ground fennel seed, toasted in a dry skillet until fragrant, then crushed or ground

1 teaspoon minced garlic

1 teaspoon minced lemon zest

Salt and black pepper

2 tablespoons olive oil

1 recipe Fennel-Sage Stuffing (page 234)

1   Preheat the oven to 350°F. Pat the chicken legs dry with paper towels, then season them generously with salt and pepper. Rub the chicken legs with the fennel seed, garlic, and lemon.

2   Heat the oil in a large skillet over medium-high heat and after a minute or so, when the oil is shimmering, add the legs skin sides down. Place another skillet (or bricks wrapped in foil) on top of the legs and cook them for 5 to 7 minutes, undisturbed, until the skin is crisped and golden brown, and the legs are no longer sticking to the pan.

3   While the legs are cooking, heat or reheat the stuffing in a foil-covered pan in the oven. Flip the chicken skin sides up, and cook uncovered 2 to 5 minutes more, until the legs are crisp and firm but not dry. Let the legs rest 1 to 2 minutes off the heat while you portion out the warmed stuffing, then serve.

The Boned Chicken Leg

Although boneless chicken legs are increasingly common in supermarkets these days (the Whole Foods around the corner from Suzanne's Los Angeles restaurant had them the day we cooked together, and my supermarket has them most of the time), they're not yet a staple. Here's how to bone a whole chicken leg.

Use a heavy knife or cleaver to chop off the knuckle of the drumstick bone. Use a paring knife to make an incision through the meat (non-skin) side of the leg running from the top of the thighbone to the bottom of the drumstick. Cut the meat away from the thick center bone of the thigh, then scrape around the bottom of the bone where it's connected to the drumstick bone.

Pull out the thighbone, then run the tip of the knife down the sides of the drumstick. The bone should pull away easily from the leg meat.

Chicken Breasts Stuffed with Prosciutto and Parmigiano-Reggiano

MARK BITTMAN | Makes: 4 SERVINGS Time: 40 MINUTES

I was inspired by Suzanne's stuffed chicken legs, and determined to produce something nearly as elegant but far less complicated. One way to do that is to turn to ingredients that already have great developed flavors, and there are none better than prosciutto and Parmigiano-Reggiano.

You could stuff boneless thighs or legs in this same manner, but it's a bit trickier to pound them out, and chicken breasts are far easier to find. The results are delicious either way. At Lucques, I served the chicken on a bed of sautéed spinach to echo the greens in Suzanne's dish, but you could serve this with almost any vegetable.

4 (6-ounce) chicken breast halves

Salt and black pepper to taste

4 slices prosciutto, preferably imported, halved

Several thin slices Parmigiano-Reggiano

Chopped fresh parsley leaves

2 tablespoons extra-virgin olive oil

2 tablespoons butter (or use more oil)

½ cup white wine or water

2 tablespoons balsamic vinegar

1 Preheat the oven to 400°F. In turn, put each of the breast pieces between two sheets of plastic wrap and pound firmly with a mallet or other object (your fist will work, too), until evenly flattened and less than ¼ inch thick. Season with salt (not too much since both the prosciutto and Parmigiano-Reggiano are salty) and pepper, then layer on a couple of pieces of prosciutto, some Parmigiano-Reggiano, and a good sprinkling of parsley. Roll up and, if necessary, skewer with a toothpick or two (if your chicken is evenly flat and more or less uniform, and you roll tightly, it will self-seal).

2 Put an ovenproof skillet, large enough to accommodate the 4 rolls comfortably, over medium-high heat and wait 1 or 2 minutes. Add the olive oil and 1 tablespoon of the butter (the butter should sizzle) and, when the butter foam subsides, put the rolls in the pan. Brown the rolls on one side, 3 or 4 minutes. Flip them, then immediately put the pan in the oven. Cook until the rolls are done, about 15 minutes (they will be lightly browned and quite firm when done, but it's safest to cut into one to be sure the meat is no longer bright pink). Remove to a cutting board and let rest.

3 Put the skillet back on top of the stove over medium-high heat. Add the wine and cook, stirring and scraping the bottom of the pan, until the liquid is all but evaporated. Stir in the vinegar and reduce by half, just a couple of minutes, then stir in the remaining 1 tablespoon butter until it melts; taste and adjust seasoning. Cut the rolls into 1-inch slices, arrange on a serving platter, pour the sauce over all, and serve.

Prosciutto and Parmigiano versus Ham and Cheese

When I was a kid, there was a dish served in fancy restaurants called veal cordon bleu, which later—as chicken breasts became a popular substitute for veal cutlets—became chicken cordon bleu. Both were made with more or less random ham and cheese; the fact that you were stuffing and rolling the meat was impressive enough a trick (and, indeed, it's pretty cool, because you get a nice pinwheel effect).

But when you use real prosciutto and real Parmigiano-Reggiano, both of which come from the area around Parma, Italy, you are doing more than creating a cool look—you are really adding some flavor. Both ham and cheese age for more than a year, so in a way this recipe began eighteen months ago, with the milking of the cows and the salting of the meat.

It's not that you couldn't use other ham and other cheese, but the point is that traditionally made and well-aged specimens of each are what's going to give you great flavor in this dish.

Grilled Quail with Bitter Greens Salad

GARY DANKO | Makes: 4 SERVINGS Time: 30 MINUTES, PLUS MARINATING TIME

Gary's Poultry Marinade will improve any bird, but quail, with their very slight gaminess and delightfully dense meat, seem to have been made for it.

Many times, quail are sold with their breastbones removed. If that's how you find them, or you have a cooperative butcher, that's great. Otherwise, removing the breastbone is a task I wouldn't wish on anyone. The alternative is to semi-bone the quail as described in the Broiled Squab with Jordan Almonds (page 124)—deboning the breast while leaving wing and leg intact. Cooking time for these half-boned birds will be just over half the time given above.

You could also use spatchcocked (split) Cornish hens or even a cut-up chicken (both will take longer to cook than the quail), marinated and served in the same way. Just make sure you're using the best balsamic vinegar you can find. In any case, you can broil the quail (or their alternatives) instead of grilling them; cooking time will remain about the same.

4 quail, breastbones removed

1 recipe Poultry Marinade (recipe follows)

1 clove garlic, peeled

⅓ cup extra-virgin olive oil

2 tablespoons good balsamic vinegar, or to taste

Salt and black pepper to taste

6 ounces assorted bitter greens, such as arugula, frisée, chicory, or endive

½ cup pomegranate seeds

1 Marinate the boned quail with the Poultry Marinade in the refrigerator for 24 to 48 hours, turning occasionally.

2 When you're ready to cook, start a charcoal or gas grill; the fire should be moderately hot, and the rack about 4 inches from the heat source. Rub a large bowl thoroughly with the garlic. Add the oil, vinegar, salt, and pepper and whisk. Check for seasoning, adjust as necessary, and leave the garlic clove to macerate in the vinaigrette while you grill the quail.

3 Grill the quail over direct heat, turning as it browns, for about 15 minutes total, until nicely browned and just cooked through. Remove the quail from the grill and allow to rest.

4 Add the greens and pomegranate seeds to the large bowl with the vinaigrette; toss them gently with your hands until evenly coated. Transfer the dressed greens to a large serving platter, arrange the grilled quail alongside, and serve.

Poultry Marinade

GARY DANKO | **Makes:** ABOUT 1 CUP **Time:** 10 MINUTES

½ cup California Cabernet
Sauvignon or Merlot

¼ cup extra-virgin olive oil

1 tablespoon minced garlic

1 tablespoon Dijon mustard

2 teaspoons ground coriander

1 teaspoon dried thyme

1 teaspoon salt

Combine all the ingredients in a medium bowl and whisk well to blend thoroughly (emulsify). Use immediately or refrigerate for up to 1 day before using it to marinate the quail or other poultry.

The Littlest Bird

At less than five ounces each, quail are the smallest commercially raised poultry available. And due to their low yield and a relatively low market demand, they can be pretty expensive as well—as much as five dollars apiece from the specialty purveyors who raise them. (You can also find them frozen in Portuguese markets and sometimes at Costco for two dollars apiece or even less.)

In any case, quail make a nice change for the home cook. Their meat is dark and lean with a subtle gamy flavor—certainly without the "liver-y" overtones common to squab, partridge, and the true game birds. High, direct heat, like grilling or deep frying, is the best way to preserve quail's natural succulence and avoid drying them out.

Figure that one bird per person with a salad like Gary's will serve as an elegant main course at lunch or a starter course at dinner. And, after you've politely eaten the breast with fork and knife, attack the rest of the bird with your fingers—it's really the only way.

Sautéed Chicken with Green Olives and White Wine

MARK BITTMAN | **Makes:** 4 SERVINGS   **Time:** 45 MINUTES

I actually cooked this in a skillet over a grill, since Gary already had the grill going for his quail, but it's truly a stovetop dish. Like Gary, I concentrated on the flavors of the California wine country and, like him, I benefited from local produce, using olives, olive oil, wine, and walnuts—all from Villa Mille Rose (see the sidebar). Of course, these are ingredients you can find anywhere these days, so the recipe is easily replicated.

3 tablespoons extra-virgin olive oil

1 (3- to 4-pound) chicken, cut up into serving pieces, for sautéing

Salt and black pepper

2 cups white wine

2 tablespoons balsamic vinegar

1 cup green olives, the flesh lightly cracked with the side of a knife

1 lemon, thinly sliced, seeds picked out

½ cup broken walnuts

¼ cup coarsely chopped fresh parsley or tarragon leaves

1   Put the oil in a deep skillet or casserole, preferably non-stick; turn the heat to medium-high and wait a minute or so, until the oil is hot. Add the chicken, skin sides down, and brown it well, rotating and turning the pieces as necessary; the process will take 10 to 15 minutes. Sprinkle the chicken with salt and pepper as it cooks.

2   With the skin sides up, add the wine, balsamic vinegar, and olives. Adjust the heat so the mixture simmers vigorously and cook until the chicken is almost done, another 10 to 15 minutes.

3   When the chicken is almost done, add the sliced lemon to the mix and cook 2 to 3 minutes more. Arrange the chicken and lemon on a platter and stir the walnuts into the sauce; taste and adjust seasoning, then spoon the sauce over the chicken, along with the parsley or tarragon. Serve hot.

Cooking in Napa

The day after Gary and I cooked in his restaurant kitchen in San Francisco, we traveled together to Napa. It was a late fall day, and a spectacular one: The view of the bay was clear, and when we turned inland, the vineyards, with the harvest just completed, were sparkling with dew. Gardens were filled with November produce and we found persimmons, figs, squash of all kinds, just-cured olives, just-pressed olive oil, walnuts, and more.

Our ultimate destination was Maria Manetti's Tuscan-style estate in Napa Valley, which she calls Villa Mille Rose—the villa of a thousand roses—and, there too, the November harvest was impressive. The four dishes we cooked there— his quail, my chicken, and the persimmon recipes on pages 204 and 206—relied almost entirely on local products, including the birds (from nearby Sonoma), lemons, parsley, olive oil, even vinegar. The walnuts, figs, pomegranates, and persimmons were all from Maria's trees (the olive oil and vinegar were also hers, but produced earlier). We cooked the birds on a grill in Maria's huge kitchen fireplace, a real treat.

Lemon-Peppered Duck Breast

GARY DANKO | Makes: 4 SERVINGS Time: 30 MINUTES, WITH PREMADE HASH,
CRACKLINGS, AND STOCK

Make sure you read through this and the accompanying recipes before tackling them; this is the kind of rustic yet beautiful presentation that is the beacon of elegant restaurants like Gary's and requires some planning. There is nothing challenging here but the time needed, and—if you prepare the recipe the way Gary intends—plenty of it. But the duck stock and confit can be made days or even weeks in advance, so when it comes to putting together the finishing touches, you won't need more than an hour or two.

1 cup chopped fresh parsley leaves	2 whole duck breasts, split and skinned (reserve skin)
2 tablespoons minced garlic	2 tablespoons extra-virgin olive oil
2 tablespoons minced lemon zest	Salt
4 teaspoons coarse black pepper	1 recipe Duck Confit and Potato Hash (page 118)
4 teaspoons dried thyme	1 recipe Gary Danko's Duck Essence (optional, page 249)
2 teaspoons fresh rosemary	

1 Combine the parsley, garlic, lemon zest, pepper, thyme, and rosemary in a shallow bowl. Roll each of the duck breast halves in the herb mixture so that they're coated on all sides. Cut the duck skin into bits and, over medium-low heat in a skillet just large enough to hold the bits in one layer, gently render the fat and let the skin cook until crisp, about 15 minutes. cool, then crumble (these are cracklings).

2 Put the oil in a large sauté pan and turn the heat to medium-high; when the oil shimmers, add the duck and reduce the heat to medium. Cook, turning once or twice, until the coating browns and the duck is medium-rare to medium, about 6 minutes. Season the meat with salt and allow it to rest while you assemble the rest of the plate.

3 Set the Duck Confit and Potato Hash cake just off center of each plate. Slice the duck breasts and fan slices of them around the hash. Drizzle with the Duck Essence and garnish with the cracklings.

Duck Legs Confit

GARY DANKO | **Makes:** 4 LEGS **Time:** AT LEAST 2 DAYS AND UP TO 2 WEEKS, LARGELY UNATTENDED

No wonder duck confit is popular: The process transforms tough duck legs into tender, savory meat, preserves them (for weeks, if you like), and allows you to recook them in minutes, achieving perfectly crisp skin.

You can confit in olive oil, and it's easy and convenient, but if you can get duck fat (which can be ordered or accumulated, see sidebar page 167), the flavor will be better. In Gary's dish, however, where there is flavor coming at you from many directions, oil-confited duck legs will be fine.

4 duck legs

4 teaspoons Confit Spice (page 120)

About 2 quarts duck fat, rendered and strained, or extra-virgin olive oil

1 Season each of the legs with 1 teaspoon Confit Spice, wrap in plastic, and refrigerate for 12 to 48 hours.

2 Preheat the oven to 250°F. Heat the duck fat over medium heat until it liquefies. Arrange the duck legs in an ovenproof baking dish and cover them with the warm fat. Cook the legs in the fat in the oven for 1½ to 2 hours or longer, until a wooden skewer stuck in the thickest part of the legs encounters barely any resistance.

3 Cool the baking dish to room temperature on a baking rack with the duck and fat still in it, then transfer it to the refrigerator, covered, for up to 2 weeks. When you're ready to use the confit, warm the dish in a low (200°F) oven and remove the legs from the fat, then cool the fat to room temperature and freeze to use the next time you make confit.

Duck Breasts as Steak

Both Gabrielle Hamilton's delicious omelet (page 132) and Gary's duck extravaganza on these pages deal with duck breast in an unconventional way. Each chef separates the breast meat from the thick skin that covers it—surprising because many people, myself included, consider the skin/fat layer the best part of the breast.

Needless to say, the chefs are well aware of this, and don't waste the opportunity. Both of them fry the skin into cracklings, which are delicious by themselves or sprinkled on just about anything (especially, it seems to me, mashed potatoes).

But it's worth pointing out that duck breasts take well to simpler treatments. They're easily cut off a whole bird (or bought individually), as fillets, and cooked that way:

Score the skin in a cross-hatched pattern about halfway through the fat, and season well with salt and pepper. Cook them on a grill, under a broiler, or in a heavy skillet over high heat, about three-quarters of the way on the skin side, until crisped and brown, then flip them and give them a minute or so on the flesh side. Serve them rosy, sliced on the bias (next to a pile of Michel Richard's Pont-Neuf Potatoes, page 194, if at all possible), and taste poultry's best impersonation of a good rare steak.

Duck Confit and Potato Hash

GARY DANKO | **Makes:** 4 SERVINGS **Time:** ABOUT 1 HOUR

This integral part of Gary's magnificent duck dish (page 116) is essentially a croquette (see the sidebar for more ideas). It makes an amazing side dish for breakfast or brunch, especially if you have guests you really want to impress.

Salt

2 large thin-skinned, waxy ("new") potatoes, skin-on

1 cup minced onion

Olive oil or duck fat, for cooking, as needed

The meat from 2 Duck Legs Confit (page 117)

½ cup heavy cream, Chicken Stock (page 249), or Duck Essence (page 249)

2 tablespoons chopped fresh parsley leaves

1 tablespoon Worcestershire sauce, or to taste

2 teaspoons Confit Spice (page 120), or to taste

½ teaspoon black pepper, or to taste

Pinch cayenne, or to taste

1   Set a medium pot of water to boil and salt it. Boil the potatoes until firm yet tender, 30 to 40 minutes for large. Cool to room temperature, then mash coarsely. (This can be done well in advance if you prefer.) Meanwhile, sauté the minced onion in 1 tablespoon or so oil, until softened and golden. Cool.

2   When the potatoes and onions have cooled, combine them with the duck meat in a bowl; beat together with a spoon, adding the cream, parsley, Worcestershire, Confit Spice, pepper, and cayenne. Cook a spoonful or so of the batter in a skillet in oil to check the seasoning and adjust as necessary. Form into patties using your hands or a 3-inch ring mold and keep wrapped in plastic in the refrigerator (for up to 1 day) until you're ready to proceed.

3   Heat 3 tablespoons oil in a non-stick skillet over medium heat and when it's shimmering, add the hash cakes. Cook them 3 to 4 minutes on the first side, until nicely browned, then flip them carefully—you'll probably need a spatula and your fingers—and brown on the second side. Serve immediately or keep warm in a low oven until ready to serve.

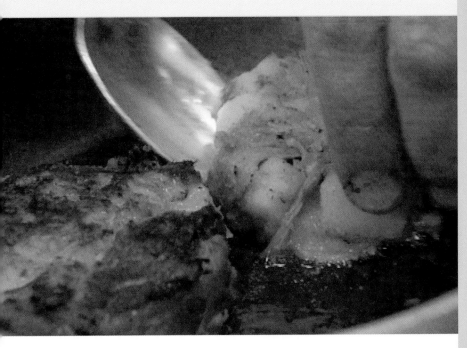

Inventing the Croquette

The eleven ingredients in the accompanying recipe—and especially the duck confit—make it seem more intimidating than it really need be.

For one thing, you can certainly serve the hash (croquettes) simply, independent of the rest of Gary's dish, with a poached or fried egg on top and a salad of bitter greens alongside. At that point, you'd have an elegant and delicious main course in scarcely more time than it takes to make the cakes—assuming, of course, you'd already made the confit.

But even if you have not, think of this as a template: Try combining any savory, salty leftover meat you have on hand—the scraps from Suzanne Goin's pork shoulder confit (page 166), crisped bits of skin and meat from a roasted chicken, some smoked salmon, or really, any pieces of cooked meat or fish—with leftover mashed potatoes. Add a little flour if the mixture seems loose, then fry it up. You've got yourself an irresistible croq uette.

Confit Spice

GARY DANKO | **Makes:** ABOUT 1 CUP   **Time:** 5 MINUTES

Kept cool and dry, Gary's Confit Spice will remain potent for several weeks. Use it to season any poultry or pork; it's a great spice rub for grilling, too.

½ cup kosher salt	1 tablespoon ground allspice
6 bay leaves	1 tablespoon ground ginger
2 tablespoons dried thyme leaves	1½ teaspoons ground nutmeg
1 tablespoon ground coriander	⅛ teaspoon ground cloves
1 tablespoon ground cumin	

1   Grind the salt and bay leaves to a powder in a spice grinder.

2   Stir all the ingredients together in a bowl, then transfer the mixture to a covered container.

SHOP TALK: Gary Danko and the Smiling Oil

Gary is not only one of the three or four most respected chefs on the West Coast, he is just about the best and most articulate cooking teacher in the country. Spend a half hour with him and you start looking at things a different way.

Like all great teachers, he has a succinct and memorable way of summarizing his knowledge. To wit:

"Cooks invented multitasking. We keep on top of things by using all five senses; cooking is about touch, taste, smell, sight, and hearing. I can hear stock talking to me; it keeps me in tune to what is going on."

"Seasoning with salt is very important; salt balances one of the yearnings of your tongue. Most people feel hungry if there's no salt in a meal. So it's important not only to season food while it's

cooking, but to finish dishes with a little bit of salt. That's one of the things that satiates your palate."

"Most of the time, you only need two knives in the kitchen: a paring knife and a chef's knife. They'll do almost everything you need them to."

And my favorite:

"You'll know oil is hot enough to cook in when it shows its dimples and smiles at you."

It's true.

Crisp-Braised Duck Legs with Aromatic Vegetables

MARK BITTMAN | **Makes:** 4 SERVINGS **Time:** ABOUT 2 HOURS, LARGELY UNATTENDED

I rarely have the time for duck confit, but I love duck legs. And though this is clearly less sophisticated than Gary's extravaganza, I get a good crisp skin on the legs, and they become quite tender, all using a recipe that takes less than two hours and requires very little work.

Many supermarkets stock duck legs these days, but it pays to call (or visit) ahead just to make sure.

4 duck legs, trimmed of excess fat	3 celery stalks
1 large onion	Salt and black pepper to taste
8 ounces carrots	2 cups Chicken Stock, preferably homemade (page 249)

1   Preheat the oven to 400°F. Put the duck legs, skin sides down, in a skillet large enough to accommodate all the ingredients comfortably; turn the heat to medium and cook, rotating (but not turning) the pieces downward into the pan as necessary to brown the skin thoroughly and evenly. Meanwhile, peel and dice the vegetables.

2   When the skins are nicely browned, turn and sear the meat sides for just 1 to 2 minutes and season with salt and pepper. Remove to a plate; remove all but enough of the fat to moisten the vegetables (there's plenty more fat where that came from). Add the vegetables along with some salt and pepper and cook, stirring occasionally, over medium-high heat, stirring occasionally, until they begin to brown, 10 to 15 minutes.

3   Return the duck legs, skin sides up, to the pan and add the stock; it should come about halfway up the duck legs but should not cover them. Turn the heat to high, bring to a boil, and transfer to the oven.

4   Cook for 30 minutes, then turn the heat to 350°F. Continue to cook, undisturbed, until the duck is tender and the liquid reduced, at least another 30 minutes and probably a bit longer. (When done, the duck will hold nicely in a 200°F oven for up to another hour.) Serve hot.

The Hard-Working, Great-Tasting Duck Leg

My recipe is neither a straight braise (in which food is poached in liquid) nor a confit (in which it's simmered in fat). This dish employs both, an odd combination and one that works not only with duck legs but with any fatty cut of meat cooked with enough vegetables to disperse the fat so that it becomes a benefit rather than a detriment—think of pork and beans, for example.

As with other animals, the dark meat of birds, which comes from the harder-working muscles, like legs, takes longer to cook—this is why when a whole turkey is cooked the breast dries out by the time the legs are done—in order to become tender. These are the strongest muscles and take the longest to break down, but they are always worth the work and the wait.

And if you compare the flavor and texture of a cooked duck breast to legs that are confited, like Gary's, or bronfited or craised, like mine, you'll become a leg fan too.

Broiled Squab with Jordan Almonds

JEAN-GEORGES VONGERICHTEN | **Makes:** 4 SERVINGS **Time:** 30 MINUTES

Jean-Georges Vongerichten, with whom I've cooked regularly for ten years, is fiercely and determinedly restless. The dishes he created in the late eighties are standards in dozens of restaurants today, and they're almost as fresh and inspired as they were back then. He could've stopped being inventive twenty years ago and he'd still be considered a top chef.

Yet he continues to invent. Some of his innovations don't work, and he's the first to admit it (I especially remember some turmeric cookies that set us both laughing). Others sound goofy but can make you ecstatic upon tasting. This combination of sweet, crunchy nuts with gamy, rich squab is just such a dish.

The simple boning technique, in which the wing is left intact, protecting the breast against overcooking, can be used with any bird, including chicken. You can substitute quail (just split them in half) or even Cornish game hens (as I do in my comparative version on page 126) for the squab; the results will be somewhat less flavorful but much less expensive.

You can buy Jordan almonds in the candy section of most supermarkets—or in a movie theater!

Jean-Georges served this with Chive Spaetzle (page 196).

4 squab, innards and excess fat removed, rinsed and patted dry with paper towels

Salt and black pepper

6 tablespoons (¾ stick) butter, softened

1½ cups (6 to 8 ounces, depending on size) Jordan almonds, finely chopped with a knife or food processor or crushed with the back of a skillet

1   Preheat the broiler; the heat should be as high as possible, the rack set 4 to 6 inches from the heat source. Place the bird on its back on a cutting board. Using a sharp boning knife, begin at the breastbone and, following the bone, cut straight down through the bird. Cut through the shoulder joint, where the wing meets the body. Using your hands, pop out the hip joint and separate the thigh from the body, then cut through the skin, meat, and tendons with the knife. You will have a half bird; handle it gently, since the leg and breast quarters are held together by nothing more than skin. Repeat the process for the other half of the bird. Reserve or discard carcasses.

2 Sprinkle the birds all over with salt and pepper. Smear some of the butter on the bottom of a roasting pan (or whatever you're using to broil) and the rest all over the birds. Put the birds skin sides up in the pan and sprinkle with the crushed almonds; broil, adjusting either the heat or the rack distance, so the almonds melt and the top of the bird browns while the meat cooks through. Squab is best medium-rare (about 125°F on an instant-read thermometer), so the cooking time usually will be between 10 and 15 minutes. Serve, spooning the pan juices over the birds.

Buying Squab

A squab is a pigeon (raised in captivity, not in your local park or roof rafters) that has never flown (and therefore never become tough from using its muscles). I once asked a producer how he knew the difference between squab and pigeon. His answer: "I take the top off the cage; if one flies away, it's not a squab."

Almost all the squab in the United States are raised by a cooperative of farmers in northern California and they, in turn, supply most retailers and wholesalers. The upshot is that if you can find squab you don't need to worry about the comparative quality of the bird, since it's all coming from the same group.

It's finding the squab at all that's usually the issue. Try any upscale market near you—Whole Foods carries squab in many cities—or order them online or over the phone from poultry and game specialists D'Artagnan (800-327-8246, ext. 0, or Orders@dartagnan.com).

Broiled Cornish Hens with Red Hots

MARK BITTMAN | **Makes:** 4 SERVINGS **Time:** 30 MINUTES

Knowing that my knife technique could never match Jean-Georges's (no one has ever made as much fun of me as he has; when I was boning my squab in the recipe on page 124 he grabbed it from me and said, "Let me put both you and the bird out of your misery."), I decided to go with a slightly bigger (and less expensive) bird, forego the boning aspect, and substitute the less subtle (by far) Red Hots (you can buy these in any supermarket or candy store) for the almonds. The recipe follows the same technique, with distinctively different results.

2 (1¼-pound) Cornish hens, split in half, excess fat removed, rinsed and patted dry with paper towels

Salt and black pepper

6 tablespoons (¾ stick) butter, softened

1½ cups (6 to 8 ounces, depending on size) Red Hots, ground to a coarse powder in a coffee grinder or food processor

1   Preheat the broiler; the heat should be as high as possible, the rack set 4 to 6 inches from the heat source. Sprinkle the birds all over with salt and pepper. Smear some of the butter on the bottom of a roasting pan (or whatever you're using to broil) and the rest all over the birds.

2   Put the birds skin sides up in the pan and sprinkle with the Red Hots powder; broil, adjusting either the heat or the rack distance, so the candy melts and the top of the bird browns while the meat cooks through; probably, you'll want high heat but at least 4 inches of distance between the heat source and the top of the bird. Cooking time will be at least 15 minutes, since the birds should be cooked through; be careful not to burn the tops. Serve, spooning the pan juices over the birds.

Candy in the Kitchen

These days, many chefs are cooking with candy—José Andrés uses both Altoids and Pop Rocks at the Mini Bar in Washington, DC, and the famous Ferran Adrià employs Fisherman's Friend at El Bulli in Spain. Jean-Georges has been crushing Jordan almonds (the candy-coated nuts served at weddings everywhere) over poultry for nearly ten years, and he gave me the idea for using Red Hots on my Cornish hens.

Though you can't always claim that you're using "the finest ingredients" when you cook with candy— Red Hots, for example, contain nothing that occurs in nature—the process is kind of fun. In Jean-Georges's dish, the sugar from the nuts caramelizes perfectly, and, for a simple dish, the crunch and flavors are unbeatable. And the Red Hots melt into a cloak over the top of the bird and then harden to a brittle, candy-like (or really, a candy) topping, that is both sweet and hot. As shortcuts to flavor, these are winners.

Braised Rabbit with Olives

ANNA KLINGER | **Makes:** 4 SERVINGS **Time:** ABOUT 2 HOURS, LARGELY UNATTENDED

Rabbit makes a nice change, but to say that it "tastes like chicken" is to acknowledge that neither, at least in their domesticated states, tastes like much of anything. They're both pretty much blank palettes on which we can layer whatever flavors we like.

So, if you can't find rabbit in your local supermarket, or you choose not to eat it, feel free to substitute a whole cut-up chicken in this classic Italian dish, which is best served—as Anna often does it—over a mound of creamy polenta.

2 tablespoons olive oil

1 (2- to 3-pound) rabbit, cut into serving pieces as you would a chicken

Salt and black pepper

5 cloves garlic, crushed

1 or 2 sprigs fresh rosemary

½ cup white wine

2 to 3 cups chicken stock, preferably homemade (page 249)

½ cup canned tomatoes, chopped (don't bother to drain)

12 black oil-cured olives

4 tablespoons (½ stick) butter

1   Preheat the oven to 350°F. Put the oil in a deep skillet or casserole, and turn the heat to medium-high. A minute or so later, when the oil is hot, add the rabbit, season it with salt and pepper and brown it well, rotating and turning the pieces as necessary; the process will take about 10 minutes. Remove the rabbit to a plate, pour off excess fat, if there is any, and return the pan to the stove over medium heat.

2   Add the garlic and rosemary and cook, stirring occasionally, until the garlic is lightly colored, 2 or 3 minutes. Add the wine and raise the heat to high; scrape the bottom of the pan to loosen any browned bits, and reduce the wine until there is just a tablespoon or two of liquid remaining in the pan.

3   Turn the heat down to medium, return the rabbit and any juices to the pan, and add the stock, tomatoes, and olives; cover and transfer the pan to the oven. Cook for 1 to 1½ hours, until the rabbit is tender but not falling off the bone (it tends to dry out at that point). Remove the rabbit, olives, rosemary, and garlic to a plate. Return the pan to the stovetop and reduce the liquid to a thick, sauce-like consistency (you want about 1 cup liquid) over high heat. Stir in the butter, pour over the rabbit, and serve.

When I asked Anna Klinger why she used Sicilian oil-cured olives in her dish (and why she specified twelve) she explained:

"You've got to be careful when you're cooking with olives—you don't want to bite into the rabbit and taste nothing but olives! And Sicilian oil-cured olives don't dominate. Instead, they're a nice surprise when you get one. I like cooking with oil-cured olives because they're less salty than brined olives, and therefore, you have more control over what's happening in the pan."

Chicken alla Cacciatora

MARK BITTMAN | **Makes:** 4 SERVINGS **Time:** 50 MINUTES

"Alla cacciatora" means "hunter's style," and Anna's delicious rabbit dish reminded me of this one, which is similarly Tuscan in spirit. It's not your mother's chicken alla cacciatora, unless your mother's a traditional Italian cook, but a simple sauté of chicken and vegetables that's quick to make and really flavorful. And mastering it will allow you to discover variations of your own. (See the sidebar.)

2 tablespoons extra-virgin olive oil

1 (3- to 4-pound) chicken, cut into 8 pieces, or 4 pounds chicken legs and thighs

Salt and black pepper

1 large onion, sliced

2 medium carrots, peeled and thinly sliced

4 ounces shiitake or white button mushrooms, stems removed and discarded (or reserved for stock), sliced

1 tablespoon minced garlic

1 tablespoon juniper berries, lightly crushed

2 bay leaves

1 cup chicken stock, preferably homemade (page 249)

1 cup chopped tomatoes

Chopped fresh parsley leaves, for garnish

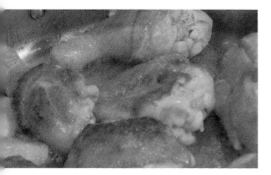

1   Put the oil in a deep skillet or casserole, preferably non-stick, that can later be covered. Turn the heat to medium-high and wait a minute or so, until the oil is hot. Add the chicken, skin sides down. Season it with salt and pepper and brown it well, rotating and turning the pieces as necessary; the process will take 10 to 15 minutes. Remove the chicken to a plate, pour off any excess fat, and turn the heat down to medium.

2   Add the onion, carrots, mushrooms, garlic, juniper berries, and bay leaves and cook, stirring occasionally, until the onion softens, about 10 minutes. Add the stock, then the tomatoes and chicken, along with any accumulated juices. Stir, then partially cover the pan; reduce the heat to low and cook about 20 minutes, or until the chicken is cooked through. Garnish with parsley and serve.

Cacciatora by Any Other Name…

Both chicken and rabbit dishes here follow a pattern for a technique that's sometimes called a "fricassee" and sometimes a "sauté." Brown the meat, add vegetables, flavoring, and a bit of liquid, and cook until the meat is done. It's about the fastest, most flavorful, and most useful way there is of cooking chicken parts.

You can follow this same technique with almost any flavors you like, and not just European ones. Try, for example, using:

• Button mushrooms, pearl (or quartered) onions, and red wine (a very informal coq au vin)

• cubed eggplant, coconut milk, and prepared Thai chile paste

• bacon chunks, onions, carrots, and dark beer

• peas, potatoes, celery, and stock or white wine

• reconstituted dried mushrooms, thyme, and cream

• olives, figs, honey (just a little), and white wine

Each of these dishes needs to be balanced with herbs or spices, and usually some acidity in the form of tomatoes, lemon, lime, or vinegar. But the pattern remains the same in every case.

Rye Omelet with Duck Pastrami

GABRIELLE HAMILTON | **Makes:** 1 LARGE OMELET, ENOUGH TO FEED 2 PEOPLE
Time: ABOUT 1 HOUR

There's something about the simple, elemental nature of this dish—essentially a duck-skin omelet, great at brunch, dinner, or supper—that speaks volumes about the appeal of Prune, Gabrielle's New York restaurant. Her menu features this, along with fried sweetbreads, marrowbones, and raw radishes with bread and butter, dishes that have a nearly Proustian appeal (to me, at least) but for some reason either aren't on the menu at other restaurants or, if they are, come to the table all tarted up.

But for all the gusto of the dish, there's a certain high-mindedness, too: The rye and pastrami flavors she employs are a salute to the history of the neighborhood Prune is in, Manhattan's formerly very Jewish Lower East Side.

Smoked duck breast is akin to pastrami in its texture and flavor. If you can't find it locally, you can find it online with no trouble at dartagnan.com—or substitute pastrami!

1 smoked half duck breast	4 eggs
2 shallots, peeled and thinly sliced crosswise	2 Ryvita dark rye whole-grain crackers, crushed or ground (you can do this with a rolling pin or your hands)
3 tablespoons fresh thyme leaves	
3 tablespoons butter	

1 Pull the duck skin away from the breast meat, using a paring knife if necessary to cut through the membrane (usually you can handle the whole operation with your fingers). Transfer the skin to a small non-stick pan and put it on the stove over low heat. Cook for 30 to 40 minutes to render its fat, turning occasionally. When the skin resembles crispy but not crumbly bacon, remove it from the pan and drain on paper towels; reserve the rendered fat and roughly chop the skin into cracklings.

2 Meanwhile, preheat the oven to 350°F. Warm the duck breast in the oven on a heatproof plate or a foil-lined baking sheet while you make the omelet.

3 Put 1 tablespoon reserved rendered duck fat in a small non-stick pan and turn the heat to medium-high. A minute later, add the shallots and thyme and cook, stirring or tossing occasionally, until softened and light-

ly colored, less than 5 minutes. Transfer the shallots to the plate with the cracklings and return the pan to the stove.

4   Turn the heat down to medium and add the butter. Whisk the eggs until frothy; when the butter foam has subsided, pour the eggs into the pan. Use a spoon or heatproof spatula to pull the cooked egg from the edges of the pan toward the center, letting the uncooked egg pool at the rim.

5   After 3 or 4 minutes, when the omelet still looks a little moist, scatter the top with the crushed rye crackers and a generous handful of the cracklings, and cook 1 to 2 minutes more, until the bottom is golden brown (you can lift up a corner to check the color while it's cooking.)

6   When the bottom has browned, slide the omelet onto a warmed serving plate, folding it in half as you do. Retrieve the smoked duck breast from the oven, thinly slice it on the bias, and serve it alongside the omelet.

SHOP TALK: The Perfect Omelet

Gabrielle and I were talking eggs during this segment, and she mentioned the "Soltner omelet," by which she meant a perfectly rolled, slightly tapered omelet with a tiny curd and just the right amount of moisture, not the more rustic style she serves at Prune. It is said that André Soltner—the much beloved former chef of New York's Lutèce—used to judge whether to hire a new cook at Lutèce by watching him make an omelet. Gabrielle then told a related story:

"My sister was doing a story on the three big French guys—Soltner, Sailhac, and Pepin. And she wanted to invite them to the kitchen for a friendly get-to-know-you, a little lunch, no big deal. So she calls me and says, 'I'm going to have Soltner over; I'm not going to do anything fancy—I'm just going to make omelets.' And I screamed, 'Melissa! He's THE omelet guy! You can't possibly make him an omelet!'"

"But she did it anyway, and she had him over and asked him to show her his technique. And instead of cracking the eggs with one hand

and throwing the shells in the trash, he cracked one and then wiped the inside of the eggshell out with his thumb."

Gabrielle was demonstrating as she told the story, and there really was a fair amount of white stuck to the shell.

"And he told her about growing up during the war and said that this technique 'Made a thirteenth egg out of a dozen.' And he's right. You don't throw anything out."

Salami and Eggs

MARK BITTMAN | **Makes:** 1 LARGE OMELET, ENOUGH TO FEED 2 PEOPLE **Time:** 10 MINUTES

This is the food I grew up eating, cooked in the neighborhood in which I grew up eating it—the Lower East Side of Manhattan; it's the ancestor and primitive soul mate of Gabrielle's dish.

The Katz's Delicatessen salami I used here was intensely spiced—loads of salt and pepper, plus the still-mysterious overtones of garlic, coriander, and who-knows-what-else—so I needed nothing other than the salami to flavor the dish. Serve with brown delicatessen-style mustard and rye bread.

4 ounces salami, or more, cut into ⅛- to ¼-inch-thick slices

4 or 5 eggs

Salt and black pepper

1 Place the sliced salami in a medium to large skillet, preferably non-stick, and turn the heat to medium. Cook the salami for 3 or 4 minutes, turning occasionally, until it begins to color and get crisp. Raise the heat to medium-high. Whisk the eggs with a pinch of salt and some pepper.

2 Just before adding the eggs to the pan, tilt the pan back and forth to coat the bottom with the rendered salami fat. Pour in the beaten eggs and cook undisturbed for 30 seconds. Then use a heatproof spatula or wooden spoon to push the edges of the eggs toward the center of the omelet while tipping the pan so the uncooked eggs from the middle of the pan can reach the perimeter.

3 Repeat until the omelet is still moist but no longer runny, 3 to 5 minutes. If you prefer, you can even stop cooking a little sooner, when there are still some runny eggs in the center; most of this will cook from the heat retained by the eggs, and you'll have a moister omelet.

4 Fold the omelet, or turn it and cook 10 seconds on the other side, or simply invert it onto a plate; serve immediately.

The Mystique of Meat and Eggs

'll always associate this combo of meat with my childhood. We had salami, bologna, corned beef, pastrami, even tongue—cured and smoked, of course—with eggs. The meat was always spicy and needed no seasoning (which was a good thing, as my family was not real big on seasoning anyway) so the whole thing was kind of foolproof; I began making it for myself was I was about ten.

There are a couple of styles possible here, and your choice can still generate arguments. One way is to chop the meat and brown it; another is to slice it. If chopped, you have the option of making an omelet-style dish as above (and either folding it or cooking it like a pancake), or of scrambling the eggs with the meat. If sliced, you're pretty much committed to the omelet style.

But one thing that no one seemed to figure out when I was young is obvious to me now: It's critical not to overcook the eggs. So make sure the meat is at the stage you want it before adding the eggs, because they'll cook quickly.

Meat

Chefs continue to seek and find new and wondrous things with meat, and although we do include a fairly simple steak dish here, even that one—James Boyce's gorgeous tenderloin—has a new-style balsamic reduction taking the place of the old-fashioned wine sauces more typically associated with steak.

All but one of the remaining pairs of dishes I cooked with the chefs overlooked beef; Kerry Simon and I did beef tartare (or nearly tartare in my case), but lamb and pork played a much larger role in the series.

The reason for this is that chefs need to present less familiar items and, though it's easy enough to satisfy carnivorous customers with a simple grilled steak, offerings like Daniel Boulud's Stuffed Saddle of Lamb (page 148), Suzanne Goin's Grilled Pork Confit (page 166), and Chris Schlesinger's classic Slow-Grilled Ribs (page 164)—and my own simpler alternatives—are more enticing to adventuresome eaters.

Steak Tartare

KERRY SIMON | Makes: AT LEAST 4 SERVINGS Time: 30 MINUTES, WITH A LITTLE ADVANCE PREPARATION

Tartare is classic, delicious, easy to make, highly flavorful… and, in these days of fear of undercooked foods, increasingly unusual. Yet this is an impressive, easy-to-execute dish, and the hardest part is finding beef you feel comfortable serving raw. (See The Raw and the Cooked sidebar).

Chop the beef with two knives (that's traditional) or in the food processor, but do not mince it; the pieces should be no smaller than ⅛ inch in any dimension.

Kerry used a Thai-inspired palate to flavor his tartare—ginger, shallots, and lime—but you could just as easily swap them out for the traditional seasonings (as in the variation) without changing the method or the watercress and horseradish cream accompaniments; see the sidebar for inspiration.

3 to 4 tablespoons prepared horseradish

½ cup sour cream

1 pound freshly cut beef tenderloin, chopped with 2 knives or in a food processor

2 tablespoons minced shallot

1 tablespoon finely chopped fresh cilantro leaves

1 tablespoon extra-virgin olive oil

1 tablespoon sesame oil

½ tablespoon peeled and minced fresh ginger

½ tablespoon sesame seeds (preferably black)

½ tablespoon roughly chopped peanuts

1 teaspoon soy sauce

¼ teaspoon Tabasco, or to taste

Salt and black pepper to taste

4 ounces watercress, thick stems removed, washed and dried

Lime wedges

12 toast points or toasted bread slices, rubbed lightly with a cut garlic clove

1   Combine the horseradish and sour cream several hours in advance or the night before; put it and the plates you'll serve the tartare on in the fridge to chill.

2   Combine the beef, shallot, cilantro, olive oil, sesame oil, ginger, sesame seeds, peanuts, soy sauce, and Tabasco in a medium bowl. Toss and season with salt and pepper to taste. If the mixture seems dry, add more sesame or olive oil as necessary.

3 Use a 3-inch ring mold or your hands to form neat portions of the tartare on the chilled plates, then surround the meat with horseradish cream, watercress, lime wedges, and toast.

Classic Steak Tartare: Combine the beef with 1 shallot, peeled and roughly chopped; 2 teaspoons Worcestershire sauce; Tabasco as above; 1 tablespoon sherry or other vinegar; 2 tablespoons chopped cornichons; ¼ cup drained capers; salt and black pepper; 1 tablespoon mayonnaise; and 2 tablespoons chopped fresh parsley. Serve as above, with or without the horseradish cream.

The Raw and the Cooked

Although from a safety perspective, there's little or no difference between raw and rare meat, getting the sort of beef you want to eat raw—and feel safe doing so—is unquestionably an obstacle for home cooks. Few of us get our meat from butchers, and the meat at supermarkets, almost always butchered off premises, has a definite air of mystery about it.

If you have access to a traditional butcher's shop, go there. Not only will you be buying better beef, you can find out where it came from. Furthermore, if you tell a butcher you're making tartare, you can make sure to get fresh-cut meat (and you'll get help with the frustrating butchering tasks that are the true challenges of otherwise relatively easy dishes, like Daniel's Stuffed Saddle of Lamb, page 148). If you're buying meat in the supermarket, check with the butcher there, and tell him you plan to eat it raw, to make sure you're getting the freshest meat possible; he may even be able to cut it for you on the spot.

Another option, and one that would work admirably with Kerry's recipe, is substituting raw salmon, tuna, or yellowtail. Of course, finding fish of a high enough quality is yet another challenge.

And the final option is to just harness the flavor of tartare and sacrifice rawness, like I did in my recipe.

Good Burgers with Tartare-Like Seasonings

MARK BITTMAN | Makes: 4 SERVINGS   Time: 15 MINUTES

It bugs me when people call things tartares or seviches or sashimi when they're cooked; it's just the sort of prejudice you acquire when you eat out as much as I do. To that end I'm not calling these "Steak Tartare Burgers," but you might—they're actually burgers made with top-quality beef and classic steak tartare seasonings.

I came up with this recipe to counter Kerry's Asian-accented steak tartare, trying to use equally strong but perhaps more familiar European flavorings and choosing to cook the beef for two reasons: one, not everyone wants to eat absolutely raw meat; and two, that's what makes it a burger.

These are good with no more than lemon juice, but of course you can add typical burger condiments like pickles, red onion, mustard, and ketchup.

1 medium onion

½ cup fresh parsley leaves

4 anchovy fillets, or to taste

¼ cup capers

Dash Tabasco or other hot sauce

Dash Worcestershire sauce

1½ pounds prime beef, like tenderloin or sirloin

Salt and black pepper

Small hamburger buns or dinner rolls

Fresh lemon juice

1   Combine the onion, parsley, anchovies, capers, Tabasco, and Worcestershire in the work bowl of a food processor and pulse them until chopped to a relatively even consistency. Then add the beef, season with a little salt and pepper, and pulse on and off again until you achieve a coarsely chopped texture. Taste and adjust the seasoning.

2   Preheat a non-stick pan or well-seasoned skillet over medium-high heat for a minute or two while you form patties from the ground meat mixture. Cook the burgers for 2 to 2½ minutes a side in the pan without any additional fat, until they have a light brown crust but are still quite rare in the middle.

3   Transfer the burgers to a plate or cutting board and let them rest for a minute while you split the buns and prepare any condiments you want to serve them with. Season with an additional pinch of salt and a squeeze of lemon juice, build your burgers, and serve.

Salt Packed?

Like just about every other home cook I know, I usually use anchovies packed in oil and jarred capers in vinegar. But Kerry Simon had salt-packed anchovies and capers on hand, so I used them in my burgers when we cooked together.

It has been a long time since I considered myself a purist, so it was interesting for me to re-assess the salt-packed varieties, which are among the current darlings of the food world.

Capers packed in salt taste like capers. This is what you'd expect, unless you've become accustomed—as have most of us—to the vinegary flavor of jarred capers. Though they're not as widely available, salt-cured capers are definitely worth stocking; you can soak most if not all the salt out of them during the time it takes you to prepare the dish they're going into. (Just let them sit in one or two changes of water.)

Salt-packed anchovies are a different story. Though they're clearly better than most tinned or inexpensive jarred anchovies, they're not better (and they're certainly less convenient) than the high-quality olive oil–packed Italian anchovy fillets that are available at most higher-end grocery stores and any decent Italian market.

But if you're fanatical about anchovies, you might check out the salt-packed kind, which can usually be purchased a few at a time at an Italian specialty store, where you can buy them individually. You do have to fillet them one by one, which is a chore, but the flesh is in great condition, and it stays that way during cooking, which is perfect for those times you don't want the anchovies to dissolve into the dish.

Seared Tenderloin with Root Vegetables and Balsamic Vinegar

JAMES BOYCE | **Makes:** 4 SERVINGS **Time:** 30 MINUTES

This is a gorgeous, richly flavored luxury dish—the kind of thing that makes you want to break out your best red wine. When James was simultaneously making this with his Lobster Salad with Corn and Tomatoes (page 144)—his "Surf & Turf"—I poked fun at the number of pans he had going. It was probably six but seemed like ten. He laughed, saying he was really "playing the pans." Few of us have a stove that can accommodate that many pans at once, let alone the presence of mind to remember what's going on in which.

Luckily, each of his two dishes is successful in its own right, and this one is quick enough to pull off on a weeknight after work.

Use any root vegetables you like here, just cut larger ones into small pieces to mimic the effect of baby vegetables.

1 cup balsamic vinegar

1 pound baby root vegetables, like carrots, parsnips, Brussels sprouts, and turnips

4 tablespoons (½ stick) butter

3 tablespoons extra-virgin olive oil

Salt and black pepper to taste

4 (6- to 7-ounce) pieces beef tenderloin ("filet mignon")

Coarse salt, for garnish

1 Boil the balsamic vinegar in a small saucepan over moderately high heat until reduced by three-quarters or so, and thick and syrupy, about 10–15 minutes. Keep warm. Meanwhile, prepare the vegetables: Peel and trim; if necessary, cut them into pieces that will cook in 15 minutes or so on the stove (no dimension should be more than ½ inch).

2 Heat 2 tablespoons of the butter and 1 tablespoon of the oil over medium heat in a pan large enough to cook the vegetables in (more or less) one layer. When the butter melts, add the vegetables and season with salt and pepper. Cook, tossing the vegetables, for 10 minutes or so, until they start to get tender and color around the edges.

3 Put the remaining 2 tablespoons oil and 2 tablespoons butter in a large sauté pan over medium-high heat. Season the steaks generously with salt and pepper. When the butter foam subsides, add the beef; it should sizzle when you add it. Sear for 2 to 3 minutes on each of the larger sides, then for 30 seconds to 1 minute on each of the smaller sides (that is, sear it while standing it on its sides), until the meat registers 130°F on an instant-read thermometer. Transfer the beef to a cutting board and let it rest 1 to 2 minutes before slicing it.

4 Portion the vegetables among 4 plates, then slice the steaks into 4 or 5 slices each and fan them over the root vegetables. Drizzle the balsamic reduction in a ring around the plate, sprinkle a pinch of coarse salt over the meat, and serve.

Aceto Balsamico or Balsamic Vinegar?

Though James is obviously a fan of expensive ingredients—check out his Lobster Salad recipe on page 144—this dish is *almost* luxury free. Okay, he did start with tenderloin and finish with countless baby root vegetables from the famous Chino Farm in southern California, but even mere mortals like us can find or substitute for those items.

I was somewhat surprised that, when it came to finishing the dish,

he didn't wheel out a bottle of *Aceto Balsamico Tradizionale di Modena,* the real, honest-to-god product from Modena that sells for $60 for a 100-milliliter bottle. Instead, he reduced an "industrial" version—the stuff we buy in the supermarket for four dollars a half-liter—down to a syrup, a brilliant way to imitate the flavor and consistency of true balsamic. Without much work, this produced a wonderful sweet-and-sour sauce

that would make a great accompaniment for simple roast chicken or grilled pork chops.

If you do end up with a bottle of the Aceto Tradizionale (or buy one; www.zingermans.com has a fine selection and loads of information), don't be tempted to use it in this or just any recipe. Enjoy it instead drizzled over pieces of Parmigiano-Reggiano or over sliced ripe pears or peaches for dessert.

Lobster Salad with Corn and Tomatoes

JAMES BOYCE | Makes: 4 SERVINGS   Time: 45 MINUTES

Touches like Minus 8 vinegar (an ultra-fancy vinegar made from ice wine; see www.minus8vinegar.com and the sidebar) and grapefruit-infused olive oil add a level of complexity to this dish that reflect James's sensibilities as a chef as well as the almost routine opulence that characterizes his cooking at Studio, his restaurant in Laguna Beach.

But beyond the fancy trappings, this is actually a simple dish, with three components—lobster warmed in butter, lightly sautéed corn, and great tomatoes accented with vinegar. If you approach it one part at a time, you can make quick work of the dish once the lobster is shelled. And, if you don't want to search for scarce ingredients, substitute the best-quality wine vinegar you've got for the Minus 8 and good extra-virgin olive oil for the grapefruit-infused oil.

1 teaspoon white vinegar

1 teaspoon crushed black peppercorns

1 bay leaf

Salt and black pepper to taste

4 (1-pound) live lobsters

Large bowl ice water

4 tablespoons (½ stick) butter

1 shallot, peeled and thinly sliced

1 clove garlic, crushed

1 sprig fresh thyme

Kernels scraped from 2 large ears corn, preferably white

1 teaspoon balsamic vinegar, preferably white

4 assorted heirloom tomatoes, cored and quartered

1 to 2 tablespoons (or to taste) Minus 8 vinegar or good red wine vinegar

1 tablespoon snipped fresh chives

Finely minced zest of 1 orange

Grapefruit-infused or extra-virgin olive oil

1   In a large pot, combine the white vinegar, peppercorns, bay leaf, and a handful of salt with 1 gallon water and bring to a boil. Poach the lobsters for 4 minutes, just until their shells start to turn bright red, then plunge them into a bowl of ice water. When the lobsters are cool, break them apart and extract their meat. Split the claw meat into 2 pieces and cut the tail meat into ¼-inch-thick slices. Reserve.

2   Put 2 tablespoons of the butter in a small sauté or saucepan over medium heat. When the butter melts, add the shallot, garlic, and thyme. Cook for 2 minutes, stirring occasionally, until softened but not colored. Add the corn and balsamic vinegar and cook for an additional 5 to 10

minutes, stirring occasionally, until the corn is browned and no longer tastes starchy. Cool briefly, taste, and season with salt and black pepper to taste.

3 Heat the remaining 2 tablespoons butter in a small sauté or saucepan (you could transfer the corn to a bowl and reuse that pan) and warm the poached lobster—you don't want the lobster to cook much further—until glazed with the melted butter. Meanwhile, toss the tomatoes with the Minus 8 vinegar and chives and season with salt and black pepper to taste.

4 Portion the tomatoes among 4 plates (cut sides down, so they lay flat), mound a few generous spoonfuls of the corn on top of the tomatoes, then top each of the corn and tomato piles with the lobster, laying the neatly sliced tail pieces on the top. Season each salad with a spoonful of the butter the lobster was warmed in, a drop of Minus 8 vinegar, and a pinch of orange zest. Drizzle a ring of oil around each salad and serve.

Esoteric Ingredients and the Modern Chef

Vinegar made from grapes frozen on the vine, honey from bees fed only anise blossoms, and extra-virgin olive oil pressed with grapefruit zest—James's kitchen was awash in esoteric (make that *very* esoteric)—specialty ingredients. Most were outlandishly expensive and none qualified as easy to find. But you don't go to Studio or many of the other restaurants we visited, where we saw things like peeled grapes, Buddha's Hand citrus, caul fat, and sea urchins, because you're looking for something run-of-the-mill. And, as snide as I am about things like $60-a-bottle vinegar, I feel like James makes honest use of these indulgences.

So if you are moved to buy this kind of exotica, do what James and our other chefs do: Work them into recipes that are part of your repertoire, letting your taste guide you. Above all, *use them*. I cringe every time someone tells me about this fabulous bottle of olive oil they paid a fortune for on their trip to Tuscany five years ago that they're waiting to find the "right opportunity" to use. Few food products improve with age, no matter how much they cost, so go ahead, anoint your weeknight salad with that oil or vinegar. Because though luxury ingredients like these aren't necessary to make great food, they sure don't hurt, and there's no time like the present to use them.

Thai-Style Shrimp and Beef Salad

MARK BITTMAN | **Makes:** 4 SERVINGS **Time:** 20 MINUTES

I think this dish went from conception to consumption in about nine minutes, but it fared well—even James deemed it "simple but elegant." Part of what made it so easy is that I was able to take advantage of the bounty available to me in his kitchen, which explains the presence of three fresh herbs, enoki mushrooms, and tenderloin instead of a fattier cut of meat. And while I stand by this recipe, you could simplify it a little by skipping one of the herbs or omitting the mushrooms, and you could certainly replace the tenderloin with sirloin or rib-eye.

4 tablespoons olive oil

1½ tablespoons sherry vinegar

2 teaspoons soy sauce, or to taste

1 shallot, peeled and minced

2 tablespoons neutral oil, like corn, canola, or grapeseed

1 (8-ounce) piece beef tenderloin

Salt

1 pound medium (31–35) shrimp, peeled and deveined, if you like

1 bunch watercress, washed, thickest stems removed

½ cup peeled and diced papaya (optional)

2 ounces enoki mushrooms, rinsed (or use thinly sliced white mushrooms)

Leaves from 4 or 5 fresh mint sprigs, washed and roughly chopped

Leaves from 2 or 3 stems fresh cilantro, washed and roughly chopped

Leaves from 2 or 3 stems fresh basil, washed and roughly chopped

1   Whisk together the olive oil, vinegar, soy sauce, and shallot. Taste and adjust the seasonings, adding more soy, vinegar, or oil to taste.

2   Put the neutral oil in an 8- to 10-inch sauté pan and turn the heat to high. Season the meat liberally with salt and, after 1 or 2 minutes—when you can't hold your hand above the pan for more than a few seconds—add the beef. Sear the tenderloin on each side for 3 to 4 minutes, until browned on the outside and rare but not raw inside (you can, of course, cook it a minute or 2 longer if you like). Transfer the beef from the pan to a cutting board and let rest while you cook the shrimp.

3   Return the same pan to the stove, add the shrimp and lower the heat to medium. Cook until the shrimp are nicely browned on the bottoms, about 2 minutes, then turn and brown the second sides, 1 to 2 minutes more, for a total of 4 or 5 minutes.

4 Meanwhile, toss the watercress with the papaya, enoki, and herbs in a large bowl. Pour the vinaigrette over the salad and toss until the greens are evenly dressed. When the shrimp are ready, add them to the salad and toss again.

5 Slice the meat as thinly as possible. Divide the salad among 4 plates, top with the sliced rare tenderloin, and serve.

SHOP TALK: Why Some Chefs Don't Use Cilantro

JAMES: I don't use too much cilantro in my cooking.

MB: You don't like it?

JAMES: No, I love it. But with customers in the restaurant it's like there's a fine line—and cilantro and lavender—either they love them or hate them. So I'd probably leave it out of here.

MB: I know—so many people think cilantro tastes like soap.

JAMES: Yes, and it's bad form to serve things that people spit out.

Stuffed Saddle of Lamb

DANIEL BOULUD | **Makes:** 4 TO 6 SERVINGS **Time:** 1½ HOURS

You could approximate this wonderful dish of Daniel's without the distinctive flavor of pre-served lemons or the novelty of Buddha's Hand citrus, but without access to a butcher who will provide you with a boneless saddle of lamb, this recipe's just here to read. Of all the lamb cuts, saddle is the most difficult to obtain and perhaps the most delicious, an exquisite combi-nation of flavor and texture, with just the right combination of fat and lean. It's possible to bone out a saddle of lamb at home, but unless you are extremely skilled with a knife, you're likely to butcher it—in the negative sense.

The technique for "filleting" Meyer lemons (or any small citrus, really), is to peel them with a knife, cutting right down to the flesh and removing all the white pith, then cutting the seg-ments away from the membrane that criss-crosses through the center of a lemon. If you can't get Meyer lemons, substitute clementines, blood oranges, or regular lemons.

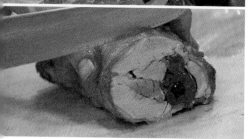

2 tablespoons extra-virgin olive oil

1 bunch Swiss chard, about 1 pound, leaves only, blanched in boiling water until tender

1 medium onion, chopped

Pinch fresh thyme leaves

1 bunch spinach, trimmed of thick stems, washed and dried

1 bunch fresh basil, stemmed, washed, and dried

1 (2- to 3-pound) boned saddle of lamb (bones reserved)

Salt and black pepper

2 teaspoons lemon zest

About 10 black olives, pitted and roughly chopped

1 confited tomato (page 243)

2 tablespoons butter, melted

4 artichokes, peeled and quartered (or 6 trimmed, halved baby artichokes)

8 cloves garlic, peeled

1 cup lamb stock or water

2 preserved lemons, zested, zest cut into matchsticks and blanched

3 Meyer lemons, "filleted" (see sidebar)

1 cup cherry tomatoes

Several thin slices Buddha's Hand citrus (optional; see sidebar, page 153)

Coarse salt, for garnish

1   Put 1 tablespoon of the oil in a large deep skillet or casserole. Turn the heat to medium-high and wait a minute or so, until the oil is hot. Add the chard, onion, and thyme and cook, stirring occasionally, until the chard is wilted, then add the spinach and one-third of the basil and cook about 5 minutes more. Set the mixture aside to cool while you stuff the saddle (you can execute this step hours or even the day before and use the mixture straight from the refrigerator).

2 Preheat the oven to 375°F. Open the saddle on a cutting board in front of you and season well on both sides with salt, pepper, and 1 teaspoon of the lemon zest. Score the flanks of the saddle with the tip of a sharp knife.

3 Toss the sautéed chard mixture with the olives, remaining 1 teaspoon lemon zest, confited tomato, and another third of the fresh basil, then arrange it down the middle of the saddle. Wrap the two flanks over the top of the stuffing, then tie the saddle tightly in 3 or 4 places using butcher's twine.

4 Put the remaining 1 tablespoon of the oil in the skillet you used previously and turn the heat to medium-high. Wait a minute or so, until the oil is hot, then add the tied saddle and the reserved bones and lightly brown them; the process will take 10 to 15 minutes. Transfer the pan to the oven.

5 After 10 minutes, brush the saddle with the butter and return it to the oven. After another 10 minutes add the artichokes and garlic cloves to the pan, baste all with the juices in the pan, and bake another 10 to 15 minutes, until the saddle is medium-rare (it should be firm but moist when you poke it and measure about 130°F on an instant-read thermometer at its thickest part).

6 Take the pan out of the oven and transfer the saddle to a cutting board; let rest for 15 minutes. Remove the artichokes and garlic to a warm plate. Strain the sauce, discard the bones, and return the pan to the stove over high heat. Deglaze with the stock, scraping the bottom of the pan with a wooden spoon to loosen any browned bits. Reduce the liquid by half or more, until it thickens and becomes saucy, about 10 minutes. Keep warm while you untie and slice the saddle.

7 Add the preserved lemon zest, lemon fillets, cherry tomatoes, sliced Buddha's Hand, and remaining basil to the pan and warm through. Transfer sliced saddle to a serving platter. Sauce the saddle, garnish with coarse salt, and serve.

A Better Lemon?

Meyer lemons owe much of their popularity to the Named Vegetables Trend that started in the eighties: the trend that means you no longer eat just, say, gremolata, but "A Relish of Flat Leaf Parsley, Meyer Lemon Zest, and Bob's Iranian Garlic." And their appearance on fancy restaurant menus across the country seems to have as much to do with the cachet of the name as the fact that Meyer lemons aren't widely available to the public, even in cities where restaurateurs can get them, imbuing them with a kind of rarefied air.

To be sure, Meyer lemons are different from the supermarket variety. They're smaller, thinner skinned, somewhat sweeter, and often less acidic. That makes them better suited to some preparations, like Daniel's dish here, where the flavors meld perfectly, and especially to desserts. When it comes to overall usefulness, however, "regular" lemons are preferable. And in general you can substitute them for the more expensive Meyer variety whenever you like.

Leg of Lamb with Beans and Mushrooms

DANIEL BOULUD | **Makes:** 6 TO 8 SERVINGS **Time:** 2 HOURS

Lamb and beans is a classic combination, and while Daniel's preparation essentially follows the traditional patterns, the addition of orange zest, sweet Mousseron mushrooms, and even butter distinguish his version.

While Daniel was working, I joked with him about how simple my lamb dish (page 156) was going to be, and he started to look a little annoyed, protesting that he could cook simply, too—he'd just make this and some Chickpea Fries (see page 198 for those gems).

The two of these together are simple, and the preparation is fantastic. This is a great dish for a dinner party at which you're going to serve your best red wine.

Mousseron mushrooms are exotic and fabulous, with a nice, firm texture and a flavor that recalls chanterelles and cèpes (porcini). But they have a short season and are imported from France, so they're not widely available. Substitute shiitakes, as suggested below, or, if you can find them, chanterelles.

1 cup cranberry beans, preferably fresh, or use dried beans

1 stalk celery, roughly chopped

2 onions, quartered (don't bother to peel)

2 carrots, peeled and roughly chopped

Salt and black pepper

1 (5- to 7-pound) leg of lamb, preferably at room temperature

About 1 tablespoon slivered garlic plus 4 whole peeled cloves garlic

1 tablespoon chopped fresh rosemary

2 tablespoons extra-virgin olive oil

8 ounces haricots verts or green beans, trimmed

8 ounces yellow wax beans (or any other string bean, or more green beans), trimmed

1 cup lamb or chicken stock, or use water

2 tablespoons butter

1 shallot, peeled and minced

1 pound Mousseron or other wild mushrooms, brushed clean, or shiitake caps, roughly chopped

1 teaspoon orange zest

1 Put the cranberry beans, celery, and half the onions and carrots in a large pot with water to cover. Turn the heat to high and bring to a boil; skim the foam if necessary. Turn the heat down so the beans simmer. Cover loosely and cook, stirring occasionally, until the beans begin to become tender (quite quickly for fresh beans, an hour or so for dried); add about 1 teaspoon salt, taste, and let the beans sit off the heat in their cooking liquid. Remove and discard the vegetables. (You can cook the beans as much as a day or two ahead of time; store them covered in their cooking liquid in the refrigerator.)

2 Preheat the oven to 425°F and put a large pot of salted water on to boil. Remove as much of the surface fat as possible from the lamb; rub the meat all over with salt and pepper. Use a thin-bladed knife to cut some small slits in the lamb and push a sliver of garlic and pinch of rosemary into each of them. Heat the oil in a roasting pan on the stove over medium heat and when it shimmers, add the lamb. Brown it lightly on all sides, 10 to 15 minutes total, then transfer the pan to the oven.

3 Meanwhile, blanch the haricots verts and wax beans in the boiling salted water. Cook them until just tender and brightly colored, about 3 minutes for the haricots verts and 5 to 7 minutes for the wax beans. Drain well and reserve.

4 When the roast has cooked for 30 minutes, add the remaining onions, carrots, and the whole garlic cloves. Baste the leg with the juices in the pan and return it to the oven. After another 15 minutes, check the internal temperature of the lamb in several places with an instant-read thermometer; when it reaches 130°F (medium-rare), transfer it to a cutting board to rest for at least 20 minutes.

5 Put the roasting pan on the stove over medium heat and add the stock, scraping the bottom of the pan with a wooden spoon to loosen any browned bits. Reduce the liquid by half or more, until it reaches a sauce-like consistency; strain and keep warm.

6 Heat the butter over medium heat in a medium skillet and, when it melts, add the minced shallot. Cook for 1 to 2 minutes, stirring, until softened, and then add the mushrooms and orange zest and season with salt and pepper. Cook, stirring occasionally, for 10 minutes or so, until the mushrooms are tender and lightly browned. Meanwhile, reheat the cooked beans.

7 Slice the leg and serve with the beans, sautéed mushrooms, and a little of the sauce.

Daniel's Lamb

Like all of the world's greatest chefs, Daniel Boulud likes to show off a little bit. His clientele can afford it, and they're experienced enough to appreciate it. When I arrived to cook with him, he announced he was doing lamb in four parts. And, almost needless to say, he treated each of the four parts in magnificent fashion.

He stuffed the saddle, a luxury cut that must be stretched to serve four, and then seared and quickly roasted it, melting its abundant fat and quickly tenderizing it. He braised the shoulder, the most common treatment (I roasted mine), and the one that best turns it meltingly delicious. The gorgeous leg was roasted, and the rack grilled in just a few minutes.

Each preparation was sublime, and each is worth making individually. Of course Daniel prepared all four at once, and served them, as he would in his restaurant, all at once—a course of four cuts of lamb each ideally prepared.

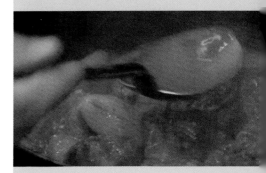

Brochette of Lamb Chops, Summer Squash, and Zucchini

DANIEL BOULUD | **Makes:** 4 SERVINGS **Time:** 30 MINUTES

This is the fastest of Daniel's four lamb dishes, although with its inclusion of orange powder and marmalade it's not exactly straightforward. It's also made with double chops from the rack, the most expensive cut; each chop is essentially one-quarter of a rack, meaning you'll need two racks to serve four. Daniel, like many chefs, "frenches" the chops, scraping the meat from the upper bones; this is not only unnecessary, though it makes for a lovely presentation, but it robs you of crispy bits to gnaw on. In any case, the cooking is quite clear-cut. Just make sure you start with zucchini and summer squash of similar diameters and that you don't discard the marinade after the skewers go on the grill.

8 double-rib lamb loin chops (frenching optional)

Salt and black pepper

Pinch orange powder (optional, see sidebar)

Juice of 2 oranges, strained

Zest of 1 orange

1 to 2 tablespoons orange marmalade (optional)

1 tablespoon fresh rosemary, chopped

2 tablespoons olive oil

2 medium summer squash, about 8 ounces, cut into 1-inch chunks

2 zucchini, about 8 ounces, cut into 1-inch chunks

Pinch cayenne

Zest of 1 lemon

1 tablespoon sugar

1 Season the meat well with salt, pepper, and orange powder, then combine it in a large casserole or resealable bag with the orange juice, orange zest (reserve a pinch for the zucchini), orange marmalade, and rosemary. Marinate for at least 20 minutes and as long as 1 hour, covered in the refrigerator. Start a charcoal or wood fire or preheat a gas grill or broiler; the fire should be moderately hot and the grill about 4 inches from the flame.

2 Heat the oil in a large sauté pan over medium-high heat and, when the oil shimmers, add the squash and zucchini. Season with salt and cayenne and cook, stirring, for 3 to 5 minutes, until the squash just starts to color.

3 Make the brochettes: Using large skewers, match up a wedge of yellow squash with one of zucchini, skewer them together, then slide a double chop on, skewering it between the bones. Add another matched zucchini-squash pair, a second chop, and finish with 1 more zucchini-squash pair. Repeat for 3 more skewers, reserving the lamb marinade.

Buddha's Hand and Other Rarities: Raising the Bar on Citrus

Daniel's arsenal of citrus and citrus derivatives is so impressive it borders on intimidating. He uses oranges, lemons, Meyer lemons, zest from all three, preserved lemons, orange marmalade (which he calls confit, and of course makes at the restaurant), and two especially unusual specimens: Buddha's Hand and orange powder.

Buddha's Hand is a type of citron with a flesh that's just faintly bitter, so you can slice and eat the whole thing, rind and all. Touch all your fingertips together and imagine your skin looks like lemon peel and you have an image of what a bizarre looking fruit it is. It hails from and is used in kitchens across Asia, though there's some debate about whether it's Japanese or Chinese in origin. In the States it's primarily grown as an ornamental plant, though not often.

The only places I've seen Buddha's Hand for sale are Berkeley Bowl market in Berkeley, and the Santa Monica and Hollywood farmer's markets, which makes them accessible to about 3 percent of the people in the country (though they are available elsewhere from time to time also). I wouldn't worry about trying to track Buddha's Hand down yourself—the dish will be great in any case—but if you come across one, grab it.

Orange powder, on the other hand, is something that Daniel makes at the restaurant and you can make, too, if you're so inclined:

Dry the peels of a few oranges, scraped clean of any white pith, either in a dehydrator or on a rack set over a baking sheet in a very low oven—at 150°F, this will probably take 10 to 12 hours. Then grind the dry skins in a coffee or spice grinder.

Or leave it out of the recipe; it is an elegant and refined touch, but a lot of work for a little impact.

4 Grill or broil the brochettes until they are nicely browned on both sides, 4 or 5 minutes per side and not longer than 10 minutes total. Allow the skewers to rest for 5 minutes after you take them off the grill.

5 While the skewers are grilling, transfer the marinade to a saucepan, turn the heat to high, add the lemon zest and sugar, and boil until reduced to a glaze, about 5 minutes. Strain and pour a little of the glaze over each of the grilled lamb chops. Unskewer and serve.

Braised Lamb Shoulder

DANIEL BOULUD | **Makes:** 4 SERVINGS **Time:** ABOUT 2½ HOURS, LARGELY UNATTENDED

Some of Daniel's professional touches here, like passing the ground spices through a sieve, and peeling the grapes, are optional refinements that marginally improve flavor and texture. But others, like adding flour to the braise to give the sauce more body or soaking his currants in sweet wine, are traditional tricks that are worth integrating into your culinary repertoire.

Though the ingredient list may be intimidating, there's not a huge amount of work here, and it produces an impressive, stunningly delicious dish.

2 tablespoons olive oil

2 pounds boneless lamb shoulder, trimmed of excess fat and cut into 2-inch cubes

Salt and black pepper

6 green cardamom pods, cracked with a mallet or the bottom of a skillet

1 teaspoon cumin seeds

½ teaspoon ground sumac

½ teaspoon ground fenugreek

2 tablespoons pine nuts

2 tablespoons butter

1 large onion, roughly chopped

1 medium carrot, peeled and roughly chopped

1 stalk celery, trimmed and roughly chopped

1 tablespoon flour

1 cup white wine

Bouquet garni (cheesecloth wrapped around 1 bay leaf, 1 sprig fresh thyme, 5 or 6 cloves garlic, and 10 black peppercorns)

1 cup lamb or chicken stock, or more as needed

20 grapes, preferably peeled and halved

2 tablespoons currants, soaked in a bit of sweet white wine

1 roasted and peeled red bell pepper (page 237), finely chopped

½ cup chopped fresh parsley leaves

1   Preheat the oven to 325°F. Heat the oil over medium-high heat in a large, deep skillet or casserole that can later be covered; season the lamb with salt and pepper. Add the lamb chunks to the pan a few at a time, removing them as they brown. (You can also do the initial browning in the oven: Preheat to 500°F and roast the lamb chunks and oil, turning once or twice, until brown all over; time will be about the same, 20 minutes. Move the casserole to the stove, carefully, and proceed.)

2   While the lamb is browning, combine the cardamom and cumin in a small skillet and toast over medium-low heat. Cook, shaking the pan occasionally, until lightly colored and fragrant, just a few minutes. Transfer the spices to a spice or coffee grinder and grind to a fine powder. Sift through a sieve into a small bowl, add the sumac and fenugreek, and toss to combine. Toast the pine nuts in a similar manner and set aside.

3   When the lamb is nicely browned, return it to the pan, lower the heat to medium, and add the butter, onion, carrot, and celery. Cook, stirring, until the vegetables soften. Add the flour and ground spices and cook, stirring, for 1 to 2 minutes. Raise the heat to high, add the wine and bouquet garni, and bring to a boil. Reduce heat to medium and simmer until the wine is reduced by half. Add the stock, cover, and transfer to the oven. Cook until the lamb is tender, at least 1 hour, stirring occasionally and checking after about 30 minutes to make certain that the mixture is not too dry. (The recipe can be prepared a day or two in advance up to this point; cool, place in a covered container, and refrigerate.)

4   Remove the pot from the oven and transfer the shoulder to a serving platter. If the braising liquid seems thin, put the pan on the stovetop over high heat and reduce to about ¾ cup. Pour the sauce into a sieve or fine-meshed strainer and strain the sauce over the lamb, pressing on the vegetables and bouquet garni to extract as much liquid as possible, then discard the spent vegetables. Garnish the platter with the grapes, currants, peppers, parsley, and pine nuts and serve.

SHOP TALK: Daniel on Lamb and Rareness

Daniel grilled his lamb brochettes until they were almost medium, which was surprising and a little uncommon, because most chefs prepare lamb racks quite rare. But as he explains it, this makes sense:

"Young lamb is like veal—neither is at its best when rare because the flesh is very chewy and too soft. When you cook it a little longer, the texture is better, and I think it has more flavor as well."

"I do serve mature lamb more rare, because the meat is aged longer, and as a result it's more tender."

"Too-Simple" Stuffed Lamb Shoulder

MARK BITTMAN | **Makes:** 6 TO 8 SERVINGS **Time:** 1 HOUR, LARGELY UNATTENDED

After two cooks helped move the three-foot sterling silver platter lavishly spread with Daniel's four lamb preparations, he handed me a dinner plate and said tongue-in-cheek, "You see the size of your platter? That represents the complexity of your dish." Then he continued to needle me almost constantly during the fifteen or so minutes I spent preparing this dish.

And, from the time my lamb shoulder hit the cutting board for trimming to the moment I served it, there was no point at which he didn't try to take the reins to his kitchen back. You could, as he suggested, add lemon zest to the mix or, as I've done in the past, chopped anchovies or rosemary or even all three. But I often believe that less is more and, in the end, Daniel conceded that he liked the dish and that maybe, just maybe, he had learned (or at least recalled) something about simplicity in home cooking.

The meat is especially lovely served with some mixed salad greens dressed with a vinaigrette made from a little of the pan juices and some sherry vinegar.

1 (2- to 3-pound) boneless lamb shoulder, in one piece

Salt and black pepper

½ cup chopped fresh parsley leaves

2 tablespoons minced garlic

2 tablespoons butter

½ cup bread crumbs, preferably fresh

1 If you're in a hurry, preheat the oven to 400°F (if you're not, wait until the meat rests at the end of Step 2). Season the shoulder well on both sides with salt and pepper. Mix together the parsley and half the garlic. Slather a couple heaping spoonfuls of the parsley-garlic mixture into the middle of the shoulder (where the bone once was), massage it in, and tie the shoulder into a roast. (Don't worry about technique—just wind some butcher's twine 2 or 3 times around the length of the roast, then a few times around the width, and tie it off.)

2 Use a thin-bladed knife to cut some small slits in the lamb and push pinches of parsley-garlic mixture into them; rub the lamb all over with any that remains. If you have the time, let the lamb sit, for an hour or more (refrigerate if it will be longer).

3 Put the lamb in a roasting pan or large ovenproof skillet and put it in the oven. Check it after 40 minutes; it's ready when slightly firm to the touch and about 130°F on an instant-read thermometer for medium-rare. Transfer the shoulder to a cutting board to rest for at least 10 minutes while you make flavored bread crumbs.

4 Pour off all but 1 tablespoon of the fat from the pan, then put it on the stove over medium heat; add the remaining garlic and the butter. When the garlic is fragrant and beginning to soften, add the bread crumbs and stir them around to color lightly and absorb the juices in the pan. (Use within a couple minutes of cooking them, or pour the bread crumbs out onto a baking sheet and reheat for 1 to 2 minutes in the oven when you're ready to carve the lamb.)

5 Serve the shoulder sliced, with the bread crumbs sprinkled over the top.

SHOP TALK: You Must Be Kidding…

The generally serious tone in Daniel's kitchen vanished after he was done and it became my turn to cook. He immediately switched gears from his intensely focused mode (which he's almost always in when in the kitchen) to a lighter, more easy side, making fun of me every step of the way:

DANIEL: So, Mark, what's your vegetable with this?

MB: Parsley is my vegetable.

DANIEL: You must be kidding. It's like my mother.

MB: I am kidding. But I do cook like your mother—she gave you a piece of lamb, maybe a little salad, and some bread, right?

DANIEL: It's just that I was expecting a little bit more from you….

MB: Don't.

DANIEL: You want to stuff it with some bread crumbs? Do you want to add some lemon zest, to cook it like me?

MB: No! I don't want to make it more complicated….

DANIEL: Is it that you don't want to make it more complicated or that you're cheap?

MB: Not cheap; lazy. Not everybody has all day to cook. There is no stopping you, is there?

DANIEL: Here, let me put a little black pepper on there for you….

MB: Do I have to throw you out of your own kitchen?

DANIEL: I just want to make sure if I have to eat this that it tastes like something…

MB: Come on, you know the flavor is going to be good. I have been cooking almost as long as you—just not as well.

Lemongrass-Grilled Rack of Lamb with Tamarind Sauce

CHARLES PHAN | **Makes:** 4 SERVINGS **Time:** 30 MINUTES, PLUS MARINATING TIME

Charles's mesquite charcoal grill at Slanted Door is a wonder—hot as heck, but with enough cool spots so food can be moved around to cook evenly. One of the best dishes he produces on it is this sweet-and-sour rack of lamb. The marinade is one his mother made when he was young, so he has a particular fondness for it, but it will have instant appeal to anyone who enjoys the flavors of Southeast Asia.

If you don't have a grill, you can broil the meat, following a similar pattern. But you could also cook it on top of the stove: Pan-grill the rack without the marinade until it's almost done, then finish it by cooking it in the marinade (but watch carefully; with this much sugar, it will burn easily).

4 stalks lemongrass, trimmed of its ends, first couple layers of outer coating peeled off (see sidebar, page 161)

4 shallots, peeled

2 Thai chiles or 1 small jalapeño, stemmed and seeded, or about 1 teaspoon crushed red pepper flakes, or to taste

½ cup sugar

1 tablespoon neutral oil, like corn or canola

2 tablespoons fish sauce (nam pla or nuoc mam)

2 small (1¼-pound) racks of lamb, trimmed and, if you like, "frenched"

Salt and black pepper

1 recipe Tamarind Sauce (page 160)

1   Mince the lemongrass as finely as you can. Combine with the shallots, chiles, sugar, and oil in a mortar and pestle or a food processor, or continue to mince until as fine as possible. Add the fish sauce. Sprinkle the lamb with salt and pepper, then marinate in this mixture (you can use a bowl or strong resealable bag) for 2 to 3 hours, refrigerated. Meanwhile, make the Tamarind Sauce (page 160).

2   Start your grill; rake the coals so the fire is quite hot on one side and cooler on the other, and place the grill rack about 4 inches from the heat source. Grill the lamb, starting on a hot part of the fire, until crusty, turning as necessary. (Move it to a cooler part of the grill if it threatens to char.) Cook until an instant-read thermometer inserted into the center of the meat measures 125°F to 130°F for rare—this will take 10 to 15 minutes. Serve hot, passing the Tamarind Sauce at the table.

Tamarind Sauce

CHARLES PHAN | **Makes:** 1 TO 2 CUPS **Time:** ABOUT 30 MINUTES

This dark brown, tantalizingly sweet-and-sour sauce will be pleasingly familiar to frequenters of Southeast Asian restaurants; it's a classic.

Tamarind is sold in many forms; Charles gets it fresh, or semi-fresh, and you can find it that way in some Asian markets. You're more likely to find dried pods, or a thick paste wrapped in plastic, still containing seeds and some hulls. (You can also buy premade tamarind sauce, and it's not bad, but this is better.) No matter what form you find, the process is the same: You cover the pods or paste with water and simmer gently, mashing until the whole thing is blended. Then you force the paste through a sieve and season it.

8 ounces dried tamarind pods or 1 pound tamarind paste

½ cup sugar, or to taste

2 tablespoons fish sauce (nam pla or nuoc mam), or to taste

1   Simmer the pods or paste in hot water to cover, stirring and mashing until soft, about 10 minutes. If you used pods, remove the husks. Press the pulp and seeds through a fine-meshed sieve.

2   While warm, stir in the sugar and fish sauce to taste. Serve hot, with the lamb. (This sauce can be refrigerated for about 1 day and reheated just before serving; add a little water or lime juice if necessary to thin it out.)

Lowdown on Lemongrass

Lemongrass has a distinctive piney, lemony flavor that's immediately recognizable. And unlike *nam pla*, cilantro, and some other Southeast Asian staples, lemongrass's aroma and flavor have universal appeal: It's widely used to scent beauty products and is big in aromatherapy.

You want the bulbous end and bottom three to four inches of the stalk for cooking. Begin by peeling away any dry outside leaves, then pound the more tender interior to a paste, or chop into thin slices, according to the recipe you're using. The trimmings can be boiled in water to make lemongrass tea or tied in a piece of cheesecloth and used to reinforce the lemongrass flavor in soup, stock, sauces, or braised dishes.

It may take a little work to track down lemongrass near you (though I've found it all over the country), but it's worth your while to buy a little extra if you see it; wrapped in plastic, it keeps well in the refrigerator for weeks.

If you live in a warm climate (or it's summer in the northern part of the country), and the lemongrass you find is even marginally fresh, stick a stalk of it in a glass of water on the kitchen counter. If it sprouts, plant it in the ground or a pot. Kept warm and moist, it will produce more lemongrass in two or three months than you can imagine. It looks, unsurprisingly, like a feathery outcropping of prairie grass, and its aroma is reputed to be an insect repellent (it's used in some proportion in some citronella candles).

You can prepare lemongrass in one of two ways—bang it a few times with the blunt side of a heavy knife, then toss the whole or chopped stalks into stews, teas, and so on; discard them before serving. Or, as in most recipes, trim the ends, then peel enough of the outer layers off (it's not unlike a scallion) until you get to the part you can actually chop—then mince.

Skewered Squid with Black Pepper and Sesame-Lemon Sauce

MARK BITTMAN | **Makes:** 4 SERVINGS **Time:** 15 MINUTES

I whipped up this dish after Charles wowed everyone with his Lemongrass-Grilled Rack of Lamb with Tamarind Sauce (page 158). Although squid and lamb are not usually considered in the same category, what these recipes have in common is that they're both grilled, and they both feature the primary flavors of Vietnam; his uses lemongrass and mine, that country's most common spice, black pepper. You see black pepper everywhere there, and it's not just an afterthought but also an important part of many dishes. It works very nicely in this quick squid dish, which can be made with shrimp or scallops as well.

Like shrimp and scallops, squid grills (or broils) very, very quickly—typically in less than 5 minutes. So as long as you're building a fire (unless you have a gas grill) you might as well grill some vegetables at the same time. Treat them the same way, including the dipping sauce.

2 pounds squid, cleaned

½ cup sesame oil

Salt and lots of black pepper

Fresh lemon juice to taste (at least that of 1 lemon)

1 tablespoon minced garlic

1 Preheat your grill or build a grill fire; the heat should be quite hot, and the grill rack should be about 4 inches from the heat source. (If you're using wood skewers, soak them in water to cover while the grill preheats.) Skewer the squid (it will be easier to turn if you use 2 skewers, parallel to one another). Brush the squid with some sesame oil and sprinkle it with salt and pepper.

2 Put the remaining sesame oil in a small saucepan over medium-low heat and cook until it is thin and hot, about 5 minutes.

3 Meanwhile, in a small, heatproof bowl, combine the lemon juice with the garlic and about 1 tablespoon black pepper. When the oil is ready, carefully pour it over this mixture and let sit. Stir to combine. Taste and adjust seasoning.

4 Grill the squid until nicely browned on both sides, about 5 minutes total. Serve immediately, with the dipping sauce.

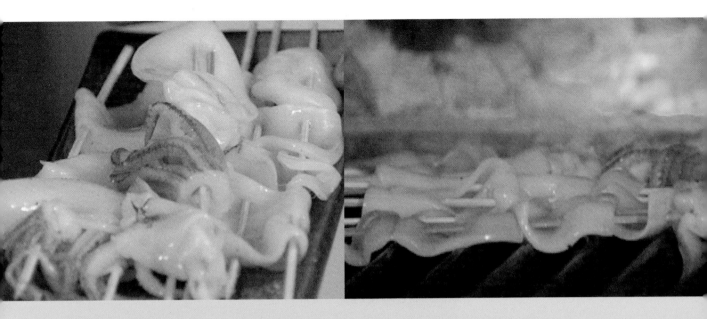

Squid 101

Unlike most fish, squid remains inexpensive and in little danger of extinction; it freezes well, too. But almost no one cooks it at home.

This is a shame. It's easy to cook, and not just as fried calamari. To get started, it makes sense to buy cleaned squid, which is increasingly common. (At one time, you could chat or read the newspaper as the local fishmonger cleaned it for you; now it's mostly precleaned, and often frozen.)

The only real trick in cooking squid involves timing. Undercooked, it has a rubbery texture. But when it spends more than a couple of minutes over heat, it becomes tough. Long, slow cooking tenderizes it, which explains the saying, "Cook squid two minutes or two hours."

That oversimplification points in the right direction: When cooking squid over high heat, it is usually done within a few minutes, less than five. (Perfection varies with the species, the time of year, and the storage conditions.) But, generally speaking, stir-fried, sautéed, or fried squid quickly loses its rubbery texture. Although it doesn't become soft, it becomes tender in the same way that a properly cooked lobster, shrimp, or piece of sirloin becomes tender. Cook it as you would pasta, and taste it every minute or so; the instant it loses its rawness, turn off the heat and serve.

In braised dishes, squid performs much more predictably. After 30 minutes to an hour of cooking (again, depending on the squid itself), toughness is no longer a concern. However, care should be taken not to cook longer than necessary because, when the squid has lost all of its water (about two-thirds of its total weight), it can become quite dry.

Chris Schlesinger's Slow-Grilled Ribs

CHRIS SCHLESINGER | **Makes:** 4 SERVINGS **Time:** AT LEAST 3 (AND UP TO 6) HOURS, LARGELY UNATTENDED

These are ribs the way they should be, but you need a day off with an empty schedule to make them. If days like those are as infrequent in your life as they are in mine, try my version—the Bittman's Faster Grilled Ribs variation. The flavor is roughly the same, but the texture is not as perfect as that you achieve with Chris's method.

Chris's reasoning is that you drink a beer every time you add charcoal to the fire, so wood fires are not only better but more fun. Mine is that you have a beer whenever you feel like it, regardless of which grill you're using.

¼ cup Chris Schlesinger's Rib Rub (recipe follows)

About 4 pounds pork spareribs

About 3 cups hickory, oak, or other hardwood chips, soaked in water to cover

1 Massage the rub into the ribs. If you have a gas grill, preheat by using the burner on only one side, on medium heat, for about 15 minutes. If you are using a charcoal or wood fire, bank it to one side of your grill and keep the fire as low as possible, starting with just enough fuel to get heat, about 15 briquettes or the equivalent in hardwood charcoal. Sprinkle a handful of wood chips onto the rack above the heat source, allowing them to fall directly onto the fire.

2 Place the ribs away from the heat source (over the unlit burner of a gas grill) and cover the grill. You want a very cool fire, less than 300°F if possible (you should be able to hold your hand right over the area on which the ribs are cooking with just a little discomfort). If you are using solid fuel, add a few lumps of charcoal or a few briquettes every hour, just enough to keep the fire going. Turn the ribs every 30 minutes or so, adding more wood chips as needed, and re-closing the grill cover.

3 Depending on the heat of your fire, after 2 to 6 hours the ribs will have lost much of their fat and developed an unquestionably cooked look. Just before you're ready to eat, raise the heat to high (or add a bunch more briquettes and wait a while) and brown the ribs on both sides. Be very careful; they will likely still have enough fat on them to flare up and burn, ruining all your hard work in an instant (believe me, I've done it several times). Watch them constantly and move them frequently. Browning will take about 10 minutes. Serve immediately.

Chris Schlesinger's Rib Rub

Makes: ½ CUP **Time:** 5 MINUTES

I've relied on this for more than fifteen years; it's the best rib rub in my repertoire, and the only one you'll ever need. Unbelievably delicious, and not at all hot.

2 tablespoons paprika

2 tablespoons sugar

1 tablespoon salt

1 tablespoon ground cumin

1 tablespoon black pepper

1 tablespoon chili powder

Stir all the ingredients together in a bowl, then transfer the mixture to a covered container. Keeps for at least one summer.

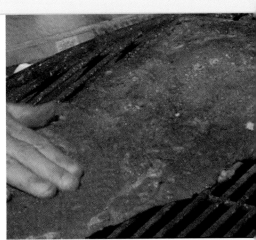

Bittman's Faster Grilled Ribs

There are certainly times I prepare Chris's ribs, but then there are times I decide to make ribs at the last moment. In those cases, I buy baby back ribs (about 1 pound per person) and rub them as in Step 1, page 164. I grill them on a covered grill, over low or indirect heat for the first 30 minutes or so, to render some of the fat, and then I finish them over direct heat for 10 or 15 minutes, watching carefully so they don't burn. That's my recipe.

Grilled Pork Confit

SUZANNE GOIN | **Makes:** 6 TO 8 SERVINGS **Time:** 3 DAYS, LARGELY UNATTENDED

Few dishes elicit quite the same animal response as this one. When I cooked it with Suzanne, friends and onlookers brandished forks like weapons and resolved to replicate it for wives, girl-friends, and/or families immediately.

And as long as you have space and time, it's not a particularly difficult dish to prepare. Just make sure you have a container large enough to brine a pork shoulder in, enough room in the fridge to store it while it's curing, and enough fat to submerge it in. None of these are insurmountable problems; you just need to do a bit of planning to make it happen. (Or, you could cut the recipe in half.)

If you don't have a grill, don't let that stop you: Just sear the meat in a cast-iron pan with a few tablespoons of the fat left over from making the confit.

This is great served with Knepfla (page 196) and Sautéed Cabbage (page 199).

¼ cup juniper berries

¼ cup allspice berries

½ cup fennel seed

½ cup sugar

½ cup salt

1 onion, roughly chopped

1 bulb fennel, roughly chopped

1 carrot, roughly chopped

¼ bunch fresh thyme

¼ bunch fresh parsley

3 cloves

2 bay leaves

2 dried chiles

Half a boneless pork shoulder, 2½ to 3 pounds, trimmed of excess fat

2 to 3 quarts rendered duck or pork fat (see sidebar)

Mustard Butter (page 245)

1   Lightly crush the juniper, allspice, and fennel in a mortar and pestle or with the back of a heavy pan (if you use a spice grinder, be sure to keep it coarse). Dissolve the sugar and salt in 2 cups hot water in a stockpot or plastic container large enough to accommodate the pork shoulder (and make a space in your refrigerator large enough to fit the stockpot). Add 2 cups cool water, and then stir in the onion, fennel, carrot, thyme, parsley, cloves, bay leaves, and chiles. Add the pork shoulder and enough water to cover the meat. Brine the pork in the refrigerator for 48 hours.

2   Remove the pork from the brine, pat it dry and clean with paper towels, and let it sit while you heat the fat; discard the brine. Preheat the oven to 300°F. Warm the fat gently in a large deep pan (if you used a stockpot for brining, that would work) over low to medium heat until it liquefies. Submerge the brined pork shoulder in the fat and transfer the pan to the oven. Cook 4 to 5 hours, until very tender (a paring knife inserted in the center of the meat should meet little resistance).

3   Cool the pork in the fat for 1 hour. (At this point you could transfer the shoulder, submerged in fat, to the refrigerator for up to 5 days. Before you grill the shoulder, transfer the pan from the fridge to a 250°F oven for 1 hour or so to re-liquefy the fat, then proceed.) Remove the shoulder from the fat and transfer it to a cutting board (strain the fat and refrigerate or freeze until the next time you make confit).

4   Start your grill; the fire should be moderately hot (you should be able to hold your hand over the hottest part for 4 or 5 seconds) and the grill rack about 4 inches from the heat source.

5   Slice the pork into ½- to ¾-inch-thick slabs across the grain of the meat (save the scraps to make great sandwiches or to sauté with eggs). Taste a little piece of the pork to make sure it is seasoned correctly. If not, add some salt and pepper. Brush the slabs with a little melted fat or olive oil and grill for 2 to 3 minutes on the first side (turning them 90 degrees after a couple of minutes if you want to serve them with cross-hatched grill marks). Turn the pork over and finish cooking for 1 minute more on the other side. You should have a really crisp, deep-golden crust. Smear each piece of grilled pork with a generous tablespoon of Mustard Butter and serve immediately.

Dork Fat: Spend or Render

You need quite a bit of fat to submerge four duck legs, as on page 117, and even more to do the pork shoulder here. Two quarts is a good starting point, depending on the dimensions of the container you're working with, but you could very well need more. And not only is fat not the kind of thing home cooks keep lying around, dunking food in fat doesn't jibe very well with the food pyramid.

Yet I implore you to try this. Even though you can make confit— good confit—with olive oil, I think it's worth your while to give duck fat a whirl, because it tastes so great. To get some, you're either going to have to pay a premium to buy prerendered duck fat from a specialty purveyor or make your own.

And here's the secret: You don't have to confit something in only its own fat. "Duck preserved in its own fat" is a term of poetic license; there are always other ducks involved in the process.

If, whenever you're cooking with duck or chicken, you buy whole birds (which are cheaper, anyway, and give you trimmings for stock), trim and collect all the skin and excess fat, then freeze these (along with any pork fat you come across); you'll eventually have quite a bit.

Once you have a couple of pounds, you start rendering. The delicious by-products of rendering poultry fat are cracklings (see page XXX) and, once the fats are rendered, you can store them together in an airtight container in the freezer until you decide to make confit.

And if you end up rendering pork and duck fat together, you get what Suzanne affectionately refers to as "dork fat."

Braised and Grilled Pork Shoulder

MARK BITTMAN | **Makes:** AT LEAST 6 SERVINGS **Time:** 1½ TO 2 HOURS, SOMEWHAT UNATTENDED

Making something easier than Suzanne's elaborate treatment of pork shoulder wasn't difficult, but maintaining the spirit of her dish and creating something really delicious put me to the test. I thought for weeks—really—about how I was going to come up with confit-like pork without confiting and still wasn't sure what I was going to do until I actually began cooking. I had vague notions, only, but more ideas—the right ones, fortunately—came to me as I was working.

I have to say I'm pretty proud of the results, and the simple parsley-garlic sauce guarantees extra flavor and juiciness.

1 (4-pound) boneless pork shoulder

Salt and black pepper to taste

Neutral oil, like corn or canola, as needed

10 allspice berries

2 or 3 (3-inch) cinnamon sticks

10 nickel-sized slices fresh ginger (don't bother to peel) or 1 tablespoon ground ginger

5 dried red chiles or a good teaspoon of cayenne

2 (12-ounce) bottles dark beer, like Guinness or any porter

1 cup chopped fresh parsley leaves, washed and left wet

2 cloves garlic, or to taste

1   Cut the pork into big chunks, at least 2 inches across, or slices about 1 inch thick. Season them with salt and pepper and put about 2 tablespoons oil in a large, deep skillet or casserole; turn the heat to medium-high and, when the oil shimmers, sear the meat on all sides until nicely browned, turning as necessary. The process will take 10 to 15 minutes.

2   Add the allspice, cinnamon, ginger, and chiles, and stir, then add the beer. Bring to a boil; cover the pan and adjust the heat so the mixture simmers steadily. Cook until the pork is tender, 1 hour or more. (When the pork is done, you can refrigerate it in its liquid for 1 to 2 days before proceeding.)

3   When the pork is done and you're ready to cook, start a grill; the fire should be only moderately hot (you should be able to hold your hand a few inches over the grill for 4 or 5 seconds) and the rack set about 4 inch-

es above the heat source. Drain the pork, dry it with paper towels, brush it lightly with oil, and sprinkle it with salt and pepper. Grill on both sides until brown and crisp, just a few minutes.

4 Meanwhile, make the parsley salsa: Combine the wet parsley leaves in the container of a blender with the garlic and some salt and pepper. Add 2 tablespoons oil and blend until combined but not pureed. You want some texture remaining. (Add water by the tablespoon as necessary to allow the machine to do its work.) Serve the meat straight from the grill, with the parsley salsa.

Cooking in Beer

In many braised recipes, the liquid in which you cook is flexible. Water can sometimes be substituted for stock; chicken stock can usually be substituted for other meat stocks; even white wine for red.

When you're cooking with beer, however, the differences in style—even between a brown ale and a porter—can make or break a dish. When I tested this recipe at home with a light pilsner instead of a porter, I saw just how different the results could be; the version I made with Suzanne was robust and flavorful, but with pilsner it was almost anemic. So stick with porter or stout here, or at least dark beer, like Guinness (the easiest to find) or even Negro Modelo.

Pasta, Rice, & Vegetables

This may sound and look like a side dish chapter, but really it's anything but. Most of the recipes here are for dishes that can easily serve as main courses, or at least share the spotlight with anything else.

Suvir Saran's Manchurian-Style Cauliflower (page 190) is one of the most enjoyable (and filling) vegetable dishes I've ever eaten. The pasta dishes, both from our chefs and me, range from quite simple (Pasta with Ham and Egg, page 180, is a personal favorite) to unusual and very impressive (I'm thinking specifically of Anna Klinger's Beet Ravioli, page 172).

There are, of course, some good side dishes here, including Jean-Georges' Spaetzle (page 196, actually his mom's recipe) and Michel Richard's best-in-the-world French fries (page 194).

Beet Ravioli with Butter and Poppy Seeds (Casunziei)

ANNA KLINGER | Makes: 3 OR 4 MAIN COURSE OR ABOUT 6 FIRST COURSE SERVINGS
Time: 1 HOUR, PLUS TIME TO MAKE THE PASTA

Dishes like this are the reason I love eating at great Italian restaurants like Al di Là—they're good eating and a ton of work to make at home. If, however, you do go through the trouble of making the ravioli, you'll need little more to round out the meal—a salad of bitter greens to start and some fresh fruit (or Anna's Chocolate Pear Cake, page 222, if you feel like gilding the lily) to finish. A bottle of good northern Italian red to wash it all down would be ideal.

If you're not going to take the time to make stuffed pasta—and I'd be the last person to blame you—you can still take advantage of these flavors, and do what many Italians would do: Roast the beets, coarsely chop them, and boil some spaghetti. When the spaghetti is ready, toss it in the melted butter with the beets for a minute and serve each portion with a dollop of ricotta and a sprinkle of poppy seeds.

4 large or 8 medium roasted beets (see sidebar)

2 eggs

½ cup ricotta, preferably fresh, drained briefly

20 tablespoons (2½ sticks) butter, melted

Salt and black pepper to taste

1 recipe Egg Pasta Dough (page 176)

2 ounces Parmigiano-Reggiano, or more to taste

4 teaspoons poppy seeds

1 Put the beets in the work bowl of a food processor fitted with the plastic blade and process until they're finely chopped (or chop them finely with a knife or pastry cutter). Transfer to a large bowl and add the eggs, ricotta, and ½ cup of the melted butter; stir to combine. Season liberally with salt and pepper, stir, taste, and add more salt or pepper if necessary. Refrigerate until ready to use, up to 1 day.

2 To make the ravioli: Lay a length of rolled pasta out on a counter lightly dusted with flour and place small teaspoonfuls of the filling evenly on half of the dough, about 1 inch apart. Brush some water between the mounds of filling so the dough will stick together, and fold the unfilled half of the dough over onto the other, carefully pressing outward from the filling to the edges of the pasta, eliminating any pockets of air. Cut between the ravioli with a pastry wheel or sharp paring knife, and keep the ravioli separate from each other until you are ready to cook.

Repeat with the remaining dough and filling. Put a large pot of salted water on to boil and turn the oven on to its lowest setting; warm 4 pasta bowls in it.

3 Drop the ravioli into the boiling salted water, cooking them in batches if necessary. They will take about 3 minutes to cook. When they're done, they will float, the filling will be firm, and the pasta tender.

4 Portion the ravioli out among the warmed pasta plates. Pour some of the remaining melted butter over each portion, grate Parmigiano-Reggiano over each to taste, and finish each plate with a large pinch of poppy seeds. Serve immediately.

On Roasting Beets

Once you try roasting beets you'll probably never boil them again—there's less work, less mess, and the results are tender rather than mushy, and not at all soggy. Think of the difference between a boiled and a baked potato and you get the idea.

The technique is a snap: First preheat the oven to 400°F. Trim the beets, leaving about 1 inch of their tops intact. Wrap each individually, still moist, in a large sheet of heavy-duty aluminum foil (or a double thickness of regular foil) and place on a baking sheet or roasting pan. Roast, undisturbed, for 45 minutes to 1½ hours—it all depends on their size and water content—until a thin-bladed knife pierces one with little resistance. (If they vary in size, they will vary in cooking time.)

Remove them from the oven, let the beets cool to a manageable temperature, and peel. (Or refrigerate in their foil until you're ready to use them; this can be days later.) Use them in the ravioli recipe or in any beet recipe; or simply cut them up and reheat them in butter or oil, or serve them, warm or cold, dressed with vinaigrette.

Pasta with Savoy Cabbage

MARK BITTMAN | Makes: 3 TO 4 MAIN COURSE OR ABOUT 6 FIRST COURSE SERVINGS
Time: 30 MINUTES

As good as Anna Klinger's beet-stuffed ravioli are, when I want pasta I usually want fast pasta and, when it comes to a simple dish of pasta and a winter vegetable, few beat this one, which is as traditional as anything.

Salt and black pepper to taste

¼ cup extra-virgin olive oil

4 cloves garlic, crushed

4 or more anchovy fillets (optional)

1 dried red chile, like serrano

3 bay leaves

1 (1½- to 2-pound) head savoy or white cabbage, cored and shredded

1 cup stock or dry white wine

1 pound dried pasta, like spaghetti

Chopped fresh parsley leaves, for garnish

1   Set a large pot of water to boil and salt it. Put the oil, garlic, anchovies, chile, and bay leaves in a large, deep skillet or casserole and turn the heat to medium. Cook just until the garlic colors, then add the cabbage and raise the heat to high. Cook, stirring occasionally, until the cabbage browns a bit.

2   Add the stock and continue to cook until the cabbage becomes tender, about 10 minutes. Meanwhile, cook the pasta.

3   When the pasta is tender but not mushy, drain it, reserving some of the cooking water. Toss the cabbage and pasta together, adding some of the cooking liquid if necessary to moisten the mixture. Taste and adjust seasoning with salt and pepper, garnish with the parsley, and serve.

Egg Pasta Dough

MARK BITTMAN | **Makes:** ABOUT 1 POUND, ENOUGH FOR 3 TO 4 MAIN COURSE SERVINGS, ABOUT 6 FIRST COURSE SERVINGS, OR 25 TO 30 RAVIOLI **Time:** 20 MINUTES, PLUS TIME FOR THE DOUGH TO REST

The best pasta contains just three ingredients: flour, eggs, and salt. It varies only in the ratio of flour to eggs and the technique. This recipe, a combination of my own experience and that of Gabrielle Hamilton of Prune and Anna Klinger of Al di Lá, can be used for Gabrielle's Pasta Kerchiefs (page 178), Anna's Beet Ravioli (page 172), or any other recipe calling for freshly made pasta.

Cook the finished pasta as soon as it's done, or allow the sheets to dry for a few hours (or even a few days) and cook them later.

2 cups (about 10 ounces) all-purpose flour, plus more as needed

1 teaspoon salt

3 eggs

½ tablespoon extra-virgin olive oil

A few drops water, if needed

1   Combine the flour and salt in the container of a food processor fitted with the plastic blade and pulse once or twice. Add the eggs and olive oil and turn the machine on. Process until a ball begins to form, about 30 seconds. Add a few drops of water if the dough is dry and grainy; add a little flour if dough sticks to the side of the bowl.

2   Turn the dough out onto a dry, lightly floured work surface and knead until it is smooth, just 1 or 2 minutes. Add water by the half teaspoonful if the mixture is dry; add flour if it is sticky. This should be an easy dough to work. Cut the dough into 6 pieces; wrap 5 pieces in plastic. (If time allows, wrap it all in plastic and refrigerate for 1 to 24 hours.)

3   Clamp a pasta rolling machine to a counter and sprinkle the counter lightly with flour; have more flour ready. Put a piece of dough through the widest setting (usually #1). Decrease the distance between the two rollers, making the strip of dough progressively thinner. Note that as the dough becomes longer, it will become more fragile. If at any point the dough sticks or tears, bunch it together and start again. You will quickly get the hang of it. Use as much flour as you need to keep the dough from sticking, but no more than necessary or the dough will become too dry.

4 When you pass the dough through setting #6 (on most machines; in any case, thin enough to see your hand through a sheet of it), set it aside on a lightly floured towel and cover it. (The rolled-out pieces will be about 5 inches wide.) Repeat the process with the remaining pieces of dough.

5 To make kerchiefs: Cut the dough into the largest squares you can (about 5 inches); you'll need 4 for 4 servings of Gabrielle's pasta.

To make ravioli or any other stuffed pasta. Leave the sheets whole and see the directions with Anna's recipe (page 172).

Pasta Kerchiefs with Poached Egg, French Ham, and Brown Butter

GABRIELLE HAMILTON | **Makes:** 3 OR 4 MAIN COURSE OR ABOUT 6 FIRST COURSE SERVINGS **Time:** 20 MINUTES, WITH PREMADE PASTA

This is Gabrielle's take on a "lazy raviolo"—fresh pasta with the "stuffing" on top—though with all the last-minute work, it's not exactly a dish I'd classify as lazy. However, once the pasta is made and your eggs are poached (both of which are steps you can take care of hours in advance), it's a pretty quick dish to assemble. It's also enormously appealing, a lovely square of pasta with ham and egg on top. Most people will salivate when they see it.

Salt

8 tablespoons (1 stick) butter

4 (5-inch) square sheets Egg Pasta Dough (page 176)

1 cup loosely packed arugula, watercress, or other bitter greens, chopped

4 slices smoked cured jambon de Bayonne or other lightly smoked, dry-cured ham

4 poached eggs (recipe follows)

¼ cup shaved Parmigiano-Reggiano cheese

Best-quality balsamic vinegar

3 tablespoons pine nuts, toasted

1   Bring a large pot of water to boil and salt it. Turn the oven on to its lowest setting; warm 4 pasta bowls in it. Cook the butter over medium heat in a medium saucepan until it browns and has a nutty aroma; keep warm.

2   When the water is again at a rolling boil, drop in the pasta sheets and cook for about 90 seconds. Use tongs to fish out the pasta sheets and transfer one to each of the bowls, laying each handkerchief flat across the bowls. Leave the water on the heat.

3   Roll about ¼ cup greens in a slice of ham, grab the little bundle with your tongs, and hold in the boiling pasta water for a few seconds, until the greens wilt a bit. Drain momentarily, then place in the center of one of the sheets of pasta. Repeat, making a bundle for each serving.

4   Put a poached egg on top of each ham and greens bundle, fold one corner of the pasta over the filling, brush the edges with water and seal two corners at the top. Pour a little of the warm brown butter over each. Garnish with a little Parmigiano-Reggiano, a tiny drizzle of balsamic vinegar, and a sprinkle of pine nuts and serve.

Poached Eggs

Makes: 4 **Time:** 10 MINUTES

Producing perfect-looking poached eggs takes practice, but the challenge is reduced if you poach the eggs ahead of time. You can make them look professional by trimming off the ragged edges once they've cooled a bit; then reheat as instructed below.

1 teaspoon salt	4 eggs
2 teaspoons white or cider vinegar	

1 Bring about 1 inch water to a boil in a deep, small skillet. Add the salt and vinegar, and lower the heat to the point where it barely bubbles. One at a time, break the eggs into a shallow bowl and slip them into the water. At this point, cover the skillet.

2 Cook 3 to 5 minutes, just until the whites are set and the yolks have filmed over. Remove with a slotted spoon. If you are eating the eggs right away, place them directly on the pasta, toast, corned beef hash, or what have you. If you are reserving them for another use, drain them on paper towels; they can sit there for up to 1 hour. Poached eggs are delicate, but they can be handled as long as you are careful. To reheat them, dip into a saucepan of simmering water for 30 seconds.

SHOP TALK: On Handmade Pasta

While Gabrielle Hamilton and I were working together, we chatted about the pleasures of making pasta:

MB: Making pasta is one of the few arduous kitchen tasks I actually like to tackle a few times a year...

GABRIELLE: It's one of those things that reminds me why people love to cook. It's very different from when you're cooking in a restaurant, which is all manual labor and pure drudgery, but making pasta, it's just something that makes your day go better. I mean you're just feeling this little...breast. It's so soft!

MB: It *is* soft.

GABRIELLE: And the flour, all silky now, and it's cool to the touch. It's so nice.

MB: You know, this dish reminds me of the saying, "The older my grandmother gets, the bigger her ravioli are." And it's true—when you're young and you've got tons of energy and plenty of manual dexterity and great eyesight you make all these tortellini and little stuffed shapes. But when you get older you're like, "What? I'm not going to stuff all these little pastas. I'll just roll out a sheet and cook it. And here we are."

Pasta with Ham and Eggs

MARK BITTMAN | **Makes:** 3 OR 4 MAIN COURSE OR ABOUT 6 FIRST COURSE SERVINGS
Time: 10 MINUTES

"Can I steal this for my menu?" is the best thing I can hear from a chef, and that was Gabrielle's response to this dish. When I was at Prune, I used her jambon de Bayonne, among France's best hams, but the kind of ham doesn't matter much—salt-cured or smoked are both fine, as long as it's of good quality.

This is also an ideal dish for one. You really can cook it in 10 minutes once the water comes to a boil—just adjust the proportions accordingly.

Salt and black pepper

1 pound spaghetti

4 to 8 tablespoons (½ to 1 stick) butter

8 slices ham (about 6 ounces), cut into ribbons

4 eggs

Freshly grated Parmigiano-Reggiano, to taste

1   Set a large pot of water to boil and salt it. Turn the oven on to its lowest setting; warm 4 pasta bowls in it. When the water is ready, add the pasta. Meanwhile, put 1 tablespoon of the butter and the ham into a medium sauté pan over medium-high heat. Cook, shaking the pan occasionally, until the ham colors, about 2 minutes, then divide the ham among the pasta bowls.

2   Add the remaining butter (the more the better, of course) to the pan and, when the foam subsides, crack the eggs into the pan. Cook them sunny side up, until the whites are nearly firm and the yolks very runny. The butter will begin to color while the eggs are cooking; if it threatens to burn, lower the heat to medium.

3   When the pasta is tender but not mushy, drain it, reserving a bit of the cooking water. Put the pasta in the bowls. Use a spatula to transfer a fried egg to each bowl of pasta and pour all the butter from the pan around the eggs onto the pasta. Slice the eggs on the pasta and toss them with the pasta, adding cheese and, if necessary, a little of the pasta cooking liquid, to make a sauce. Add salt if necessary, and lots of black pepper, and serve.

Ham and Eggs…and Pasta

Adding ham and eggs to pasta is a traditional preparation that takes many forms; the most famous is carbonara, in which cooked pancetta (or bacon or bits of ham) are combined with raw eggs, a load of Parmigiano-Reggiano, and lots of black pepper.

I love the nutty, buttery flavor of fried eggs, but you can also substitute raw egg yolks for the fried eggs in this recipe; just toss the pasta with the sautéed ham and butter and serve piping hot with an egg yolk right on top of the pasta. Stir the egg into the pasta while still warm. Or beat a couple of whole eggs and stir them into the pasta when it's still very hot. (Warmed bowls are important in this recipe, or the egg will cool the dish too much.)

Almost any cured meat can be substituted for the ham—cooked bacon, pancetta, *guanciale,* chorizo, or other sausage are all good.

Or, you can incorporate vegetables. For example, cook large cut pieces of red onion as you do the ham in Step 1 until it softens, and a handful of frozen peas, rinsed and drained, to warm through in the butter just before serving.

Mushroom and Chicken Paella (Paella de Setas y Pollo)

JOSÉ ANDRÉS | Makes: 4 TO 6 MAIN COURSE OR AT LEAST 8 FIRST COURSE SERVINGS
Time: 1 HOUR

During the hour José and I spent around his huge paellera—a paella pan—he made a number of outrageous claims. A certain chef (surprisingly, a friend of his) was "the best chef in the world, no question." The salt in Spain was saltier because Americans, you see, are savvy entrepreneurs who put less "salt" in the salt so you have to buy more. And his paella was cooking unevenly, not because the stovetop it was on was uneven but "because here in Washington we have a problem with the soil. In Spain, the ground is perfectly flat."

Those quips, plus his vociferous knife-in-hand defense of the pelicula—*the glossy residue of evaporating liquid that develops on the paella as it cooks—kept me in stitches.*

When he wasn't making outlandish claims, José gave me some great pointers about paella making: For one thing, he said—and it's probably true—that a thin layer of rice across the pan produces rice with the best texture; it never becomes soupy. He also believes in oversalting slightly, because rice soaks up so much salt. And, finally, he nearly killed me when I threatened to touch, or even breathe on, the paella during the last 10 minutes of boiling, when the precious pelicula formed, claiming I would ruin the dish.

This last one seemed apocryphal, but whatever; his paella is great. For a less rigid—and by José's standards, less authentic—paella, see my Fast and Easy Shrimp "Paella" (page 184).

2 tablespoons extra-virgin olive oil

2 or 3 bone-in, skin-on chicken thighs

1 yellow onion, chopped

3 cloves garlic, chopped

1 bay leaf

½ cup dried porcini, reconstituted in 2 cups hot water

8 ounces fresh mushrooms, preferably mixed

8 ounces chorizo, chopped

1½ to 2 teaspoons pimentón (Spanish paprika; see sidebar), or to taste

½ cup dry white wine

½ cup tomato sauce

2 cups Spanish or Arborio rice

4 to 6 cups chicken stock, preferably homemade (page 249)

Pinch saffron

Salt to taste

1   Heat the oil in the widest pan you own (or use a roasting pan straddling two burners) over medium-high heat. When the oil shimmers, add

the chicken thighs skin sides down and cook them, flipping once or twice, until the skin is deeply browned, about 10 minutes.

2 When the meat is browned, add the onions and cook them, stirring occasionally, until they soften and start to take on a little color, then add the garlic and bay leaf and cook 1 minute more, until the garlic is golden.

3 Drain the soaked mushrooms and add them, along with the fresh mushrooms, to the pan; cook, stirring, until the mushrooms have wilted slightly and begun to give up some of their liquid. Add the chorizo and pimentón and cook, stirring, for a 30 seconds more. Add the wine and reduce by half, about 10–15 minutes. Add the tomato sauce and cook for 5 minutes, stirring occasionally.

4 Add the rice, scattering it across the pan in as even a layer as possible. Add the stock and saffron and season heavily with salt. When the stock reaches a boil, set a timer for 20 minutes, and adjust the heat so the paella cooks at a gentle simmer. When the timer rings, check the rice—if it's still crunchy on the top, add a little more liquid and cook a few minutes longer. When the rice is ready, turn the heat off, let the paella rest for 2 minutes, and serve immediately.

Pimentón, NOT Paprika

I liked to tease José by nonchalantly referring to *pimentón,* Spain's beloved smoked paprika, as simply "paprika." His eyes lit up in astonishment, and he immediately began lecturing me about the provenance and flavor of "real" pimentón. He seems to oscillate between being angry at the Hungarians for producing something that could be confused with Spain's noble spice and being angry at what he feels is the food world's carelessness in thinking that paprika can mean just any "ground dried pepper."

José's jingoistic proclivities aside, pimentón is a great ingredient with a distinctive flavor that makes some Spanish food taste "right." It's made from certain types of peppers, which are picked ripe and then dried over the smoldering ashes of an oak fire, a process that reportedly takes up to two weeks and clearly imbues the peppers with a strong, smoky flavor.

There are three types of pimentón, hot, sweet, and bitter, but I've seen them used pretty interchangeably. If you can't find a local source, try the Spice House, www.thespicehouse.com.

Fast and Easy Shrimp "Paella" (Arroz de Gambas)

MARK BITTMAN | **Makes:** 4 SERVINGS **Time:** 30 MINUTES, SOMEWHAT UNATTENDED

José protested repeatedly that my dish was "an arroz, not a paella," the distinction in his mind being that paella must be cooked in a paella pan. Fine. Although I believe paella is almost any rice-and-anything-else-dish from Spain (and I know plenty of non-fussy Spaniards who'd agree), let's call this Arroz de Gambas, a dish that not only bears a distinctive resemblance and similarity in flavor to paella, but tastes great. Got that?

4 cups shrimp shell stock (see sidebar) or chicken stock

Pinch saffron (optional but very nice)

3 tablespoons olive oil

1 medium onion, minced

About 1 teaspoon pimentón (Spanish paprika; see sidebar, page 183) or other paprika

1 teaspoon ground cumin

2 cups Spanish (or other) short-grain rice

2 cups raw peeled shrimp, cut into ½-inch chunks, shells reserved for stock

Salt

Minced fresh parsley, for garnish

1   Preheat the oven to 450°F. Warm the stock in a saucepan along with the saffron, if you're using it. Place an ovenproof 10- or 12-inch skillet over medium-high heat and add the oil. A minute later, add the onion and cook, stirring occasionally, until translucent and soft, about 5 minutes. Add the paprika and cumin and cook 1 minute more.

2   Add the rice and cook, stirring occasionally, until glossy, just 1 or 2 minutes. Stir in the shrimp, season liberally with salt, and add the warm stock, taking care to avoid the rising steam. Transfer the skillet to the oven.

3   Bake about 15 minutes, until all the liquid is absorbed and the rice is dry on top. Taste for salt, then garnish with parsley and serve immediately.

Shrimp Shell Stock

By extracting great flavor from something you'd ordinarily throw out, making stock from shrimp shells is one of the smartest things a home cook can do. All it takes is this:

Put whatever shells you have in a saucepan and add water to cover. Bring it to a boil, then take the pan off the heat and let the shells steep until you're ready to use the stock, or until the water cools.

Put the stock through a strainer; discard the shells and use or refrigerate (up to two days) or freeze (up to a month). Nothing easier, and often the best stock to use in seafood dishes.

Parathas Stuffed with Lamb, Chiles, and Cilantro (Keema Ke Parathe)

SUVIR SARAN | Makes: 12 PARATHAS; 6 TO 12 SERVINGS   Time: 1½ HOURS

If you've never had parathas before, you're in for a treat. These are India's great griddle-cooked flatbreads—puff pastry–like, but without quite so much work—and stuffed with any number of highly seasoned fillings. Hot from the pan, it's hard not to fill up on them alone, though they're usually served in the context of a larger Indian meal.

Once you get the hang of the technique, you can vary the filling however you like. Suvir, who is a vegetarian, acknowledges the wide appeal of this traditional version, but also tells stories of growing up eating his grandmother's potato-stuffed parathas. You can use my potato filling (page 183), with Suvir's technique here to make these, and see why he loves aloo paratha—potato-stuffed breads—so much. Look for carom or ajwain seeds in Indian markets or on spice websites.

1 cup whole wheat flour plus 1 cup unbleached all-purpose flour or 2 cups all-purpose flour, plus additional for dusting

Salt

1 pound ground lamb or beef

½ cup finely chopped red onion

1 fresh, hot green chile, minced

1 teaspoon minced garlic

½ teaspoon cayenne pepper

½ teaspoon fennel seeds

½ teaspoon carom seeds (ajwain, optional)

2 tablespoons chopped fresh cilantro

½ teaspoon Garam Masala (page 248)

The juice of ½ lime

Canola oil, for cooking

Butter, for serving

1   Mix the flour(s) and 1 teaspoon salt in a large bowl or in the bowl of a standing mixer fitted with the dough hook. Add ½ cup water to the flour mixture and stir to incorporate, then add another ¼ cup water and mix again. Continue adding water a little at a time while stirring the mixture with either your hands or the dough hook, until it starts to coalesce into a smooth dough.

2   Increase the mixer's speed or knead the dough by hand until it is smooth and clears the sides of the mixer bowl. If the dough is dry, sprinkle it with a few drops of water. Put the dough into a clean bowl, cover with a clean damp kitchen towel pressed directly onto the surface, and let rest from 10 to 30 minutes.

3 Meanwhile, put a heavy medium skillet over medium-high heat for 1 or 2 minutes, then add the lamb to the pan. Sauté the meat in its own fat, breaking it up with the side of a wooden spoon, and cook until it has lost its color. Add the onion, chile, garlic, cayenne, fennel, and carom, if you're using it; cook, stirring frequently, until the meat is browned, about 5 minutes more.

4 Stir in the cilantro, Garam Masala, lime juice, 1 tablespoon flour, and salt to taste; cool completely. (The meat filling can be made 2 to 3 days in advance and kept in the refrigerator; bring to room temperature before using.)

5 When the dough has rested, set out a bowl of flour and a small bowl of canola oil, with a spoon or brush, on your work surface. Lightly flour your work surface and a rolling pin. Break off a piece of dough about the size of a golf ball. Toss it first in the bowl of flour and then roll it in your hands to make a ball. Flatten it into a 2-inch disk, then roll into a thin round, about 5 inches in diameter, dusting with flour as necessary.

6 Mound about ¼ cup of the filling in the center of the round of dough. Bring the edges of the round up over the top of the filling and press them together to make a pouch. Press down on the "neck" of the pouch with the palm of one hand to make a slightly rounded disk. Turn the disk in the bowl of flour and roll it out again into a round about 6 inches in diameter. Pat it between your hands to brush off the excess flour. Put the paratha on a plate and cover with a sheet of plastic wrap. Continue to roll all of the remaining dough into parathas and stack them on the plate with a sheet of plastic wrap between each one.

7 Heat a non-stick skillet or griddle (like you'd use for pancakes) over medium-high heat for 1 or 2 minutes, then put a paratha (or two, if they'll fit) on and cook until the dough darkens slightly, 30 seconds to 1 minute. Flip the paratha with a spatula and cook another 30 seconds on the second side. Use the back of a spoon or a brush to coat the top of the paratha with oil. Flip and coat the other side with oil. Continue cooking the paratha until the bottom of the bread has browned; flip and repeat. Do this a few times until both sides of the paratha are golden brown and very crisp, 2 to 3 minutes total for each paratha. As the parathas finish, remove them from the pan and spread with butter. Serve immediately, or as soon as possible.

SHOP TALK: Indian Breads

SUVIR: In India, just like we have gods for different days of the week, we have a different bread for almost every day. And some people who fast won't eat wheat flour, so we have breads made from different flours—buckwheat, chickpea, rye, even melon seed flour.

MB: I guess one thing you have to get past if you're used to European breads is that when I say flour I'm usually talking about something that has gluten, that has the power of being able to be leavened. And I doubt that you can do much with ground melon seeds. It's just a dry powder that just somehow....

SUVIR: ...holds together. Yes. And we use fats for that; potato starch also helps. In southern India they'll ferment the dough and make crêpe-like dishes.

MB: Those great dosas....

SUVIR: Right, dosas. And *utthapam*, which are like pancakes. And then you have *besaratu*, which are made with lentils. And so there are all kinds of breads.

MB: Like fried, griddled....

SUVIR: ...and made in the tandoor. And which is your favorite?

MB: Next to paratha, I like *sheermal*, the sweet one made with saffron, and cooked on the back of the thing that looks like an upside-down wok. I could eat that all day...but let's get cooking.

Faux Potato (Aloo) Paratha

MARK BITTMAN | Makes: 4 **Time:** 20 MINUTES

There is an ancient street known as Paratha Street in Old Delhi where a man sits, cross-legged, on a counter and rolls aloo parathas (potato parathas) one after the other, while his partner cooks them. This is street food at its best. And, really, unless you're an anti-carb fanatic, how can you go wrong stuffing bread with spicy mashed potatoes? Although I thought my creation was inauthentic, Suvir assures me it resembles a "frankie," sold on the streets of Bombay. In any case, this combination crêpe/knish/burrito/paratha has both good flavor and texture. And it's easy.

One technical point: Use "baking" (Idaho or russet) potatoes here; their mealiness will give you just the right texture when mashed.

3 or 4 baking potatoes, boiled, peeled, and mashed, or at least 2 cups leftover mashed potatoes

About ½ cup yogurt

1 tablespoon peeled and minced fresh ginger

1 tablespoon dried mint

Salt, black pepper, and cayenne to taste

¼ cup chopped fresh cilantro leaves

4 large whole wheat or white flour tortillas

2 tablespoons butter

1 Combine the mashed potatoes, half the yogurt, the ginger, mint, and seasonings in a large bowl and mash with a spoon or fork until fairly smooth. Taste the mixture and adjust the seasoning; add additional yogurt as necessary to smooth it out and give it a refreshing acidity. Stir in the cilantro.

2 Put a non-stick skillet over medium heat. Meanwhile, divide the potato-yogurt filling among the 4 tortillas, spreading the filling over the bottom third of each; fold up the bottoms of the tortillas over the filling, then fold in the sides and roll up like burritos.

3 Add the butter to the skillet and turn the heat to medium-high. When the butter melts, cook the filled tortillas a couple at a time; do not crowd. When they're nicely browned, turn, then brown the other sides. Repeat until all are done, then slice in half or thirds and serve hot or warm.

SHOP TALK:
The Faux Paratha

After telling me a lovely little story about his grandmother's potato parathas—how, after making them, she split them open and drizzled melted butter onto the inside—Suvir started in on mine:

SUVIR: My god, it looks like a knish gone wrong.

BITTMAN: To me it looks like a crêpe.

SUVIR: That's a stretch of the imagination. What would your grandmother think of this?

BITTMAN: I don't really remember my grandmother making knishes—but if she saw this, she'd be rolling over in her grave.

SUVIR: Yes, mine too.

Manchurian-Style Cauliflower (Lahsuni Gobi)

SUVIR SARAN | Makes: 4 TO 6 SERVINGS Time: 30 MINUTES

After hearing about Suvir Saran for a few years, I finally made it to his then-new restaurant in New York, Amma. And this was one of the dishes that really wowed me. I kept telling people about his food, "...and he makes this great dish of fried cauliflower cooked in ketchup...," which netted more than a few puzzled looks. But you gotta try it, and please don't be intimidated by the deep frying; it's not that big a deal.

This recipe is part of a pantheon of Sino-Indian fusion dishes created by Chinese immigrants who now live in India. According to Suvir, it's closely associated with the Chinatown in Calcutta, where it's sold on the street, to be eaten off toothpicks.

Neutral oil, like corn or canola, for frying

3 eggs

⅔ cup cornstarch

1 teaspoon salt, for the batter, plus additional to season the sauce

1 teaspoon black pepper

1 large or 2 small heads cauliflower, trimmed and separated into florets

2 teaspoons finely minced garlic

1 cup ketchup

½ teaspoon cayenne, or to taste

1   Put at least 2 inches oil in a countertop deep fryer or in a pan on the stove and turn the heat to medium-high; bring to 350°F (you can check this with a deep-fry or instant-read thermometer; a pinch of flour will sizzle but not burn when added).

2   Beat the eggs and cornstarch together until well blended in a bowl large enough to accommodate the cauliflower. Season the batter with salt and pepper, then add the cauliflower. Use your hands to toss until the florets are evenly coated.

3   Fry the cauliflower in batches small enough not to crowd your pan or fryer, and make sure to let the oil return to temperature (350°F) between batches. Fry until the florets take on a pale, sandy color, with a little brown mottling, about 5 minutes; transfer to paper towels to drain.

4   Warm 1 tablespoon oil in a large non-stick pan or wok over medium heat and immediately add the minced garlic. Cook the garlic for 1 or 2 minutes until fragrant but not colored, then add the ketchup. Cook, stirring, for about 5 minutes, until the sauce bubbles, thickens, and starts to caramelize around the edges of the pan. Add the cayenne; taste and add salt as necessary. Toss the cauliflower in the sauce until evenly coated and serve.

On Ketchup and India

As a matter of course, Indians serve hot or sweet or sour (or sometimes hot, sweet, and sour) chutneys, made from all kinds of fruit and vegetables, with many meals. This practice may strike many people as "foreign" or even bizarre. But I'd bet there's a bottle of sweet and tart fruit jam in your refrigerator right now; you slather the contents on meat loaf and serve it with French fries and even eggs. Ketchup, anyone?

Interestingly enough, ketchup is as familiar and common in India today as it is in the States. Many people eat it instead of or with traditional chutney—so much so that Suvir grew up eating samosas with ketchup.

Indian-Style Cauliflower Stir-Fry

MARK BITTMAN | **Makes:** 4 SERVINGS **Time:** 15 MINUTES

For as much guff as Suvir gave me while I was cooking this dish, in the end we both ended up very happy with it. And after tasting it, he said it reminded him of gobi tataki, a dish made on a flat griddle on the streets of India, where they use knives to mince the cauliflower as it sautés. (The dish's onomatopoeic name alludes to the tak-tak-tak sound of two knives simultaneously mincing and tossing the cauliflower as it sautés.)

1 tablespoon neutral oil, like corn or canola

1 small red onion, chopped

1 large or 2 small heads cauliflower, trimmed and separated into florets

2 teaspoons Garam Masala (page 248) or curry powder

Salt and black pepper

Pinch cayenne

¼ cup chopped fresh cilantro leaves

1　Put the oil in a non-stick skillet and turn the heat to medium-high. A minute later, add half the onion and the cauliflower. Add the Garam Masala and season with salt, black pepper, and cayenne.

2　Cook, stirring or tossing, until the onion has caramelized and the florets are lightly browned, 3 to 5 minutes. Add ½ cup water and continue to cook, stirring occasionally, until the cauliflower is tender and browned all over (add another ½ cup water if necessary to prevent burning).

3　Add the cilantro to the pan, toss once, and transfer to a serving platter. Garnish with the remaining raw onion and serve.

SHOP TALK: On Browning Spices

MB: Many Indian cookbooks call for you to brown the garam masala in the pan, which, to me, seems like it might be a mistake. Don't some spices burn if you're not careful?

SUVIR: I think it's an absolute mistake. These spices are very delicate to begin with, very aromatic, almost floral. And if you start cooking them in the oil in the beginning, unless you do it perfectly, it's going to make them bitter and the aroma you're trying to catch by adding it will die. It kills a dish; makes it bitter. It's better to add the spices after the dish has cooked for a while.

MB: And what about fresh spices? Is it worth it?

SUVIR: Absolutely. In India we have a person called a *masalsee*, who would grind spices for the next meal. Of course, few people do that any more; but I've got a little blender that I use to grind spices daily. A coffee grinder works great too.

For more on garam masala and a recipe, see page 248.

Pont-Neuf Potatoes

MICHEL RICHARD | **Makes:** 4 SERVINGS **Time:** 1½ HOURS (30 MINUTES ACTIVE TIME)

Michel serves these magnificent—and, yes, that is the right word—fries with his Lobster Burger (page 74). Called Pont-Neuf because they're arranged in the form of a bridge, and although the presentation (made possible by careful cutting of the potatoes) is lovely, that's not what makes these special.

Although all of the best French fries are cooked twice—once for tenderness, once for crispness—Michel cleverly decided to do the second frying in clarified butter. A lot of work and a lot of expense, obviously, but these are the best conceivable French fries. Simply incredible.

If you want to build a bridge with the potatoes, you will need nine or twelve fries per serving. Make a base of three (or four) parallel potatoes, then lay three or four across those, then finish with another layer.

Strain the clarified butter afterwards and use it again—either for fries or anything you want to sauté—and you won't feel like you're being quite as wasteful.

1 quart neutral oil, like corn or canola, or more as needed

4 russet potatoes

1 quart clarified butter (see page 75), or more as needed

Salt and black pepper

1   Put at least 2 inches oil in a countertop deep fryer or in a pan on the stove and turn the heat to medium-high; bring to 275°F (you can check this with a deep-fry or instant-read thermometer).

2   Meanwhile, peel the potatoes. Cut lengthwise into ½-inch sections, then cut again lengthwise into ½-inch sticks, making them as even and rectangular as possible. If you're making a larger batch or want to do this step ahead of time, keep the cut potatoes in a bowl of water; dry them well with towels before proceeding.

3   Fry the potatoes in batches small enough not to crowd your pan or fryer, and make sure to let the oil return to temperature (375°F) between batches. Fry them until they just begin to take on the barest amount of color, then transfer them to a paper towel–lined platter or baking sheet to cool. Let them cool to room temperature before proceeding. You can allow them to rest here for up to 2 hours before going on to the next step.

4 When the oil is cool, remove it from the fryer (reserve it for another use) and replace it with the butter; heat to 300°F. Again, fry the potatoes in small batches, making sure to let the oil return to temperature between batches. Cook until they are deep golden in color and crispy, about 8 minutes. Carefully lift the fries out of the oil and onto a plate lined with paper towels, then toss with salt and pepper and serve immediately.

Chive Spaetzle

JEAN-GEORGES VONGERICHTEN | **Makes:** 4 SERVINGS **Time:** 20 MINUTES

Spaetzle—fast dumplings, probably the quickest pasta-like dish you can make—are usually formed with a dull grater-like tool called a spaetzle maker. It's messy and tricky to use.

But Jean-Georges remembers his mother simply dropping the batter off the end of a small spoon. This technique doesn't produce the tiny, odd-shaped nuggets you might think of as spaetzle, but it's obviously easier and results in lovely little dumplings that taste just as good. I'd be hard-pressed to think of things I wouldn't like to see them next to, though he serves them with his Broiled Squab with Jordan Almonds (page 124).

Once you get the hang of making spaetzle, feel free to experiment; these would be great with mustard or poppy seeds, or almost any herb substituted for the chives.

Salt and black pepper	2 eggs
½ cup milk	Large bowl ice water
1 bunch (about 2 ounces) fresh chives	4 tablespoons (½ stick) butter or olive oil
2 cups flour	

1   Set a large pot of water to boil and salt it. Combine the milk and chives in a blender and process until they're smoothly pureed. Transfer to a bowl and stir in the flour, eggs, and a large pinch of salt; beat well.

2   Drop the batter in oval lumps off a small spoon into the boiling water; cook until the dumplings rise to the top, just a couple of minutes. Drain and plunge into ice water to stop the cooking. Drain again. (You can prepare the noodles a day in advance up to this point; refrigerate, covered, until you're ready to cook.)

3   Melt the butter or heat the oil in a large skillet, preferably non-stick, over medium-high heat. Add the spaetzle and some salt and pepper and cook, stirring occasionally, until heated through, about 5 minutes.

Suzanne Goin's Knepfla: Knepfla are closely related to spaetzle, but are richer and tangier thanks to the addition of sour cream. Serve them any time you'd serve spaetzle; Suzanne served them with her Grilled Pork Confit (page 166). Omit the chives, replace the milk with 2 cups sour cream and add another egg; otherwise, proceed as above.

Chickpea Fries

DANIEL BOULUD | **Makes:** ABOUT 60, ENOUGH FOR 6 TO 8 PEOPLE **Time:** SEVERAL HOURS, LARGELY UNATTENDED

This is essentially chickpea polenta, cooled, shaped, and fried. The amazing results are a real crowd-pleaser. Daniel serves these with Leg of Lamb (page 150), but I can hardly think of an occasion when they wouldn't be welcome at the table.

Chickpea flour can be found in natural food stores and Indian and some other ethnic markets.

1 quart whole milk	Salt and white pepper
2 tablespoons extra-virgin olive oil	2¼ cups chickpea flour, sifted
1 tablespoon unsalted butter	Peanut oil, for frying
1 tablespoon fennel seeds, toasted for 2 or 3 minutes in a dry skillet	Semolina flour or finely ground cornmeal, for dredging

1   Line a 9 x 13-inch baking pan with parchment paper or plastic wrap. Put the milk, olive oil, butter, and fennel seeds in a medium saucepan, season with salt and pepper, and bring to a boil. Lower the heat so that the milk simmers steadily and, stirring constantly with a wooden spoon, add the chickpea flour in a fine stream. When all the flour is incorporated, continue stirring over low heat for about 10 minutes.

2   Pour the thickened chickpea mixture into the prepared baking pan and cover the paste with another sheet of parchment or plastic, pressing against it lightly to smooth the top of the paste and create an airtight seal. Refrigerate 2 to 3 hours or, better still, overnight.

3   Pour 3 to 4 inches peanut oil into a deep pot or casserole and turn the heat to medium-high; bring to 350°F (you can check this with a deep-fry or instant-read thermometer). Peel the top sheet of parchment or plastic off the chickpea paste. Cover a plate with an even layer of semolina. Cut out ½ x 3-inch lengths of the paste, dipping the knife in water occasionally. Roll the pieces in the semolina or cornmeal to coat them evenly and gently tap off any excess.

4   Fry in batches—you don't want to crowd the pan—until they're golden brown, 2 to 3 minutes. Carefully lift the fries out of the oil and onto a plate lined with paper towels. Pat off excess oil, sprinkle with salt, and serve immediately (these can also be reheated in a 300°F oven for 5 to 10 minutes).

Sautéed Cabbage

SUZANNE GOIN | **Makes:** 4 SERVINGS **Time:** 25 MINUTES

Suzanne prepared this as part of her pork confit extravaganza (page 166), but this simple mid-European classic would be at home alongside simple grilled pork chops, Gary's Duck Confit and Potato Hash (page 118), or Suzanne's "Much Easier" Chicken Legs (page 108, minus the stuffing).

The bacon will be easier to cut up if it's partially frozen. Alternatively, cut it into small cubes.

About 5 ounces slab bacon, cut into 1-inch matchsticks

1 medium red onion, thinly sliced

1 dried hot chile

½ teaspoon caraway seeds, toasted

Salt

3 cloves garlic, sliced

½ head red cabbage, cored and sliced into ¼-inch-thick ribbons

1   Put the bacon in a large sauté pan over medium heat and cook, stirring occasionally, until the fat has rendered and the bacon is crispy but not brittle, about 5 minutes. Remove the bacon (but not the fat) from the pan and drain on paper towels, then add the onion, chile, and caraway.

2   Season with salt and cook until the onions are tender but still hold their shape, 5 to 10 minutes, then turn up the heat to high and add the garlic. Cook 1 minute, stirring, then add the cabbage. Toss the contents of the pan and cook, stirring regularly, until the cabbage is tender, 5 to 10 minutes. When the cabbage is ready, stir in the crisped bacon, taste and adjust seasoning, then serve warm or at room temperature.

Tomato Rice

SUVIR SARAN | **Makes:** 4 TO 6 SERVINGS **Time:** 20 MINUTES

Suvir makes several varieties of nicely flavored and scented basmati rice, and they're all quite simple, not unlike what we think of as fried rice. (Note that you need precooked rice for this recipe, page 201.) He likes this one served with akoori, *the classic spicy scrambled eggs of India (essentially, scrambled eggs with minced chiles, scallions, and cilantro), and a raita (page 81).*

The tomato paste gives this a little more flavor but, more importantly, guarantees a rich red color.

¼ cup unsalted, dry roasted peanuts

3 tablespoons canola oil

2 teaspoons black mustard seeds (optional)

6 whole cloves

6 dried red chiles

1 teaspoon cumin seeds

1 large red onion, cut into ½-inch dice

Salt to taste

2 large tomatoes, chopped, or 1 pound cherry tomatoes, halved

1 (6-ounce) can tomato paste

½ teaspoon curry powder

1 recipe (about 7 cups) cooked Perfect Basmati Rice (page 201), drained, spread out on a baking sheet, and cooled to room temperature

1   Combine the peanuts, oil, mustard seeds, if using, and cloves in a large non-stick skillet or wok over medium-high heat. Cook, stirring, 1 to 2 minutes, until the spices are fragrant, then add the chiles and cumin, and cook, stirring, until the peanuts take on a light golden color, another 2 minutes.

2   Add the onion and a large pinch of salt and cook, stirring, until the onion begins to soften, then add the tomatoes, tomato paste, and curry powder and cook, stirring often, until the sauce is slightly thickened, about 5 minutes.

3   When the sauce has thickened, add the cooked, cooled rice and toss to coat it with the tomato sauce, scraping the bottom of the pan or wok to loosen the spices or caramelized bits that might be stuck to it (you can add a few tablespoons water to the pan to help loosen them if necessary). Cook just until the rice is warmed through, 2 or 3 minutes, taste for salt, and serve hot.

Perfect Basmati Rice

SUVIR SARAN | **Makes:** ABOUT 7 CUPS **Time:** 15 MINUTES

Basmati, the queen of rices, is long-grain, intensely aromatic, and a staple of Indian cuisine; you can buy it everywhere in the United States now. This is Suvir's technique, and it's an interesting one—the rice is cooked like pasta, which works perfectly and further proves my contention that plain rice can be made, successfully, about ten different ways.

10 cups water   2 cups basmati rice

1   Bring the water to a boil over high heat in a large saucepan, add the rice, and stir a few times so it doesn't stick to the bottom of the pan.

2   When the water returns to a boil, reduce the heat so it simmers vigorously, and cook, with the pan partially covered, for 10 minutes. Drain the rice and return to the pan off the heat where it can rest, covered, until ready to serve (or spread it out onto a rimmed baking sheet to cool if you're making Tomato Rice, page 200).

Desserts

Dessert kitchens—usually called pastry kitchens—are a separate arena in fine restaurants, almost always run by a different, autonomous chef who works for the head chef but independently of him or her. Head chefs usually approve desserts but don't often create them.

But though a couple of our chefs called their pastry chefs in for help when we turned to desserts, most were comfortable cooking sweet things with me. People like Gary Danko and Jean-Georges Vongerichten are so experienced in all facets of kitchen work that it was, I suspect, a pleasure to delve into something outside of their daily routines. Michel Richard, who began his professional life as a pastry chef, is close to a genius in this realm. And some of the other chefs merely turned to old personal favorites, or dishes that had become so standard in their restaurants that they'd outlived the reign of more than one pastry chef.

Although I've never considered myself a dessert person, like many cooks I began with desserts, because (like many cooks) I began young, and (like many young people) sweet things were most appealing in those days. So I'm well grounded in dessert making, but not especially creative. Still, my desserts held up well against those of most of the chefs (and a good time was had by all eating them!). These recipes are mostly based on fruit, which is my favorite way to create dessert—we use pears, persimmons, apricots…and loads of apples (we made these recipes, as you may guess, in the fall).

Suzanne Goin uttered perhaps the best line ever about desserts: "Desserts should be slutty." Not all of these are quite that, but most are pretty showy, and all are delicious.

Persimmon Pudding

GARY DANKO | Makes: 8 INDIVIDUAL SERVINGS OR 1 LARGE PUDDING CAKE
Time: 1½ HOURS, LARGELY UNATTENDED

Persimmon trees are a little like zucchini plants: One day your comment is, "Oh, look honey, the persimmons are finally ripe enough to eat!" Then the moment passes, and there's a quick and loveless transition to, "What the heck are we going to do with all these persimmons?"

Gary's Persimmon Pudding is a terrific answer (but don't discount my dead-easy recipe for Frozen Persimmons, page 206. If you don't feel like making Crème Anglaise, use the home cook's venerable shortcut: softened vanilla ice cream.

1½ pounds very soft Hachiya persimmons (see sidebar, page 207)

1½ cups all-purpose flour

1 teaspoon cinnamon, preferably freshly ground

1 teaspoon baking soda

½ teaspoon salt

½ teaspoon freshly grated or ground nutmeg

2 eggs

1 cup packed brown sugar

1 cup light cream or half-and-half

4 tablespoons (½ stick) unsalted butter, melted

1 teaspoon vanilla extract

Crème Anglaise (recipe follows)

Pomegranate seeds, for garnish (optional)

1　Peel the persimmons and transfer their flesh to the container of a food processor (a blender will also work). Process until pureed, then transfer to a large bowl. (Or put in an airtight container and freeze for up to 3 months.)

2　Preheat the oven to 350°F. Butter a 9 x 3-inch springform cake pan or 8 (6-ounce) ramekins and set aside. Sift the flour, cinnamon, baking soda, salt, and nutmeg together into a medium bowl. Beat the eggs, sugar, cream, butter, and vanilla into the persimmon puree. Stir the flour mixture in and whisk well to combine.

3　Pour the batter into the springform pan or ramekins, and cover tightly with foil, shiny side down. Create a water bath for the pudding(s) by setting the pan or ramekins into a large casserole or baking dish and filling it up with hot water about halfway up the height of the cake pan or ramekins.

4　Bake for 30 to 50 minutes, until a toothpick inserted into the middle of the pudding comes out clean. Let cool. Invert ramekins to release the individual puddings (loosen them by running a knife around their sides if necessary), and serve the puddings (or slices from the larger pudding cake) on plates with a little Crème Anglaise and a sprinkle of pomegranate seeds.

Crème Anglaise

Makes: ABOUT 1½ CUPS, ENOUGH FOR 8 SERVINGS **Time:** 20 MINUTES

Crème Anglaise, the sauce that accompanies Persimmon Pudding at Restaurant Gary Danko, is a thin custard, easy to make and a valuable addition to your repertoire because it pairs nicely with so many desserts. If you're in the mood, flavor it with a tablespoon or so of cognac or rum, stirred into the eggs along with the hot cream.

1 cup light cream or half-and-half	¼ cup sugar
½ vanilla bean	Pinch salt
4 egg yolks	

1   Put the cream in a small saucepan and heat just until steam rises. Cut the vanilla bean in half the long way and scrape the seeds into the cream; stir and let sit off the heat for a few minutes. Meanwhile, in a heavy, medium saucepan, combine and whisk the egg yolks, sugar, and salt.

2   Whisk the hot cream into the egg mixture. Place over medium heat and cook without boiling, stirring constantly, thoroughly, but gently, until the custard coats the back of a spoon (when you drag your finger over the back of the spoon it will leave a distinct trail).

3   Remove from the heat, stir gently once or twice to smooth, and strain through a fine-meshed sieve. Let cool, then serve or refrigerate until needed (bring to room temperature before serving).

Frozen Persimmons

MARK BITTMAN | **Makes:** 4 SERVINGS **Time:** ABOUT 2 HOURS, UNATTENDED

This dessert is literally a persimmon, frozen. But it's amazingly delicious—much like a sorbet, but with zero work. Getting your hands on ripe persimmons (see sidebar) is actually the hardest part, but they make a wonderful, rare dessert. I wish I could take credit for the recipe, but it was actually Gary Danko's idea. It wouldn't work too well in a restaurant, because it is just too simple, but it's perfect for the home cook.

If you overfreeze the persimmons, just temper them in the refrigerator or at room temperature for a few minutes before serving.

4 very ripe Hachiya persimmons

1   Wash the persimmons carefully, then place on a tray or individual plates, stem sides down. Freeze for about 2 hours, until very firm but not rock-hard.

2   Serve, using a spoon to scoop out the stem and dive into the contents.

Persimmons

There are two types of persimmons commonly found in this country, and though to the uninitiated eye they look quite similar, with their brilliant orange color and thin skin, they might as well be different fruits, because substituting one for the other is like substituting an apple for a banana.

The two varieties are Hachiya and Fuyu, whose names probably don't help you tell them apart. Both come into season in very late summer or early fall, and stick around until early winter. The Fuyu, which looks like a flattened tomato, is suitable for out-of-hand eating; it can be quite firm and crisp, yet still be sweet and delicious, like a stone fruit. You could use it in a salad.

The Hachiya is taller, with a more elongated shape; it's the one you want for both dessert recipes. But it's a deceptive fruit, and one that takes judgment and patience. When you're shopping for a Hachiya persimmon (Asian markets stock them most reliably), look for the softest ones you can find, but with no bruising. It's unlikely you'll find them very soft, so you will have to let them sit, undisturbed on your counter, until they become very, very soft and practically translucent, like an overripe tomato. If you try one before it's ready, you'll quickly become convinced to wait longer next time; the astringency is unparalleled.

Apple Confit

JEAN-GEORGES VONGERICHTEN | **Makes:** 10 SERVINGS OR MORE **Time:** AT LEAST 24 HOURS, LARGELY UNATTENDED

This is a dish I fell in love with years ago at JoJo, Jean-Georges's first independent New York restaurant. It's a dense millefeuille (the word means "thousand leaves") of caramelized apples that's tart, sweet, unctuous, and lean, just the sort of thing you want at the end of a rich meal. Thinly sliced apples are layered with sugar and citrus, then macerated overnight before being cooked very slowly—think about six hours—so that they miraculously retain their individuality while melting into an irresistible cake-like mass.

Making this confit is a long and undeniably tedious process—it's wise to start it the morning of the day before you wish to serve it—but it yields 10 servings, which helps amortize the labor. Serve it if you like, as Jean-Georges does, with Green Apple Sorbet (recipe follows), or simply with a piece of pound cake and a dollop of crème fraîche or sour cream.

2 cups sugar

5 oranges

15 Granny Smith apples

1   Melt 1 cup of the sugar in a sauté pan over medium heat, stirring only occasionally, until it bubbles and turns golden brown, 5 to 10 minutes. Immediately pour it into a standard 9 x 5-inch loaf pan. Swirl it around so that it coats the bottom, then set it aside.

2   Use a zester to remove the zest from the oranges, then put the zest in a saucepan with water to cover. Bring to a boil, cook 1 minute, drain, then refresh under cold running water for a minute or 2. Drain again.

3   Peel the apples, then halve and core them. Cut them by hand or with a mandoline into slices about ⅛ inch thick. Using only flat pieces (discard or eat the rounded ends), place a single layer of apples neatly in the bottom of the loaf pan. Cover with another layer, keeping the layers as level as possible. Sprinkle with a bit of the remaining 1 cup sugar, then some of the zest. Repeat, adding sugar and zest every 2 or 3 layers.

4   When you get to the top of the pan, keep the lines straight and continue to build layers beyond the top, going about 3 or 4 inches above the pan. Cover the top with plastic, then wrap the whole pan in aluminum foil. Place it in a shallow tray; the apples will "weep" liquid—and refrigerate at least overnight, preferably for 24 hours.

5   Preheat the oven to 300°F. Drain the juice from the tray (use it to replace some of the juice in Green Apple Sorbet, if you're making it) and unwrap the pan. Drain the excess liquid from the pan, then wrap it in a double layer of aluminum foil. Place the pan in a large, deep roasting pan, and fill the roasting pan with water halfway up its sides.

6   Bake for 5 hours, then check the confit. It is done when all the apple slices are dark brown, it has shrunk to fill only about three-quarters of the mold, and a thin-bladed knife pierces it easily. Cooking time is usually between 5 and 6½ hours. Unwrap, cool, and chill for several hours or up to 2 days. Slice thinly and serve.

Green Apple Sorbet

Makes: 4 TO 6 SERVINGS   **Time:** 15 MINUTES, PLUS TIME TO FREEZE

This is a lightly sweetened and quite subtle sorbet. If you do use green apples, like Granny Smiths, freeze the sorbet immediately after making the base, or it will turn brown instead of its distinctively lovely pale green. Like all sorbets, this should be eaten as soon as possible after freezing.

½ cup sugar

Large bowl ice

8 Granny Smith apples

The juice of 1 lemon

1   Place the sugar in a small saucepan with ½ cup water. Turn the heat to high and cook, stirring, until the sugar dissolves, just 1 or 2 minutes. Chill by placing the saucepan in a bowl of ice.

2   Wash the apples and put them through a juicer. (Alternatively, puree them in a blender and squeeze them in a clean towel over a bowl to extract the juice.) Combine with ½ cup of the sugar syrup and the lemon juice.

3   Freeze in an ice cream maker according to the manufacturer's directions.

Tartless "Tarte Tatin"

MARK BITTMAN | **Makes:** 6 TO 8 SERVINGS **Time:** AT LEAST 1 HOUR, LARGELY UNATTENDED

This recipe—essentially a ton of caramelized apples—is my version of a tarte tatin without the crust. It contrasts perfectly with Jean-Georges's Apple Confit (page 208), because the results are similar—sweet, soft, intensely flavorful apples—except my dish, as you might expect, takes less work and less time (it also has more added fat, but cooking is often about trade-offs).

I am pleased to say that Jean-Georges showed obvious delight in eating my little creation.

6 tablespoons (¾ stick) unsalted
butter

1¼ cups sugar

4 to 5 pounds crisp, not-too-sweet
apples, like Granny Smith, peeled,
cored, and sliced

½ teaspoon ground cinnamon
(optional)

Crème fraîche, sour cream, or ice
cream (optional)

1 Preheat the oven to 400°F. Combine 4 tablespoons of the butter with 1 cup of the sugar and 1 tablespoon water in a 10- or 12-inch non-stick ovenproof skillet and turn the heat to medium. Cook, shaking the pan occasionally, until the sugar melts into the butter and the mixture bubbles. Turn off the heat and add the apples in layers; it's okay if they overlap. About halfway through layering the apples, dot with some of the remaining butter and sugar. Use the rest of the butter and sugar on top of the last layer, along with the cinnamon, if you like.

2 Put the skillet in the oven. Bake, undisturbed, until the apples give up their liquid and it evaporates and the sides of the mass are dark brown and sticky looking. This will take around 45 minutes, but it could be considerably longer or shorter depending on the moisture content of your apples. Remove and let cool. Serve straight from the pan or, for a more attractive presentation, invert onto a plate. Serve, if you like, with a scoop of crème fraîche, sour cream, or ice cream.

The Un-American Apple Pies

Both Jean-Georges's and my apple desserts are made without crusts, which may be seen as un-American. But I find many pies entirely too bready, and the two-crusted variety of apple pie is really the worst offender—apples steaming in their own juices, becoming apple chunks in their juice at best and hard, undercooked chunks at worst—sitting between two crusts. An applesauce sandwich.

The most important part of apple pie should be the apples, so rather than throwing some apple slices between crusts and hoping for the best, Jean-Georges's and my recipes focus on nurturing and enhancing the flavor of the apples.

In both of these dishes, the apples are caramelized and candy-like. Jean-Georges's version may be a lot of work, but it's really pretty much foolproof. Mine is quicker, but may take some practice to get just right. For this, you need to learn the ideal texture and appearance when it is done: tender apples surrounded by a bubbly mahogany glaze.

Once you put the "pie" in the oven and the liquid given up by apples begins to evaporate, the edges begin to caramelize. From then on you are walking a fine line. Undercook the dish, and it's not bad—tender apples on a sweet, buttery glaze—but neither is it

glorious. (Still, it's not a mistake to play it safe the first time you make it.) Overcook it, and the apples may not release, even from a non-stick pan, and the caramel may have become sticky enough to weld your teeth together when you bite into it. (Still, even the time I screwed up, my friends loved it this way.)

Hit it right, however (and even a novice can do this, or I wouldn't be sharing the recipe), and you have a dark, slightly chewy bottom (or top; you can invert the apples onto a plate if you like) with sweet, tender apples on top. Un-American, perhaps, but delicious.

Banana Bread with Caramel Sauce, Toffee, and Tempura Bananas

KERRY SIMON | **Makes:** AT LEAST 8 SERVINGS **Time:** 1 HOUR

I like the attitude of Justin Nilsson, Kerry Simon's pastry chef, which goes counter to the often necessarily compulsive personalities of many of his peers. He said, "If you want to end up with a light-hearted dessert, you've got to approach baking more light-heartedly."

This is definitely a light-hearted dessert (as is my frozen chocolate-covered banana on a stick, page 216): a rich banana cake (muffins, really) topped with rum sauce and fried bananas. When made Justin's way, it's a pretty complicated affair—the cakes are topped with chopped English toffee, fried bananas, and rum sauce. But even without the trimmings, this is a very good banana cake—super-rich, laced with cardamom (a traditional dessert spice, now underappreciated), and tempered by the slight sourness of buttermilk.

6 eggs, separated

1¼ cups plus 2 tablespoons sugar

16 tablespoons (2 sticks) unsalted butter, softened, plus extra for greasing the pan

1 cup packed brown sugar

½ tablespoon vanilla extract

1½ teaspoons baking soda

1½ cups buttermilk

1 teaspoon ground cardamom

3 cups all-purpose flour

3 bananas, peeled and mashed

Caramel Rum Sauce (page 213)

English Toffee (page 214)

Tempura Bananas (page 215)

1   Preheat the oven to 350°F. Whisk the egg whites and the 2 tablespoons sugar together in the bowl of a stand mixer fitted with the balloon whip attachment, until shiny with soft but defined peaks, just a few minutes. Scoop them out with a spatula into another bowl; switch to the mixer's paddle attachment. Cream the butter together with the remaining white and brown sugars. Let the machine beat the mixture for at least 2 minutes (you could actually walk away for a few minutes because you can't overbeat this). Stir in the egg yolks and vanilla extract and blend.

2   Meanwhile, whisk the baking soda into the buttermilk and sift (or stir) the cardamom together with the flour. Then, while the mixer is running, alternately add portions of the buttermilk and flour mixtures to the butter and eggs in the work bowl. When you've added all the buttermilk and flour, add the mashed bananas and process a few seconds longer, until the batter looks even.

3   By hand, fold the egg whites into the batter. Portion the batter out into a buttered muffin pan, filling each cup about two-thirds of the way. Bake for 15 to 20 minutes, until golden brown. Serve the little cakes warm on a plate dressed with the caramel rum sauce, chopped toffee, and 2 tempura banana halves perched on top of each.

Caramel Rum Sauce

Makes: ABOUT 1 CUP   **Time:** 15 MINUTES

The addition of buttermilk to this sauce makes it unusual, lending an intriguingly tart flavor dimension. In finishing the sauce, use real dark rum, not spiced rum that is dark as a result of added spices you probably don't want here.

1 cup sugar

½ cup buttermilk

8 tablespoons (1 stick) unsalted butter

1 tablespoon light corn syrup

½ teaspoon vanilla extract

½ teaspoon baking soda

2 tablespoons dark rum

1   Combine the sugar, buttermilk, butter, corn syrup, vanilla, and baking soda in a large pot and bring to a boil (this will foam up a great deal, so be sure that your pot is 2 or 3 times larger than it needs to be to comfortably hold the ingredients). Once the foam subsides, lower the heat and cook the sauce until it's a medium caramel color, stirring periodically, about 10 minutes.

2   Turn off the heat, add the rum, and cool slightly; use immediately.

English Toffee

KERRY SIMON | **Makes:** ABOUT 1 CUP TOFFEE **Time:** 30 MINUTES, PLUS TIME TO COOL

People are often surprised when they learn that they can make candy at home. But why would there be fudge shops in every hamlet in America if it took a cooking school diploma to learn how to make it? Like fudge, English toffee is a candy that's easy to make; just take care when it's nearing that hard crack stage, because molten sugar is hot and sticky.

½ cup sugar

¼ cup light corn syrup

¼ cup heavy cream

8 tablespoons (1 stick) unsalted butter

1   Dissolve the sugar and corn syrup in the cream in a small saucepan over low heat. Add the butter to the mixture and refrain from stirring until it takes on a light caramel color, about 10 minutes. Then stir constantly, using a heatproof spatula or wooden spoon, until the mixture has the consistency of peanut butter, or when it reaches the hard crack stage on a candy thermometer (just over 300°F), about 10 minutes.

2   Immediately and carefully pour the toffee onto a non-stick baking sheet (or one lined with parchment paper or Silpat) and spread with an oiled spatula to an even thickness. Cool to room temperature. Break the toffee into pieces and store in an airtight container indefinitely (but do not refrigerate; the sugar will "melt").

Tempura Bananas

KERRY SIMON | **Makes:** 4 STAND-ALONE SERVINGS, OR 8 WHEN SERVED WITH THE CAKE

Time: 15 MINUTES

This is the essential, basic tempura preparation; you could easily adapt it to shrimp or small vegetables by treating them the same way and seasoning them with salt at the end. Like most fried foods, tempura deteriorates rapidly, so cook it at the last possible minute before serving.

Neutral oil, such as canola or grapeseed, for deep frying

1 cup ice-cold water

1 to 1½ cups rice flour or all-purpose flour

1 egg

4 bananas, halved lengthwise

1　Heat the oil in a deep fryer or deep saucepan; use a thermometer to hold the temperature between 350° and 375°F. Do not prepare the bananas until the oil is ready.

2　Beat the ice-cold water very lightly with the flour and egg; the batter should be lumpy. Dip the banana halves briefly in the batter and immediately transfer to the hot oil. You can probably cook 4 to 6 pieces at a time, depending on the size of your fryer. Cook 1 minute, or until nicely crisped.

3　Drain the fried banana halves for a moment on paper towels and use immediately.

Frozen Chocolate Banana on a Stick

MARK BITTMAN | **Makes:** 4 SERVINGS   **Time:** 20 TO 30 MINUTES

This was perhaps my most inspired dish of the series, or at least the funniest. In any case, it was delicious, fun to eat, and everyone in the room loved it. Don't let my version limit what you do at home: You could toast the coconut or substitute cashews or crushed peanut brittle for the peanuts.

4 ripe but not brown bananas, cut in half lengthwise and impaled lengthwise on wooden skewers

1 cup packaged chocolate shell, chocolate ganache, or Chocolate Sauce (recipe follows)

½ cup salted peanuts, roughly chopped

½ cup shredded coconut

1   Put the skewered banana halves in the freezer for 15 minutes or, alternatively, put the bananas in a airtight container (or wrap tightly in foil) and freeze them for as long as 2 days (just allow them to defrost for 10 to 15 minutes at room temperature before using them).

2   Have the chocolate, salted peanuts, and coconut out in 3 separate shallow plates or bowls and let your kids (or your guests) dip and garnish their frozen bananas to their liking.

Chocolate Sauce

Makes: ABOUT 2 CUPS **Time:** 15 MINUTES

This is a good all-purpose chocolate sauce (you could use it for my Poached Pears, page 224, also). Spike it with a splash of liquor like Grand Marnier or rum, if you like, just before you lower the heat, to let it blend in.

¾ cup (3½ ounces) chopped bittersweet chocolate

½ cup heavy cream

¼ cup sugar

Combine all the ingredients with ¾ cup water in a small saucepan over high heat and bring to a boil. As soon as the mixture boils, turn the heat down as low as it will go and cook, stirring frequently for 10 minutes or more, until the mixture thickens. Cool briefly and use. (Or store in the refrigerator and use within 3 or 4 days.)

Brioche Bread Pudding

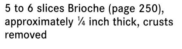

SUZANNE GOIN | **Makes:** 8 TO 10 SERVINGS **Time:** 2 HOURS, LARGELY UNATTENDED, WITH PREMADE BRIOCHE

Bread pudding is essentially a custard with bread suspended in it, and Suzanne's is sublime because the bread she begins with is homemade brioche. You could substitute any good bread, of course (or make my version, which is simpler). But this is really the ultimate, especially if you include the roasted apples.

5 to 6 slices Brioche (page 250), approximately ¼ inch thick, crusts removed

2 tablespoons unsalted butter, softened

1½ cups heavy cream

1¼ cups whole milk

¼ cup packed brown sugar

3 eggs

2 egg yolks

1 teaspoon vanilla extract

½ teaspoon cinnamon, preferably freshly ground

¼ teaspoon salt

¼ teaspoon nutmeg, preferably freshly grated

1 to 2 tablespoons sugar, for caramelizing

Caramelized Apples (optional, recipe follows)

Cinnamon or vanilla ice cream (optional)

1   Preheat the oven to 325°F. Cut the Brioche slices into triangles and butter them lightly on both sides. Lay the slices, slightly overlapping, in the bottom of a 2-inch-deep gratin or soufflé dish, about 9 inches in diameter.

2   Whisk together in a large bowl the cream, milk, brown sugar, eggs, yolks, vanilla, cinnamon, salt, and nutmeg and pour over the Brioche slices. Press down on the bread a bit so it soaks up the liquid. Put the pudding in the oven (use a water bath if you prefer; see sidebar, page 221) and bake for 50 to 60 minutes; the top should jiggle slightly when you shake the pan.

3   Let cool for at least 30 minutes. Scatter the remaining sugar over the top and caramelize with a butane torch or under the broiler. Serve with a generous scoop of Caramelized Apples, if using, and, if you like, some ice cream.

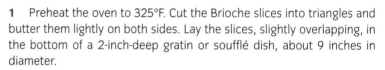

Caramelized Apples

SUZANNE GOIN | **Makes:** 8 SERVINGS AS PART OF THE BREAD PUDDING,
OR 4 TO 6 SOLO SERVINGS **Time:** 1 HOUR

One of the first things Suzanne said to me when we started cooking was, "Desserts should be slutty." Drenched in browned butter and spiked with apple brandy, this is about as slutty as fruit gets. Serve with her Brioche Bread Pudding (opposite), or simply with vanilla or cinnamon ice cream.

8 tablespoons (1 stick) unsalted butter

1 vanilla bean, split and scraped

2 tablespoons sugar

2 tablespoons packed brown sugar

4 apples, preferably Braeburn, Cortland, Rome, McIntosh, or another good cooking variety

½ teaspoon ground cinnamon

¼ teaspoon ground nutmeg

¼ teaspoon salt

1 tablespoon apple brandy, preferably Calvados

1   Preheat the oven to 400°F. Combine the butter and vanilla bean in a saucepan and cook over medium heat, swirling the butter in the pan occasionally, until the butter browns and smells nutty. Set aside off the heat while you proceed (discard the vanilla pod just before using the butter).

2   Mix the 2 sugars together in a small bowl and set aside. Cut the apples in half through the core and scoop out the seeds with a melon baller or small spoon. Toss the apple halves with the cinnamon, nutmeg, and salt, then arrange them cut sides up in a roasting pan. Top each with some of the mixed sugars, a splash of Calvados, and a drizzle of the vanilla brown butter.

3   Bake for 40 or more minutes, basting with the pan juices every 10 minutes, until the apple flesh has pulled away from the skin and is softened and browned. Serve the apples warm.

SHOP TALK: The Value of Timers

SUZANNE *(while making the brioche):* So you want to work this dough for five minutes—a real five minutes. We should set a timer.

MB: I'm surprised to hear you suggest using a timer. Most chefs I know are a little more cavalier about how long things cook. But I know I use them now. I've had some near catastrophic accidents, especially when baking. I try to check all the time, but then I forget—like everyone else.

SUZANNE: I'm definitely pro-timer, because when the pastry chef tells you to beat the dough for five minutes, she means five minutes. But you know a lot of savory cooks avoid it like the plague until they burn their nuts—er, walnuts. Or croutons. Oh come on, don't look at me like that.

Easy Bread Pudding

MARK BITTMAN | **Makes:** 6 SERVINGS **Time:** ABOUT 1 HOUR, LARGELY UNATTENDED

Suzanne's gorgeous bread pudding is a perfect restaurant dessert, and doable at home, as long as you have plenty of time. But if you want a great and very simple bread pudding, try this one. If you start with challah bread, which you can purchase in almost any neighborhood with a Jewish population, the results will be great; you can also use brioche, of course, or any other bread.

Chocolate is a perennial favorite flavoring, but I've added the chocolate chips as a variation because I honestly prefer my bread pudding unadorned.

3 cups milk

½ cup plus 1 tablespoon sugar

4 tablespoons (½ stick) unsalted butter, plus extra for greasing the pan

Pinch salt

8 (½-inch) slices challah, brioche, or white bread, crusts removed if they are very thick

3 eggs

1 teaspoon vanilla extract

1 teaspoon ground cinnamon

Sweetened whipped cream or ice cream (optional)

1   Preheat the oven to 350°F. Over low heat in a small saucepan, warm the milk, ½ cup sugar, butter, and salt, just until the butter melts. Meanwhile, butter a 1½-quart or 8-inch square baking dish (glass is nice), and cut or tear the bread into bite-sized pieces.

2   Cool the milk slightly and beat in the eggs and vanilla. Place the bread in the baking dish and pour the milk-egg mixture over it. Let it sit for a few minutes, occasionally submerging any pieces of bread that rise to the top. Mix together the remaining 1 tablespoon sugar and the cinnamon and sprinkle over the top.

3   Bake 30 to 45 minutes, or until a thin-bladed knife inserted in the center comes out clean, or nearly so; the center should remain a little wobbly. Run under the broiler for about 30 seconds if you like, to brown the top a bit. Serve warm or cold, with or without sweetened whipped cream or ice cream.

Chocolate Chip Bread Pudding: In Step 2, scatter 2 ounces chocolate chips over the bread mixture before you sprinkle it with cinnamon and sugar. Proceed as above.

Why Bathe?

Suzanne insisted that bread pudding, like other custards, must be cooked in a water bath, a pan of water surrounding the pan of custard. The theory (which is true for many custards) is that the eggs will overcook—essentially scramble—around the pan's edges before the interior is cooked. I disagreed in this case; some custards, if cooked slowly and carefully (and not overcooked), don't really need a water bath.

Then came the test: Her bread pudding went into the kitchen, where it was to be put in a water bath; mine went in unshielded from the oven's heat.

And when the moment of truth was upon us, we went to fetch our respective puddings and, incredibly, someone had forgotten to put water in the pan around Suzanne's dessert. But, far from the tragedy she would have predicted, both puddings were fine and the results were in: You can skip the water bath when you're making bread pudding.

Chocolate Pear Cake

ANNA KLINGER | **Makes:** 1 (9-INCH) CAKE, ABOUT 8 SERVINGS **Time:** 1½ HOURS, LARGELY UNATTENDED

The secret to having this pear cake come out as light as it does at Al di Là, Anna's restaurant in Brooklyn, is beating the eggs until they double in volume, which takes a long time if done by hand—at least 8 to 10 minutes. For that reason, make the cake with an electric mixer (a powerful stand mixer is best) as Anna did, or make sure you've got a partner in baking to relieve you when your arm gives out.

If you don't have bread crumbs on hand or you'd just like a change, use crushed almonds, panettone, or amaretti to yield a good, crunchy crust.

8 tablespoons (1 stick) unsalted butter, melted, plus softened butter, as needed

1 cup fine plain bread crumbs

1 cup all-purpose flour

1 tablespoon baking powder

3 eggs

¾ cup sugar

3 ripe pears, peeled and cut into 1-inch pieces

¾ cup (3½ ounces) roughly chopped bittersweet chocolate

1   Preheat the oven to 300°F. Liberally butter a 9-inch springform pan. Add the bread crumbs to the pan and swirl them around to coat the bottom and the sides. Tap out any excess bread crumbs and reserve. Sift or stir the flour and baking powder together.

2   Put the eggs in the bowl of a stand mixer and beat them at high speed until they're light, frothy, and pale yellow, 8 to 10 minutes. Then, with the machine still running, add the sugar in a slow steady stream. Beat for another minute, then beat in the flour–baking powder mixture and melted butter.

3   Pour the batter into the springform pan, arrange the pears in a single layer over the batter, and scatter the chocolate over the pears. Bake for 1 hour, or until a knife inserted into the center of the cake comes out clean. Allow the cake to cool for 10 minutes, unmold, and serve warm.

Poached Pears with Chocolate Sauce

MARK BITTMAN | **Makes:** 4 SERVINGS **Time:** 20 MINUTES, PLUS COOLING TIME

This was the one occasion in all of the challenges where my dish, a gorgeous poached pear with a lovely homemade chocolate sauce, looked fancier than the chef's. But as you can see from the list of ingredients, there's not really that much to it. And it's a perfect way to use the flavorful but firm pears that are pretty much the only type available outside of prime pear season. I used Bosc pears for their dramatic shape; you can use any pear you like as long as it's not overripe.

4 (6-ounce) pears, peeled

3¼ cups sugar

2 vanilla beans

½ cup unsweetened cocoa powder, like Valrhona or Hershey's

½ cup heavy cream

Splash Grand Marnier or other orange liqueur (optional)

1 Core the pears using a melon baller or small spoon. The idea is to burrow out the seeds from the center of the fruit, leaving the shape of the pear and as much of the flesh as possible intact. If you'd like to serve the pears standing up, slice a little off the bottom of the fruit to yield a level surface.

2 Combine 2½ cups of the sugar and 5 cups water in a saucepan large enough to hold the pears. Split the vanilla beans the long way and scrape out the seeds; add both seeds and pods to the water. Turn the heat to medium-high and bring to a boil, stirring to dissolve the sugar. Add the pears and adjust the heat so that the mixture bubbles gently. Cook 8 minutes, or until a thin-bladed knife inserted into the pears meets with little resistance. Let the pears cool in the liquid off the heat for 30 minutes, or more if you like.

3 Meanwhile, combine 1 cup water with the remaining ¾ cup sugar in a small saucepan; bring to a boil, stirring to dissolve the sugar. Turn off the heat and whisk in the cocoa, along with the cream and Grand Marnier. Return to very low heat and cook, stirring until just slightly thickened.

4 When you're ready to serve, drain the pears from the poaching liquid and serve them with the chocolate sauce spooned over.

"Fried Egg"
(Apricots with Sweet Cheese)

MICHEL RICHARD | Makes: 4 SERVINGS Time: 30 MINUTES

The trickiest part of this dessert is finding something round and roughly the size of a fried egg to serve your "eggs" in. Michel had perfect little silver sauté pans, but if your collection of tiny silver faux kitchen tools isn't as well developed, you'll probably do what I did—use round ramekins or little rimmed saucers.

Make sure to start with sulphured dried apricots, or you'll wind up with a dark brown yolk instead of an orange one.

2 tablespoons sugar	Squeeze fresh lemon juice
½ cup milk	1 cup dried apricots
4 ounces cream cheese	2 teaspoons peeled and minced fresh ginger

1 Warm the sugar and milk in a double boiler. Add the cream cheese in 3 additions, stirring until the cheese is melted each time. Remove from the heat, stir in the lemon juice, and cool to room temperature.

2 Soak the apricots in hot water for 10 minutes, until plumped and softened. Drain the apricots and put them and the ginger in a blender; process to a puree, adding a little warm water if necessary to get them going. Pass the puree through a fine-meshed strainer and put in a pastry bag, or a zip-lock bag with a corner snipped out.

3 Fill 4 small, round saucers or ramekins each with a ¼-inch-thick layer of the cheese mixture to form an "egg white"; pipe circular "yolks" of apricot puree onto the middles of them. Refrigerate for up to 6 hours or serve immediately.

"Breakfast at Citronelle": A Suite of Desserts

"Breakfast at Citronelle" is a creative tour de force that shows just what a calculating fiend my friend Michel is (he knows it, too). There's a second of hesitation when the dessert first arrives at your table because it really does look like a plate of breakfast food, and it's that moment of disbelief that Michel loves to watch.

What appears before you is a fried egg, bacon, home fries, ketchup, and coffee. (There are a couple of other elements Michel rotates in and out of the breakfast, but this is enough.)

Though your eyes are fooled, at least momentarily, nothing is what it seems to be: The "egg" is an apricot puree in a sweet cheese sauce; the "bacon" is a layered cookie made from two separate puff pastry doughs (this is a ridiculously difficult element, and one I've chosen to omit); the "home fries" are sautéed apples; the ketchup is raspberry jam (seeds strained out, of course); the "cappuccino" is a mousse with whipped cream.

Each of these individual desserts is pretty straightforward. The challenge, of course, is preparing them all at once. They all could be done in advance, though, because none is served hot. You're going to have to do some pretty fancy footwork to serve this as Michel does, but if you pull it off you'll astonish the beneficiaries. Rest assured, though, that each element is worth making on its own.

"Hash Browns"
(Sautéed Apples with Maple Syrup)

MICHEL RICHARD | **Makes:** 4 SERVINGS **Time:** 20 MINUTES

These sautéed apples really do look like hash browns in the context of Michel's dish, but they're also great on their own, with vanilla ice cream. You can substitute sugar for the maple syrup if necessary.

3 tablespoons unsalted butter

3 Granny Smith apples, peeled and cut into ½-inch cubes

2 tablespoons maple syrup

½ teaspoon cinnamon

1 Heat the butter in a large non-stick skillet over medium-high heat. When the foam subsides add the apples and maple syrup. Cook, stirring occasionally, until the apples are lightly browned but not mushy, 3 to 5 minutes.

2 Sprinkle the cinnamon over the apples, toss once, and serve warm.

"Cappuccino"
(Coffee Mousse with Whipped Cream)

MICHEL RICHARD | **Makes:** 4 SERVINGS **Time:** 20 MINUTES

A simple and delicious coffee-flavored mousse that, with the whipped cream topping, looks just like a cappuccino.

2 cups good, strong, hot coffee (espresso is best)

½ cup sugar, or to taste

1 envelope (1 tablespoon) unflavored gelatin

1 tablespoon rum

¼ cup heavy cream, whipped

Bittersweet chocolate shavings

1   Nestle a medium bowl in a larger bowl filled with ice. Put the coffee, sugar, gelatin, and rum into the medium bowl (taste and add more sugar if you like). Whisk (or whip with a handheld mixer) until the mixture is light and fluffy.

2   Spoon, pour, or pipe the mixture into espresso cups or coffee mugs. Top the coffee mousse with the whipped cream and a sprinkle of chocolate, and serve.

Spanish "French" Toast (Torrijas Castellanas)

JOSÉ ANDRÉS/MARK BITTMAN | **Makes:** 4 SERVINGS **Time:** 20 MINUTES

To counter Michel's optical illusion dessert suite, I thought I'd try a little breakfast as dessert of my own, making "French" toast in the Spanish style, which is super rich, laden with cinnamon and sugar, and cooked, in part at least (and sometimes entirely), in olive oil, adding a bitter component that offsets the sweetness nicely.

Although I thought my torrijas successful, I had yet to try those made by José Andrés, a chef supreme from Spain, who prepared it when we taped in his restaurant a couple of weeks later. This is a combination of José's recipe and my own, and I do believe it is the ultimate.

1 cup milk

1 cup heavy cream

3 eggs

Pinch salt

¼ cup ground cinnamon

¼ cup sugar

4 thick slices Brioche (page 250) or good bread (8 slices if the loaf is small)

8 tablespoons (1 stick) unsalted butter

2 tablespoons extra-virgin olive oil

Maple syrup or Apple Compote (optional, recipe follows)

1 Combine the milk, cream, eggs, and salt in a broad, shallow bowl. Combine the cinnamon and sugar on a plate.

2 Soak a piece or two of bread in the egg mixture (do not crowd) while you put the butter and oil in a large skillet over medium-high heat. Turn the bread in the egg mixture so it soaks well; when the butter melts and its foam subsides, add the soaked bread, again without crowding (it's likely that this process will have to be done in two batches).

3 Brown the bread nicely on both sides, then transfer each piece in turn to the cinnamon-sugar mixture; turn to coat both sides evenly and serve hot, plain or with maple syrup or Apple Compote.

Apple Compote

JOSÉ ANDRÉS | **Makes:** 4 SERVINGS **Time:** ABOUT 1 HOUR

4 apples, peeled, cored, and thinly sliced

½ cup sugar

The juice of ½ lemon

2 tablespoons unsalted butter

1 tablespoon rum

1 teaspoon vanilla extract

1   Combine the apples, sugar, and lemon juice in a saucepan and cook over medium to medium-low heat, stirring occasionally, until the apples break down, about 15 minutes.

2   Add the butter, rum, and vanilla and cook over low heat until saucy, stirring occasionally, another 30 minutes or so. Serve hot or at room temperature.

Sauces, Condiments, and Other Basics

This is a collection of some of the building blocks that the chefs and I used to build or balance our recipes. They have multiple uses and can stand alone, so they are presented here.

Fennel-Sage Stuffing

SUZANNE GOIN | Makes: ABOUT 4 CUPS Time: 1 HOUR

When I was cooking with Suzanne at Lucques, I was tempted to skip making my dish—the Chicken Breasts Stuffed with Prosciutto and Parmigiano-Reggiano (page 110)—and simply take Suzanne's leftover stuffing and serve it alongside a roast chicken. It's just that good and, if her grand Stuffed Chicken "Poule au Pot" (page 104) is scaring you off, I'd recommend you try the "Much Easier" Chicken Legs with Stuffing (page 108). Or—maybe an equally good idea—use this recipe any time you want stuffing. (You can prepare this the afternoon of the night you plan to use it.)

One point Suzanne made while we were working on this is that most croutons are too dry. She advocates soaking the bread in a fair amount of olive oil (if the ¼ cup called for seems insufficient), then squeezing the excess out before crisping them in the oven. That way the croutons really stand out—they're crisper and tastier than any you've ever had.

12 ounces good white bread

¾ cup extra-virgin olive oil, or more as needed

1 sprig fresh rosemary

2 dried chiles or about ½ teaspoon crushed red pepper flakes

2 cups diced onion

1 bulb fennel, trimmed and diced

2 cloves garlic, minced

1 tablespoon ground fennel seed

½ teaspoon minced lemon zest

1 tablespoon fresh thyme leaves

Salt and black pepper

4 fresh sage leaves, minced

⅓ cup dried currants or small raisins

8 ounces Swiss chard, cleaned, dried, and roughly chopped, stems reserved for another use

8 ounces chicken livers, cleaned

2 tablespoons balsamic vinegar

1   Preheat the oven to 400°F. Cut the crust off the bread and tear or cut it into roughly 1-inch pieces; don't worry about making them uniform. Toss with ¼ cup of the olive oil. Squeeze the croutons to shed any excess oil, and toast on a baking sheet for about 15 minutes, until crisp and lightly colored on the outside but still tender inside. Cool, then transfer them to a large bowl where you'll assemble the stuffing. (You can make these up to a day in advance if you like.)

2   Put another ¼ cup olive oil in a wide-bottomed pan and turn the heat to medium-high. When the oil shimmers, add the rosemary and chiles;

10 seconds later, add the onion, fennel, garlic, fennel seed, lemon zest, thyme, and about ½ teaspoon salt. Cook, stirring occasionally, until the vegetables soften and brown slightly, about 10 minutes. Turn off the heat and stir in the sage and the currants. Pour the whole mixture over the croutons and toss well.

3   Return the same pan to the stove over medium-high heat; add 2 tablespoons more olive oil and quickly cook the Swiss chard, stirring. As soon as the chard is wilted, add it to the stuffing.

4   Again return the pan to the stove over medium-high heat; add the remaining 2 tablespoons olive oil and the chicken livers, seasoning them with salt and pepper. Cook them quickly and lightly—they shouldn't go past the medium-rare stage. Remove the livers to a cutting board to cool.

5   Return the pan to the heat one last time and deglaze it with the balsamic vinegar, scraping the bottom of the pan with a wooden spoon to loosen any of the browned bits. Reduce the vinegar slightly, until it thickens a little, and add to the bread mixture.

6   When the livers have cooled slightly, coarsely chop and toss them in the bowl. Mix the stuffing with your hands, gently mashing the ingredients together so they are well blended. Taste for seasoning and adjust with salt, pepper, and olive oil accordingly.

Sticky Rice

Makes: 4 SERVINGS   **Time:** ABOUT 2 HOURS, LARGELY UNATTENDED

Probably the most challenging thing about sticky rice is buying it—it's not usually called sticky rice in the store, but glutinous (and sometimes sweet) rice. In fact, the best sticky rice is from Thailand (or at least is sold to a mostly Thai market), labeled as broken-grain jasmine rice. It's a very short grain and, unlike most rices, has a special cooking technique: It must be soaked before steaming.

1 cup broken jasmine rice

1   Rinse the rice, then soak it in water to cover for at least 1 hour (up to 24 hours is fine) at room temperature or in the refridgerator.

2   Drain, then wrap in cheesecloth and put in a steamer above boiling water. Steam for about 30 minutes, or until tender. Serve immediately.

Roasted Red Peppers

Makes: 4 **Time:** ABOUT 1 HOUR, LARGELY UNATTENDED

These peppers play a role in Daniel Boulud's Braised Lamb Shoulder (page 154), but they should be a part of everyone's repertoire, because they are useful in so many different ways.

You can grill bell peppers, broil them, or as some people do, roast them over an open flame on the stove. Grilling and broiling them is intuitive: Put them on a grill or under the broiler and blacken them on all sides. Roasting is a bit easier and neater.

You can grill twelve peppers just as easily as four, of course, and they keep well, refrigerated, covered with a little olive oil.

4 large red bell peppers, about 2 pounds

1 Preheat the oven to 500°F. Line a roasting pan with enough aluminum foil to fold over the top later. Place the bell peppers in the pan and the pan in the oven. Roast, turning the peppers about every 10 minutes, until they blacken and collapse, about 40 minutes.

2 Fold the foil over the peppers and allow them to cool. Working over a bowl, remove the core, skin, and seeds from each of the peppers. Use immediately, or store at room temperature (if you will serve them the same day) or refrigerated, covered with a bit of olive oil.

Santorini "Lentils" (Yellow Split Peas)

JOSÉ ANDRÉS | **Makes:** 6 SERVINGS **Time:** 45 MINUTES, LARGELY UNATTENDED

Sometimes simplest is best. Once, when we were taping with José at Zaytinya—his Greek/Middle Eastern restaurant—he sent the crew just about every small dish on the (very large) menu for lunch. Of the literally forty or fifty small plates scattered on the table, this was among the most appealing, a simple bowl of cooked yellow split peas (he calls them lentils) well flavored with olive oil, lemon juice, and crunchy shallots. It's a snap to make, and even José acknowledges that it's good when made with ordinary lentils or split peas; of course if you can find Santorini split peas, use them. (They may be labeled Santorini fava.) You can substitute Indian yellow dal or ordinary yellow or green split peas.

¼ cup extra-virgin olive oil	2-inch piece carrot, peeled
¼ onion, chopped	Salt and white pepper, to taste
1 bay leaf	¼ cup capers, drained
2 fresh thyme sprigs	2 or 3 tablespoons minced shallot
¼ tablespoon black peppercorns	¼ cup minced fresh chives or parsley leaves
1 pound Santorini fava, yellow split peas, or yellow dal	2 tablespoons fresh lemon juice, or to taste

1 Put 1 tablespoon of the olive oil in a wide-bottomed pan and turn the heat to medium-high. When the oil shimmers, add the onion and cook, stirring occasionally, until golden brown, about 10 minutes. Bundle the cooked onion with the bay leaf, thyme, and black peppercorns in a piece of cheesecloth and tie securely.

2 Wash the "lentils" thoroughly, then put them, the cheesecloth-wrapped aromatics, and the carrot in a medium saucepan. Add water to cover by about 3 inches. Bring to a boil and cook at a lively simmer, uncovered, until most of the water is absorbed, about 30 minutes. Turn the heat down to a minimum and cover. Cook another 10 minutes or so, then turn off the heat.

3 Discard the spice bag and the carrot, drain the lentils if necessary, and mash or semi-puree them, using an immersion blender, blender, or food processor. Season to taste with salt and white pepper. (The recipe may be made up to 1 day in advance to this point; cover and refrigerate.)

4 Warm the puree before serving, and serve warm or at room temperature, garnished with capers, shallots, chives, the remaining olive oil, and lemon juice.

Coconut Mint Chutney

SUVIR SARAN | **Makes:** ABOUT 2 CUPS **Time:** 10 MINUTES

Suvir uses this chutney to make a flavored rice dish much like the Tomato Rice (page 200). This isn't used in the book recipes, but you'll be glad I included it. It's great on its own, paired not only with Indian food but also with simply grilled chicken, pork chops, or firm white fish.

About 2 cups loosely packed fresh mint, thick stems removed

1 cup whole buttermilk or yogurt

½ cup unsweetened shredded coconut

2 inches fresh ginger, peeled and cut into 2 or 3 pieces

3 dried red chiles

¼ teaspoon coarsely ground black peppercorns

Salt to taste

Combine all of the ingredients in a food processor or blender and puree until smooth; use within a few hours. (Refrigerate if it is made more than 1 hour or so in advance.)

Fresh Mango Chutney

KERRY SIMON | **Makes:** ½ CUP **Time:** 5 MINUTES

Bottled chutney is usually little more than spicy jam; Kerry's version uses fresh mango and seasonings. It's more like a sweet and tart salad and would nicely grace many Indian or Asian grilled meat or fish dishes. Kerry serves it with his Salmon Tandoori (page 78).

2 ripe mangoes, peeled and diced

½ cup chopped fresh cilantro leaves

1 tablespoon maple syrup

The juice of 2 limes

Salt to taste

Toss all the ingredients together in a bowl; serve within 1 hour.

Fried Sage

SUZANNE GOIN | **Makes:** ABOUT ¼ CUP **Time:** 15 MINUTES

Fried herbs are quite the thing in some restaurants, to the point where they can become overkill. But this garnish for Suzanne Goin's Stuffed Chicken "Poule au Pot" (page 104) is perfect, and it goes nicely with other dishes as well. I wouldn't break out the frying apparatus solely for this, but if you have it going for something else, the herb will only take a minute or so.

Like most fried foods, fried sage is best eaten immediately; the intense flavor and crisp texture deteriorate quickly. Once you get the hang of these, you may start experimenting with frying other leafy herbs, like parsley or cilantro; the technique remains the same.

Neutral oil, like corn, grapeseed, or canola, as needed

1 bunch sage leaves, rinsed, stemmed, and well dried

1 Put 2 inches of oil in a small saucepan and bring to about 350°F on a deep-fat thermometer over medium heat.

2 Add the sage leaves in batches and fry until crisp, 1 minute or less. Remove with a slotted spoon and transfer to paper towels to drain. Reserve until ready to use, but not more than 30 minutes or so (and preferably less).

Homemade Pickled Ginger (Gari)

CHRIS SCHLESINGER | **Makes:** ABOUT 1 CUP **Time:** 30 MINUTES (PLUS 2 WEEKS)

Chris serves this ginger with his signature Grilled Tuna (page 82), figuring as long as he's got the best tuna going, he may as well use perfect pickled ginger. And this isn't the same as the ginger you get in Japanese restaurants: It's better. But don't expect it to be pink, unless you add some food coloring (or a little shredded beet) to the mix. Try it with any Asian dish, if you like.

⅔ cup rice wine or white vinegar

⅓ cup sugar

1 teaspoon salt

4 ounces peeled fresh ginger, thinly sliced

1 Bring the vinegar, sugar, and salt to a simmer. Stir, then drop in the sliced ginger and count to ten. Remove the pan from the heat and allow the ginger to cool in the liquid.

2 Transfer the ginger and the liquid to a glass jar or plastic container; cover loosely (plastic wrap is fine) and refrigerate. The pickled ginger will be ready in about 2 weeks, and will keep, refrigerated, for up to 3 months.

Tomato Confit

MICHEL RICHARD | **Makes:** ENOUGH TO GARNISH 4 BURGERS (AND IS EASILY MULTIPLIED) **Time:** 40 MINUTES, LARGELY UNATTENDED

Halfway between fresh and sun-dried tomatoes, these delicious, highly seasoned tomatoes will improve any sandwich or salad and are a good way to help along the pale flavor of out-of-season tomatoes.

Though Michel peels his tomatoes before doing this, I wouldn't bother. However, it's not that difficult: Make an "X" in the bottom of each, drop it into boiling water, and count to ten; the skin will slip off easily (if it does not, repeat).

If you're using the tomato confit for Daniel Boulud's Stuffed Saddle of Lamb (page 148), cut the tomato into quarters instead of slices and proceed.

1 large, red, ripe tomato or 2 plum tomatoes, peeled and sliced ¼ inch thick

Salt and black pepper

1 clove garlic, peeled and thinly sliced

1 sprig fresh thyme

Pinch sugar

1 tablespoon extra-virgin olive oil

1 Preheat the oven to 250°F. Lay the tomato slices out on a parchment- or Silpat (silicone)-lined baking sheet. Season with salt and pepper, then sprinkle with the garlic, thyme, and sugar. Drizzle with olive oil.

2 Bake the tomatoes for 30 minutes, until barely wilted; cool to room temperature before using.

Ginger Mayonnaise

MICHEL RICHARD | **Makes:** 1 CUP   **Time:** 10 MINUTES

The perfect spread for Michel's Lobster Burger (page 74), but great with canned tuna also. With a food processor or blender, you can make perfect mayonnaise the first time you try it.

½ cup extra-virgin olive oil	½ teaspoon soy sauce
2 tablespoons fresh lemon juice	Salt and black pepper
1 tablespoon peeled and grated fresh ginger	½ cup neutral oil, like grapeseed, corn, or canola
1 egg or egg yolk	

1   Combine ¼ cup of the olive oil, the lemon juice, ginger, egg, soy sauce, and a pinch each salt and pepper in the container of a blender or food processor. Turn on the machine and, with the machine running, start to add the remaining olive oil, followed by the neutral oil, in a thin, steady stream.

2   After you've added about half the oil, the mixture will thicken; you can then begin adding the oil a bit faster. (If, when you're done, the mixture is thicker than you'd like, add a little warm water, with the machine still running, or stir in a little cream or sour cream by hand.) Check the seasoning and serve or store in the refrigerator for up to 1 week.

Aioli: This is what Charles Phan uses on his Summer Roll (page 42). From the above recipe, delete the soy and ginger. Add, along with the egg, a pinch of cayenne, at least 2 peeled garlic cloves, and about ½ teaspoon dry mustard. Proceed as above.

Herb-Garlic Butter

SUZANNE GOIN | **Makes:** ABOUT ½ CUP **Time:** 15 MINUTES

Having a little compound butter around is great insurance on a weeknight when your energy's sapped. A tablespoon of this (or of the Mustard Butter variation) immediately dresses up a piece of grilled or roasted fish, chicken, or pork. Suzanne uses it in her Stuffed Chicken "Poule au Pot" (page 104), but it would be equally good tucked under the skin of any chicken you were about to roast, broil, or grill.

8 tablespoons (1 stick) butter, softened

1 tablespoon roasted garlic or 1 teaspoon minced garlic

1 tablespoon fresh thyme leaves

1 tablespoon chopped fresh parsley leaves

½ tablespoon chopped fresh sage leaves

½ teaspoon salt

¼ teaspoon minced lemon zest

1 Combine all of the ingredients in a medium bowl and mix together thoroughly with the back of a spoon. Gather the beaten butter and wrap in a sheet of plastic wrap, then use the plastic wrap to form the butter into a uniform cylinder.

2 Refrigerate until firm, about 1 hour, then use or freeze; slice off pieces as needed.

Mustard Butter: Suzanne spreads this on her Grilled Pork Confit (page 166), just before serving. From the above ingredient list, omit the lemon, garlic, thyme, and sage. Instead, add 2 tablespoons whole-grain mustard, ½ teaspoon honey, and 2 teaspoons Calvados or any brandy. Proceed as above.

Cornichon Sauce

SUZANNE GOIN | **Makes:** ABOUT 1 CUP   **Time:** 10 MINUTES

Suzanne uses this spirited, piquant sauce with her Stuffed Chicken "Poule au Pot" (page 104), but it would also be a good counterpoint to grilled pork chops, a roast pork loin, or any simply roasted bird. Make as close to serving time as possible for best flavor.

2 shallots, peeled and minced

1 tablespoon sherry vinegar or other wine vinegar

Salt and black pepper

10 cornichons, minced

1 hard-cooked egg, sieved or minced

½ cup extra-virgin olive oil

½ cup chopped fresh parsley leaves

1   Mix the shallots, vinegar, and a pinch of salt in a small bowl and let sit for 5 minutes.

2   Add the cornichons, egg, and a few turns of black pepper; gently stir in the olive oil and parsley. Taste and adjust seasoning, then serve or let sit for up to 2 hours (do not refrigerate).

Peanut Dipping Sauce

CHARLES PHAN | **Makes:** ABOUT 1 CUP **Time:** 10 MINUTES

A must for Summer Rolls (page 42), and a good dipping sauce for almost any dumpling.

1 cup roasted unsalted peanuts

2 tablespoons fresh lime juice

1 tablespoon red or other miso paste

About 1 tablespoon cooked rice, preferably Sticky Rice (page 236)

Combine all of the ingredients in the container of a small food processor and blend, stopping the machine to scrape down the sides if necessary and adding a little water to allow the machine to do its work. You want a fairly smooth consistency, but some chunks are okay. Refrigerate and use within 1 day.

Garam Masala

SUVIR SARAN | **Makes:** ABOUT ¼ CUP **Time:** 10 MINUTES

This is a version of the most common type of garam masala—the antecedent of "curry pow-der"—used throughout northern India. You can add the cayenne if you want more heat, but it isn't necessary; there's plenty of flavor, and a fair amount of heat from the black pepper.

Chip pieces off a whole nutmeg with the blunt edge of a heavy knife, or crack the whole thing by pressing on it with a heavy skillet. You can use ground spices in place of any of these (and you can use whole mace if you can find it); just add them at the end.

2 bay leaves	1 rounded tablespoon black peppercorns
1 cinnamon stick, broken into pieces	¼ teaspoon nutmeg pieces
¼ cup cumin seeds	8 to 10 cloves
¼ cup coriander seeds	⅛ teaspoon ground mace
1 rounded tablespoon green or black cardamom pods	¼ teaspoon cayenne, or to taste (optional)

1   Crumble the bay leaves. Combine any whole spices in a heavy skillet over medium heat. Toast, shaking the pan occasionally, until very fragrant, 2 or 3 minutes. Cool.

2   Grind in a spice or coffee grinder, then blend in the mace and any other preground spices. Store in an airtight container for up to 4 months.

Chicken (or any other Meat) Stock

MARK BITTMAN | **Makes:** 1 GALLON **Time:** 2 HOURS OR MORE, MOSTLY UNATTENDED

There was a time when chefs made stock out of scraps and even leftovers; mostly, those days are past, because chefs make so much stock every day that, although scraps may contribute, most of the base is fresh meat and vegetables bought expressly for the purpose. It makes sense for you to freeze chicken pieces, parsley stems, bits of carrot and onion, and so on, but, really, when it comes time to make stock, unless you're on a very strict budget, you might as well start with just what you need.

Some chefs swear by chicken wings; some use legs only; some add feet. Some cook stock for an hour or two; some for a day. Jean-Georges Vongerichten once admonished me against overcooking stock, saying, "You want to taste meat and vegetables, not bones." Bones give stock richness, but their flavor should not be up front. So cooking times for most stocks should be relatively short, about 1½ hours (or 6 to 8 hours in a slow-cooker, which does a great job here).

About 4 pounds chicken parts, mostly dark meat (or use turkey, beef, lamb, rabbit, or duck)

2 carrots, peeled and trimmed

1 onion (peeling is unnecessary)

1 celery stalk

4 cloves garlic (optional)

2 bay leaves

Several sprigs fresh parsley (stems alone are fine)

10 peppercorns or a few gratings black pepper

1   Combine all of the ingredients in a stockpot or slow cooker. Bring to a boil and reduce the heat to a simmer. Cook for 1½ to 2 hours in a stockpot, or 6 to 8 hours in a slow-cooker, until the broth is fragrant and flavorful.

2   Cool, then strain, pressing on the solid ingredients to extract as much liquid as possible. Refrigerate, then skim excess fat once it hardens. Taste and adjust seasonings. Ladle into containers and refrigerate (for up to 3 days, or longer if you bring to a boil every third day) or freeze.

Gary Danko's Duck Essence: In a deep skillet over medium-high heat, brown 6 or 8 pieces of duck wings or other meaty pieces in about 2 tablespoons olive oil or duck fat. Brown well, turning as necessary. Add 2 cups good stock, chicken or duck. Cook until reduced by about half, then strain; this will take about 15 minutes. Then pour the liquid into a saucepan and reduce, stirring frequently, until thick and glossy, 10 minutes or more. Season and use by the spoonful as a sauce.

Brioche

SUZANNE GOIN | **Makes:** 2 LOAVES **Time:** 1½ DAYS (ALMOST ENTIRELY UNATTENDED)

You only need half a loaf of this brioche for Suzanne's bread pudding (page 218), which is a good thing because you'll probably want to eat the rest as soon as it's cool enough to cut into. Try it spread with good French butter and good coarse salt.

1 teaspoon active dry yeast	5 eggs
2¾ cups pastry flour	¼ cup sugar
¾ cup bread flour (or use 3½ cups all-purpose flour total instead of the 2 flours)	16 tablespoons (2 sticks) butter, softened, plus extra as necessary to grease the loaf pans
1 tablespoon salt	

1   Dissolve the yeast in ¼ cup lukewarm water. Sift the flours and salt together in the work bowl of a stand mixer. Beat the eggs and sugar together in a separate bowl, then turn the mixer on low and gradually pour in the flour. When all is just combined, pour in the yeast-water mixture. Turn the mixer up a notch or two and let it knead the dough together for 5 minutes, at which point the dough should hold on to the hook.

2   Add the softened butter in 2 or 3 additions. Beat on low speed until the butter is incorporated into the dough each time, then turn the speed up to high and knead for 5 minutes more, until the dough is fairly smooth and not sticking to the sides of the bowl at all. Transfer the dough to a lightly oiled or buttered bowl, cover with plastic, and let rise at room temperature until doubled in size, about 2 hours.

3   Punch the dough down, return it to the bowl, cover, and let the dough rise overnight in the refrigerator.

4   Split the dough in half (use a scale if you have one), then using only enough flour to keep the dough from sticking to your hands or the work surface, flatten each piece into a rectangle, and shape the rectangles into loaves. Butter 2 (9 x 5-inch) loaf pans. Place the loaves in the pans, flattening the top of each. Cover and let rest for 1 hour, or until the top of the dough is nearly level with the top of the pan.

5 Preheat the oven to 350°F. Bake 35 to 45 minutes, or until the tops are golden brown and the bottoms of the loaves sound hollow when you tap them (they will fall easily from the loaf pans when done) or the internal temperature reads about 200°F. If they're not done, return to the oven for about 5 minutes more.

6 Remove them from the pans and cool completely on a wire rack before slicing.

INDEX